ation

THE CULTURES AND PRACTICE OF VIOLENCE SERIES

Series Editors
Neil L. Whitehead, University of Wisconsin, Madison
Jo Ellen Fair, University of Wisconsin, Madison
Leigh Payne, University of Wisconsin, Madison

The study of violence has often focused on the political and economic conditions under which violence is generated, the suffering of victims, and the psychology of its interpersonal dynamics. Less familiar are the role of perpetrators, their motivations, and the social conditions under which they are able to operate. In the context of postcolonial state building and more latterly the collapse and implosion of society, community violence, state repression, and the phenomena of judicial inquiries in the aftermath of civil conflict, there is a need to better comprehend the role of those who actually do the work of violence—torturers, assassins, and terrorists—as much as the role of those who suffer its consequences.

When atrocity and murder take place, they feed the world of the iconic imagination that transcends reality and its rational articulation; but in doing so imagination can bring further violent realities into being. This series encourages authors who build on traditional disciplines and break out of their constraints and boundaries, incorporating media and performance studies and literary and cultural studies as much as anthropology, sociology, and history.

Vampire
Nation

VIOLENCE AS
CULTURAL IMAGINARY

Tomislav Z. Longinović

Duke University Press
Durham and London   2011

© 2011 Duke University Press

Printed in the United States of America on acid-free paper ∞

Designed by Heather Hensley

Typeset in Chaparral Pro by Keystone Typesetting

Library of Congress Cataloging-in-Publication Data appear
on the last printed page of this book.

For Didi

CONTENTS

ACKNOWLEDGMENTS

The idea for *Vampire Nation* came to me as I was preparing a lecture on temporality in Eastern Europe, after the invitation of Linda Hutcheon and Mario Valdez of the University of Toronto, who directed *The Literary History Project* sponsored by the Canada Council. The vampire was an imaginary figure so anciently original that it defied the temporal cycles marked by beginnings and endings, remaining alive-yet-dead forever, in a time-space continuum shared by its unsuspecting victims. Its violent and parasitic nature was tied to blood, the old aristocratic prerogative that it helped disseminate into the new age of modernity and enlightenment. The sign of blood, providing sustenance for the vampire and the nation alike, was to mark this everlasting temporality with images of violence. I extend my sincere gratitude to Linda and Mario for inspiring me to consider the figures of history, literature, and culture in a comparative perspective.

Yet, what sustained my work on this volume for the past few years was the support of my colleagues at the University of Wisconsin, Madison. I am grateful for the continuous support from the UW, Madison, Graduate School, CREECA, the Institute for Research in the Humanities, and the Department of Slavic Languages and Literatures. My special thanks goes to the UW, Madison, International Institute that provided funding for the Cultural Translation Project, which I directed from 1999–2001. This book is a case study of the vampire within the emergent field of cultural translation studies.

Having a colleague like Neil Whitehead of the UW, Madison, anthropology department has been a blessing, since our work within the university's research circle on violence and sexuality led to the publication of this manuscript. My friendship with Ron Radano has made me include popular music in my research agenda on nationalism and violence. My work on masculinity has been inspired and supported by Anne McClintock, a dear friend and colleague. Susan Buck-Morss of Cornell University has offered insightful comments on my broader argument, which allowed me to place the vampire nation in the political context of global power relations. My colleagues at Harvard were always a great source of support and inspiration, especially Svetlana Boym and Julie Buckler. Scholars from the Belgrade Circle, who supported the pilot version of this research, are also to be commended for their politics of friendship, especially Branka Arsić, Vesna Bogojević, and Obrad Savić. My colleagues who have been kind enough to sustain the collaboration with me in the area of comparative Balkan and Slavic studies include Milica Bakić-Hayden, Dušan Bjelić, Marcel Cornis-Pope, Eric Gordy, Radmila Gorup, Robert Hayden, Dragan Kujundžić, Nada Petković-Đorđević, Mihai Spariosu, Maria Todorova, and Larry Wolff, as well as countless other friends and students. They are all deserving of my most profound gratitude.

Finally, if there is a future, it belongs to my beloved children, Una and Nina, and I hope they will draw inspiration and insight from their father's work. Dijana Mitrović Longinović has not only offered great support and love throughout the writing of this book, but has also provided invaluable editorial comments after reading the manuscript several times. My love and gratitude will always be extended to her, in life and work.

VIOLENCE IN TRANSLATION

The Vampire Metaphor in the Age of Nationalism

> At once part, cause, effect, example, what is happening there translates
> what happens here, always here, wherever one is and wherever one
> looks, closest to home. Infinite responsibility, therefore, no rest allowed
> for any form of good conscience.
> —Jacques Derrida, *Specters of Marx*

Jacques Derrida's call for infinite responsibility envisions a horizon of translation beyond the liberal concern based on "good conscience," a convenient epistemological mask for the global hypocrisy constructed around a clear distinction between the *Heimlich* "here" and the *Unheimlich* "there." The responsibility of the translator is located "wherever one is and wherever one looks," both "here," in the secure hostility of the Unites States, and "there," in the chaotic multiplicity of ethnic wars that terrorize the global political scene with increasing intensity. The general failure of responsibility in answering the infinite call of ethics beyond the territorialized location of "our own" identity in the West has been the prime force for resurrecting the fantasy of the bloodthirsty other at the end of the twentieth century in Europe.

For Derrida, being may not be infinite, but responsibility must retain infinity as its ever present modifier. Each performance of cultural translation takes place against the shrinking horizon of humanist ideology envisioning the possibility of opening to the foreign and the other. There can never be enough responsibility for the weight of that task; neither "there," in the glorious ruins of Europe, nor in the colonial extensions of the new global empire. There can never be enough responsibility "here," in the very center of the U.S.-led West, closest to home, where the violence touches the American viewer by the mediated gaze worn out by the compassion fatigue of the Bosnian War (1992–95) and tired after the aggressive humanitarianism of the Kosovo intervention (1999) and the switch to the democratic invasion and unsuccessful pacifications of Afghanistan and Iraq initiated in 2001. The violence creating the burden belongs to the cultures both "here" and "there," since the Yugoslav scene used to serve as a political backdrop for the replay of historical performances contrasting the identity of "new Europe" against that of the old one, still embroiled in the violent dramas of blood and soil. The sacrificial logic of identity outlined by René Girard for any type of communal becoming required a metaphysical justification for these violent conflicts, as well as for its surrogate victims. Contrary to that fatalistic view of culture, Derrida invokes the messianic orientation conceived as "a structure of experience," opening up the disciplines of humanities and social science to transform the practice of thinking and writing against the infinite horizon of translation between the proper and the alien as particular cultural idioms and their singular locations undergo the inevitable process of displacement and translation.

In Werner Herzog's film *Nosferatu the Vampyre* (1979), the real-estate agent Jonathan learns that the notorious bloodsucker lives in Geistschloß, the castle that not only is haunted by the ghosts of past centuries but also represents a virtual location where the contradictions of the emergent—one might even say post-human—identity are being articulated. The intangible location of that common chronotope tied to the vampire's time and space is no less imaginary than the violence enveloping the post–Cold War realities of East Central Europe, the preferred residence of the bloodthirsty creature haunting the past of our common humanity. In fact, the literary genre of the fantastic, in whose horror subgenre the vampire continues its seemingly timeless haunting, has been gradually transformed into a cultural mirror held in front of the human being searching for its own elusive reality. Not unlike Lacan's infant, the post-human subject has constructed its own sense of identity by developing an imaginary based on the reflections in this vast mirror of popular culture. Since the 1970s, fantasy has stopped serving the escapist impulse that characterized early Gothic literature's fascination with the foreign, alien, and evil originating in those less than civilized territories of that other Europe one is tempted to call Oriental.

The postmodern turn provided the fantastic genre in literature and cinema with a new cultural function in defining the vampire's location in the glossary of global culture as one of the possible avatars of the human subject in its final dissolution under the violent assault of its own making. Plagued by the horrors of twentieth-century world wars, the post-human subject of civilization had already transformed its habitat into a spectral castle whose inhabitants accept violence as a necessary condition for the very survival of their particular national imaginary, rooted in common fantasies of blood and soil so dear to the Gothic revenant of past centuries. The exploration of the cultural parallels between the rhetoric of the nation and the shifting incarnations of the vampire's blood and soil is the main preoccupation of this work, inspired by the radical reevaluation of psychoanalytic theory initiated by the nomadic philosophies of Gilles Deleuze and Félix Guattari.

The burden of the national imaginary plagued by unacknowledged violence found an outlet in the realm of popular culture, especially in such lowbrow genres as horror. Beyond the parody of good conscience visualized by the global media news networks and the constant noise of violent explosions around the globe, horror literature and cinema seem more and more the only viable avenues for the subject to articulate its truth and reality in a postmodern universe marked by simulation and unreality. The vampire as a metaphor for the unacknowledged sinister side of post-human civilization becomes normalized under the new regime of mass cultural production. This new cultural hybrid speaks the truth in the habitually trivial formulas of the horror genre, while its discourse underscores the guiltless gaze from the secure distance of the only remaining empire, which tends to displace all of the responsibility for its violence "there," into the realm of cultural alterity, where the forbidden dreams and violent desires of Europe proper flourish unabated. Is the imaginary location of the Nosferatu not perhaps indicative of the post-human attempt to reflect on the monstrosity of the global civilization in its apparent impotence to contain the destructive forces it has itself unleashed through the technological taming of the biological habitat and the political hunger to dominate those outside the realm of its current power?

Personally, I was fascinated by the ability of the media's gaze to translate random acts of genocidal violence in the name of territorial identity throughout my own former home (the former Yugoslavia) into similarly trite formulas of "ethnic cleansing." This fascination was extremely painful, since the Gothic timbre of reporting from the Yugoslav war zones was also classifying its varied peoples as the reincarnations of the ancient creature residing in their own particular versions of the Geistschloß. The fantasy of the immaculate national body fed by the blood of those who stood in its way was projected by the media onto the events, fueled by the same global hunger for "one's own" territory and resources, as Yugoslav politicians abandoned the common socialist dream in favor of ruthless privatization that concentrated all of the wealth in the hands of a few post-communist clans and families. Focusing on a particular nation that marks my own belonging to explore the connection of identity and its multiple and often paradoxical representations, I examine the legacies of violence, blood, and soil to account for the shifting of these Gothic themes between the realms of culture and politics.

Redeploying the move of Jean-François Lyotard in his essay "Heidegger and 'the jews,'" I am using the common noun and quotation marks in an attempt to disarm the warring cultures in both their local and their global articulations. On the one hand, 'the serbs,' the largest Balkan ethnic entity, are called to surrender the cultural weapons imagined as the essence of its being and belonging during the national emergence from slavery to Islam during the course of the nineteenth century. On the other, the public within the U.S.-led West are called to comprehend the manner in which the military–media complex used the specter of the bloodthirsty 'serbs' as a simulacrum for the target practice of its own strategic performance of military humanitarianism. The use of the common noun and quotation marks to qualify the collective identity of an ethnic group marks my departure from any notion of the nation as an essential, monumental, and historically stable category. The use of these markers serves to distinguish 'the serbs,' an imaginary assemblage of dubious veracity, from the practice of everyday life of those humans who happen to be born under that particular sign of national belonging. Without attempting to excuse any of the real war crimes committed during the Wars of Yugoslav Succession in 1991–95 and the intervention in Kosovo by the North Atlantic Treaty Organization (NATO) in 1999, this work analyzes different cultural mechanisms responsible for the framing of 'the serbs' as post-communist vampires after the end of the Cold War.

The global media identified the largest ethnic group of the former Yugoslavia as the biggest culprit for the ethnic violence in the Balkans, as well. It was 'the serbs' led by the vampire-in-chief, Slobodan Milošević, who enforced the rigid historicist model of collective identity by ensconcing the monumental past of the people as the very origin and essence of the linguistic, racial, or cultural origin of the nation. In fact, the largest appeal to each particular nation of the former Yugoslavia was not ethnic purity but "freedom," a state imagined along the lines of the unspoken American-style consumer culture in its local Balkan articulation. But alongside freedom to consume and be consumed, 'the serbs' faced ethnic profiling as the war went on: the largest nation rated the worst in the eyes of the world, while the Croats, for example, were deemed to have suffered enough during the 1990s that the uncomfortable facts of their Nazi past could quite easily be overlooked. The Bosniaks and Kosovar Albanians were considered the greatest of victims in the conflict, but also the most prominent suspects because of their Islamic roots. The Gothic ingredient was present in every single one of these global imaginings, yet the most radical breach of the protocols of human dignity was assigned to 'the serbs.' To account for the complexities of communal becoming, the fantasy structure inherent in the global media's gaze featured the communal identity as a monument erected through the blood of the people. Violence was the essential ingredient in enforcing the project of national emergency, inciting "the people" to commit acts of almost ritual violence to ensure their own survival. This mode of parasitic existence was previously characteristic of vampires, drawing fresh blood from their victims to sustain their life beyond death.

Exemplary Violence and 'the serbs'

Until the Bulldozer Revolution in October 2000, global media networks and the public relations industry profiled 'the serbs' as avatars of postcommunist violence in the Balkans. Despite the burden of all too real war crimes committed during the 1990s in the name of collective survival of their own territorial identity, global media excessively emphasized 'the serbs' as the incarnation of an exemplary and exceptional form of evil not proper to Europe, a vision that gradually excluded this imaginary assemblage from the sphere of civilization. Despite the fact that 'the serbs' belong geographically to the very core of Europe, symbolically and territorially, their borderline position was constructed as a projection of the Eurocentric fantasy about a cruel Orient in Europe.

In fact, since the nineteenth century, leading Romantics (Goethe, Scott, Pushkin) have recognized a vast array of literary and cultural practices in 'the serbs' to ensure that the communal becoming of that nation paralleled the similar processes of identity formation in Europe proper. To transform themselves into a recognizable nation after the proverbial "Ottoman yoke" was crushed with a medieval vengeance, the literate classes set out to write down their nation. It is instructive how the trajectory of their self-representation, just like that of the vampire in the postmodern universe, has gradually become a medium for self-reflection in the West. Yet, the process of discovering the vampire as the dark other of the Enlightenment during the eighteenth century is exactly the reverse from the emergence of 'the serbs' as a national formation; while the vampire was gradually normalized as a medium for self-contemplation along the lines of Werner Herzog's *Nosferatu*, the global media representation of 'the serbs' has been defamiliarized to exemplify the violence that presumably is no longer tolerated by the Western understanding of civilization.

By connecting the European legacy of modern nationalism as a foundation for the territorial notions of identity to the ancient bloodsucker, this work explores the role of violence and its cultural representations in the narratives provided by oral tradition, literature, and cinema. The central role of affect in generating and assimilating particular cultural practices replaces the emphasis on the rational and transmissible meaning of certain texts and performances. The primal bond to the national community is rooted in the imaginary relationship between identity as property and position, paired with the vague but real anxiety related to threatening others who are poised to rob the precious blood and drain the communal wellspring of imaginary unity. In fact, the writing down of this imaginary assemblage is constantly mediated by the cross-cultural movement between 'the serbs' and an array of imperial powers that took part in their invention—first, as the scientifically classified vampires of the eighteenth century; then as the glorious people fighting Islam in the nineteenth century; and finally, as the last European vampires in their return to the global scene at the end of the twentieth century.

Other Europeans

The implosion of Yugoslavia has turned 'the serbs' into a population without a common territory, since their position as the "ethnic glue" of the Yugoslav federation was no longer possible in the global political imaginary after the end of state communism in Europe. Since 1991, 'the serbs' have been tried in the media and found collectively guilty of ethnic intolerance; forced displacement of their enemies; mass rape, torture, and massacres of civilians; use of detention camps; and the creation of an endless stream of refugees. These crimes were often spiced with an excess of meaning worthy of the best of the horror genre, creating a collective image of the vampire nation in the new world order. Serbian adversaries were most often excused of crimes, due to their projected smallness and weakness when compared with 'the serbs' and their seemingly superhuman capacity for violence and evil. Within the community of 'the serbs,' the transformation of ethnic pride into a tool of neo-nationalism, coupled with an undecided cultural status of a border region between the "Orient" and Europe proper, resulted in real political, economic, and cultural isolation from the global community before the overthrow of Milošević in October 2000.

Within the context of the former Yugoslavia and its tragic end, the global media complex has constructed the specter of 'the serbs' as a doubly Orientalized other of the U.S.-led West, a nation that thwarted the aspirations for independence of other Yugoslav ethnic groups due to their propensity for the indiscriminate use of violence. The strategic decisions of NATO were based on Samuel P. Huntington's phantasms about the "clash of civilizations," whereby 'the serbs' have been treated as if they were miniature Russians, a nation that has never departed culturally or politically from the imaginary monolith of Orthodox Christianity. Serving as a metaphor for the bloody past Europe proper is striving to forget, this marginal population was transformed into a cultural mirror reflecting past traumas of the old continent. 'The serbs' were relegated to the East, both communist and "Oriental," after the end of Yugoslavia, where they were assigned the role of European civilization's other within throughout the 1990s.

On the one hand, the struggle of 'the serbs' to hold on to the chimera of Yugoslavism has linked them to the legacy of communism; on the other, by using the rhetoric of sacrifice, which will be explored in detail later, their own irresponsible leaders dragged the civilian population into a confrontation with the most powerful global force: the U.S.-led NATO. Since the role of the Western other usually implies stereotypical representations driven by the psychological-warfare guidelines supported by the global news networks and the mainstream press, 'the serbs' were often profiled as less-than-human subjects whose actions stemmed from the automatism of irrational hatred and intolerance of their own ethnic others. This approach tended to obscure the guiding principles of territorial domination and military rationality that operate universally as part of the modern logic of any state organization. This common logic based on the sanctioned deployment of violence inspired the performances of both 'the serbs' and the U.S.-led West in their collective actions but were represented through the strategic use of mass media in a different and diametrically oppositional manner as a struggle between barbarity and humanism. Using the vampire as a shared metaphor between the opponents occupying different locations in the hierarchy of Western civilization, I intend to show how the reach of this Gothic creature of imagination undermines the Eurocentric notion of the nation based on blood and belonging.

Western Interventions

The unraveling of the Yugoslav state saw a confrontation between two returning versions of totalitarian politics. On the one hand, the separatist declarations of the non-Serbian republics saw the triumph of the return to one's own religious and ethnic heritage as a foundation of new national identity. Although not in the vanguard of ethnic separatism, 'the serbs' merged their own messianic propensities with the logic of the decaying post-communist state embodied in the leadership of Slobodan Milošević, who died in prison while being tried for war crimes in The Hague. Trying to preserve remnants of the common state, the military-party apparatus of the common state lingered under the shield of "Yugoslavia" and 'the serbs' as a metaphor for an undying desire for community based on avenging past injustices.

Since Milošević's brutal yet doomed effort to patch together a nation-state out of the ruins of communist Yugoslavia has been countered effectively by the U.S.-led West and by local separatist movements based on anticommunist nationalism (Slovenia in 1991; Croatia in 1991–95; Bosnia-Herzegovina in 1992–95; and Kosovo in 1999), the weapon of "ethnic cleansing," which supposedly belonged exclusively to 'the serbs,' has been used against them as a nation of latent war criminals and crazed gunmen riding a war machine powered by other civilizational outcasts—or, in the words of George Bush Sr., a pariah nation. Indeed, underlying the pariah was the specter of the vampire nation ready to feed on others' blood and territory to sustain itself.

The acts of violence against 'the serbs' during Operation Storm in Croatia in 1995 and after the bombing of Kosovo in 1999 largely have been ignored or downplayed by a media complex guided by the vampire metaphor. In early 2001, the *New York Times* quoted an internal United Nations document that openly stated that the human rights of 'the serbs' in Kosovo after NATO's occupation of the region were not to be taken too seriously: "Human rights principles should not be viewed as operating to dogmatically bar action which must be taken to address urgent security issues."[1] It is needless to say that Milošević shared this ethical standard by invoking security concerns that obscured the infinite dimension of responsibility and transformed the idea of universal human rights into a selectively used political weapon determined by the national interest of the global player with greatest ability strategically to inflict violence on its weaker opponents.

Both the self-glorification of the nation in the writings of a large number of Yugoslav intellectuals and politicians during the 1980s and the political principle of "ethnic balkanization" applied to the entire population of the former Yugoslavia by the Gothic imaginary of the U.S.-led West have participated in imagining 'the serbs' as a vampire nation that began to haunt Europe during the 1990s. This phantasm emerged simultaneously as a figure and as a reflection of a new form of localized racism that demands distance and separation between the protagonists of different cultural currents within the common (European) territory of the former Yugoslavia. Between the struggles for independence from Islamic rule of the nineteenth-century and the current impasse in the Balkans in the wake of ongoing military tensions and conflicts, this construct altered significantly within the context of imaginary networks of signification structuring both the local and the global narratives about a particular national articulation of 'the serbs.'

Global Vampires

The first chapter of this book focuses on the vampire as a figure of Gothic imaginary in Bram Stoker's *Dracula*, which set the stage for later perceptions of the entire Balkan region. The discourse of stolen blood reveals how the imaginary lens crafted by Stoker persists in the West as a cultural filter that defines alterity: Eastern Europe is a location where sex and violence know no limits. The image produced in British popular culture at the end of the nineteenth century has traveled to the end of the twentieth century to establish political discourses that the U.S.-led West sustains when it deals with new yet old types of revenant nationalisms: the specter of 'the serbs' as the global vampires who deserve a well-guided stake of democracy.

This Gothic vision defines the boundaries of proper identity and its civilizational other within Europe, a location where bad but sharp teeth, carnage, and fornication abound. The other Europe is an extension of the notorious count's ruined castle, where excessive passions and "old centuries" conspire to halt the progress and enlightenment proper only to the superior technology of the West. One of the most symptomatic returns of this Gothic vision is the mediated emergence of 'the serbs' as a phantasm of a vampire community governed by an excess of malignant historical imagination that is alien to the values of Europe and the "civilized world."

Firmly rooted in political and cultural ideals inherited from the best European traditions of nationalism and liberalism, 'the serbs' share military rationality and territorial logic of the nation-state with Europe proper. In fact, the Yugoslav tragedies of the 1990s are a legacy of the violence that formed the foundation of modern Europe: the political and cultural ideals made flesh and blood in the uncanny law binding the nation-state. The temporal disjunction between the "other" Europe steeped in old centuries of its historical imagination and the hyper-modern amnesia of the U.S.-led West is at the root of this interpellated subjectivity structuring the Gothic emergence of 'the serbs.'

Kosovo as a Metaphor

The second chapter traces the invention of 'the serbs' as a collective national re-territorialization during the transition from the dominantly oral popular culture of the common folk to the edification of literacy based on local interpretations of a belated but volatile mix of Enlighten-ment and Romanticism. The writing down of the nation centralizes the notion of "sacrificed blood" as a historical legacy of externally imposed victimization as torturers and victims continue to switch places in the reinvention of the legacy of Kosovo.

The sense of proper identity is gained through perpetual sacrifice, as a violent rupture with the values in the immediate temporal and spatial proximity. Vuk Karadžić's transcription of the oral tradition into the newly reformed Cyrillic alphabet monumentalizes the popular literacy emerging among 'the serbs' as a vision of the past that constantly overwhelms the present and directs the future backward. The aura of holiness that surrounds writing in Church Slavic is transferred from the evangelical to the everyday as Europe is regained and Turkey is ex-pelled from the native realm. The emergence of secular culture through the newly founded educational system is marked by a simultaneous displacement of the aura of holiness and the internalization of the post-Oriental wound. The force of national progress is envisioned as the triumph of dominant masculinity over its treacherous others.

I do not discuss the life and work of Vuk Karadžić, a peasant's son who transformed himself into a founder of modern literacy and who is often credited with creating modern culture for 'the serbs.' Instead, I analyze the consequences of his cultural reforms assimilated by the common folk to what he imagined to be a properly European iden-tity. By expunging the Islamic master, 'the serbs' emerge from slavery through the discourses of domination and submission, continuing to motivate their struggles for "the honorable cross and golden freedom" through this binary logic of the *ethnos*. The agonistic vision is per-formed by the "singers of tales" (*guslars*) as a ritual catharsis of the collective burden meant to tell the story of the injured yet heroic mas-culinity of the people. This ritual lamentation mourns the past glory of the medieval empire before the Kosovo defeat of 1389. The heavenly realm of the national imaginary is suffused with the eternal mourning of those who died for the glory of the nation, marking each of 'the serbs' as dead from birth. The inability to mourn this symbolic loss of life after deliverance from Islamic domination properly prepares the national males to actualize this death in life through the endless repeti-tion of the ritual sacrifice of both the self and the designated others on the altar of the nation.

Going beyond the earlier "civic models" of communal identity developed by Dositej Obradović among the exiled middle classes in the Habsburg empire, Vuk's emphasis on the Herderian model of collective identity as a populist construct developed around the "spirit of the people" (*Volksgeist*) triumphs through its appeal to the "organic" existence of the nation. This vision of illiterate peasant culture as the foundation of modern national identity is paired with the memory of "old centuries" before Kosovo to mobilize 'the serbs' in their struggle to reinvest the newly re-conquered national territory with a sense of belonging to the world beyond the grave. This affinity with death and its perpetual return in life lays the foundation for the cult of the masculine war machine that does not respond to the boundaries of mundane life and its laws, but acts as a vampire in search of fresh blood and territory to sustain itself.

The performance of this version of masculinity has continued among the peasants of the Dinaric highlands, marked with violent returns of the submission and domination narratives. While the developing city dwellers take the written, monumental version of oral epics as a source of ethnic pride and identity, those who inhabit the rural and transitional zones of the nation nurture the burden of past injuries alongside their desire to emerge from backwardness.

The process of mourning tied to oral performance of the epic is repressed as the melancholic sense of recurrent victimization by the great powers is reinforced through the cultural production of the pre-Romantic and Romantic periods. Petar Petrović Njegoš's epic drama *Gorski vijenac* (The mountain wreath; 1847) narrates the conflict between 'the serbs' of Montenegro and Slavic converts to Islam, with the messianic logic of Christians fighting for emancipation by all means necessary. Those who convert to Islam become "Turks" and are cast in the role of traitors to their birth community through service to their imperial masters. 'The serbs' see themselves as defenders of Europe and Christianity who rebel against slavery as they exterminate their own brothers who have converted to Islam. The pain of this choice between being a proper European and collaborating with the imperial Islamic ruler constitutes the tragic ethos of *The Mountain Wreath*. Both Vuk and Njegoš see themselves as doing their best to rejoin the West, using the Kosovo legacy to fight against the "backwardness" imposed by Islamic suzerainty. Modernization through literacy comes to 'the serbs' as a transcription of a fluid oral tradition into a fixed national narrative that features permanent violence, genocide, and de-teritorrialization imagined as a traumatic network that forms the web of national identity.

This perception of victimization creates a collective identity with a communal torturer–victim complex at its core. Ever since the emancipation from bondage to the Islamic master, 'the serbs' nurture the righteous privilege of the liberated slaves to lash out against injustice and avenge past suffering. This shifting between the slavish and the imperial, as well as the ability to alternately see oneself both as a small nation victimized by the great powers and the greatest of Balkan nations, manifests the disjunctive temporality of the 'the serbs' as a national construct. When they are not in the position of the victims, 'the serbs' apply the imperial codes of domination assimilated through liberation and are quick to lash out against surrogate victims who remind them of the death they are already living.

Brothers No More

Chapter 3 explores transformations that the collective identity of 'the serbs' underwent during and after the creation of the two common South Slavic states—one after the First World War, and the other after the Second World War. The discontents of Yugoslavism as a civilizational framework are made visible in the ways Vladimir Dvorniković, a self-styled Yugoslav ethno-psychologist, imagines a common Yugoslav identity based on the unrecognized superiority of the Dinaric race. The "heavenly" dimension of oral epics is transferred from 'the serbs' onto the raw power of the newly imagined Yugoslav masses, whose origins are visualized as the pagan foundation of the nation's vitality in popular culture. The artistic avant-garde largely approximated this neo-pagan turn from the social sciences and incorporated it into its vision of the nation. Dvorniković posited the triumph of the "Dinaric race" within Yugoslavia as a counterweight to the emergent discourse of Nordic superiority among the Germans. During the Nazi-sponsored extermination of 'the serbs' as a lower race within Yugoslavia in the Second World War, the collective identity once again endured the trauma of extermination, re-establishing the victim within as a fundamental category of national identity.

Freud's postulations on the repressive function of civilization were made fully visible as Yugoslavia continued to implode and crumble. The cross-cultural construct of the citizen-warrior of the National Army fell apart along ethnic lines, especially in the Slovenian north, where Janez Janša began his successful cooperation with the West to put an end to the common South Slavic state. Other symptomatic theoretical figures of the latest Yugoslav end, such as Slavoj Žižek, provided a cultural apology for the breakup of the post-Tito Yugoslavia with a new species of performance art philosophy and theory.

While Dvorniković imagined a Yugoslav cultural prototype inspired by the avant-garde vision of the Balkan *Barbarogenije* (Barbaro-genius) at the end of the 1930s, Žižek intentionally misreads 'the serbs' as a centrifugal factor that has ended the common framework of the Yugoslav community. In fact, the Slovenes led the move away from the common state, motivated not only by the simplistic vision of the superior "Central" Europe dominating the lowly Balkans, but as a calculated cover-up for the responsibility of separatist intellectuals for pulling the plug on the common South Slavic state. This narrative was never presented in the West, as Slovenes became one of the best allies in the strategic vision of a "new Europe" based on ethnic rather than workers' solidarity.[2] The multiplicity of interests and narratives surrounding the most recent Yugoslav end was reduced to a schematic vision of a good nationalism that was inherent in Central Europe and a very bad one that was embodied in the specter of 'the serbs' as the postmodern vampires of the new world order.

Destroying the In-between

Chapter 4 presents the works of Ivo Andrić and Meša Selimović, the two most prominent Bosnian writers of the twentieth century. Analyzing the literary representations of hybrid identities and their violent destruction, the chapter traces the manifestations of sacrificial logic that underlie the conflicts between different geopolitical formations inside the peripheral territory of Bosnia. Finding themselves at the edge of the "Oriental" world, due to its Ottoman heritage, and of the equally elusive European West, these writers engage literary modernity by seeking metaphors for the loss of proper identity inherent in their post-Oriental predicament. Without the framework of the Yugoslav state, Bosnia has been transformed into an independent republic under international protectorate since 1995, a process that is strangely reminiscent of its past traumas under the domination of the Ottomans and the Habsburgs.

Representing incommensurable alterity of hybrid identities born on the boundaries of major civilizations, Bosnians are transformed into the most prominent example of a nation's inability to tolerate ambiguity. The imaginary identity of Bosnia as the land of perpetual transition was countered in the political practices of both local and global leaders. The post-Yugoslav leaders, led by Milošević, attempted to insert themselves as replacements for the authoritarian socialism of Josip Broz Tito, by dealing a decisive blow to the hybrid identity of this most indeterminate republic of the former Yugoslavia. The recycling of the Kosovo covenant to end the endless suffering of 'the serbs' appropriated national myths to pre-empt the dangers embodied in the rise of specters that belonged to the ethnic others: Croatianism and Islamism. The rendering of its own imperial myths has turned 'the serbs' into a local version of the vampire nation prone to feeding itself on the body of the disappearing South Slavic state.

Bosnia, as a metaphor for the limitless fall of humanity, raises the question of identity as an entity that constantly needs to overcome the simplified political forms that appropriate narratives of a nation sacrificed for the sake of differentiation between its dominant ethnicities. The literary process of national articulation present in the works of both Andrić and Selimović does not envision a Bosnia with a defined ethnic profile; instead, it appears as a fiction whose homogeneity can be achieved only at the expense of one or the other of its constituent groups. The projects to form various ethnic homelands that have haunted Yugoslavia in the aftermath of communism appear to bear the mark of a common European obsession with the eternity of communal blood and soil, parallel with the vampire's insatiable hunger for life that will never have a natural ending. The appropriation of the Kosovo myth by 'the serbs' of Bosnia and other Yugoslav lands is part of that imaginary heritage, rooted in the fear and hatred of those others who could endanger the boundaries of the proper identity by ruining the dream of eternity for the nation and its bloody being.

One of Selimović's characters calls Bosnians "the most complex people in the world" exactly because the scars of history have left them with a less-than-clear sense of belonging to such a community. Their self-destructive tendencies are tied to a certain repetition compulsion engendered by past injuries that one has to relive to remember. This scar tissue of identity, always in transition from the torturer to the victim, marks the body and life caught up in the narratives of submission and domination. Always between the destiny of the slave and the memory of the king, the identity of those who inhabit and share diminutive territorial domains such as Bosnia find in their literary flights a means of reaching for the soiled legacy of "universal humanism." The predicament of the nationalist is much simpler and requires only war and violence to enforce the vision and terror of common blood on those who dare separate from it.

Memoryscapes of Hope

The overwhelming need for truth and reconciliation among the Balkan nations must begin with a candid apology for the crimes committed during Milošević's rule. Since no politician will risk his masculine image by bowing in front of the former enemy, the process must begin with those who dare to take the position of intellectuals after the disaster caused by the Academics (which I capitalize to denote the concerned intellectual body of the Serbian Arts and Sciences), who imagined 'the serbs' as a race modeled on vampires to survive, and who sustain monolithic narratives about the ancient sacrifice of and for the people. The Academics have acted as neo-guslars attempting to mobilize their ethnic collective in a struggle against the rest of the world.

A first, risky step was taken in 2007 by Serbian President Boris Tadić, who apologized to the Croatian nation during a television interview. The ongoing struggle for truth and memory of the violence committed is best analyzed through the actions of different artists and activists whose works are gradually transforming the vampiric burden caused during the Age of Slobism. Starting with the first attempts to "quiet the vampire" in the 1978 novel *Kako upokojiti vampira* (How to quiet a vampire) by Borislav Pekić, countercultural movements within the former Yugoslavia have been stuggling to redefine the national identity away from narratives of blood and soil.

In randomly selecting different strategies of cultural resistance to the rigid and unforgiving logic of ethnic terror, the concluding chapter locates voices of difference who were struggling to redefine the collective memory and rectify its abuses by abandoning the lure of the Gothic imaginary. The loss of Kosovo in 1999 opened a new trajectory in the national imaginary of 'the serbs,'—one that still relies on some trace remnants of Yugo-nostalgia, as well as on different forms of both the national and the transnational identity. Note the uncanny appearance of the number 9 in the timeline leading from one loss to another—1389–1989–1999—with Milošević and the Academics briefly resurfacing during the late 1980s to incite the final destruction of the symbolic core of the national imaginary. The need for an identity without Kosovo as its figurative source requires non-sacrificial forms of everyday life motivated by performances founded on a culture of responsibility, trust, and even laughter.

The literary imagination reborn from the latest diasporic movements has yielded new work from David Albahari, one of the Yugoslav writers who chose to leave his native realm as a consequence of the country's implosion. His *Kanadska trilogija* (Canadian trilogy) rethinks the entire notion of time and identity and interrogates the limits of alterity after immigration from the disappearing homeland. His time in the new country is measured by the calendar of horror from the old one: bombings of religious buildings, shelling of civilians, and proclamations of neo-Nazi states. Memories travel along the unpredictable trajectory of the immigrant as identity is placed in the process of constant translation between the native and the adopted culture. The core of the national is transposed into the new semiotic environment, forcing a redefinition of community based on blood and its territorial extensions.

Besides flight, there are those who invent new forms of nationalism as they watch in horror the moral and material decay of their own people. Goran Marković, a film director who wrote a testimonial about the last gasps of Slobism, confronts the legacy of the perverted mass media with a vision of his own grandmother and her irreducible civic goodness from a pre-communist epoch. The imaginary excess of Professor E., whose patriotic fervor prompts him to conclude that all Indo-European races originate from 'the serbs,' causes the narrator of the testimonial to wake up from his passive posture of moral voyeurism and imagine his nation in a different framework of civilization. Marković's ironic comparison of nationalism to pornography reveals the common ground of the shameless performance of those aspects of identity better left disguised.

The last segment looks at the uses of the new media to parody the vampire nation and its state institutions. Cyber-Yugoslavia is an electronic country constructed around an interactive website launched after the NATO intervention in 1999 to enact a different form of collectivity. Reaching beyond narratives of blood and soil, this electronic form of communication gathers people around the world who have never given up on the ideal embodied in the cultural promise of Yugoslavism. Positioning both 'the serbs' and their multiple others in a global interaction, this state moves between the native realm of the truncated state, the diasporic communities, and those subjects who chance on it in their cyber-navigation. This imaginary state offers possibilities for overcoming the extreme patriotic figuration of the native ethnoscape by ridiculing the political organization of the nation-state as such. The fact that each citizen of Cyber-Yugoslavia must choose his own ministry upon joining the website parodies the morbid hunger for power embedded in contemporary political practices witnessed by those misfortunate former Yugoslavs.

This type of less-than-serious movement away from the rigid forms of national identity posits Internet surfing as a substitute for a lost homeland. The nostalgic dimension is not conflated with violent appropriations of the other, since the computer-literate generations resist easy assimilation by the sacrificial forms of identity. Both the local and the global resistance to the vampire as a metaphor of an undying past whose life depends on the blood of real humans will be the primary task of those who would help 'the serbs' resist the phantasm of the eternal life of the nation, as well as that of the global victims of the new imperial power.

THE GREAT VAMPIRE SWINDLE

Global Cultural Imaginary and the Violence of 'the serbs'

SERBIA. The cradle of vampirism in Europe.
—Matthew Bunson, ed., *The Vampire Encyclopedia*

And yet, unless my senses deceive me, the old centuries had, and
have powers of their own which mere "modernity" cannot kill.
—Bram Stoker, *Dracula*

The perception of pathological fixation of Eastern Europe in general, and of the Balkans in particular, on the "old centuries" voiced by Stoker at the end of the nineteenth century through the persona of Dracula is symptomatic of a cultural vision based on an interesting intersection of local and global discourses of violence. The past and its bloody memories define a refusal to yield to modernity imputed to the countries of the Balkan region, whose resistance to civilization and its laws are naturalized as inherently evil to oppose the advances of the Enlightenment and its technologies of mediation. The narrative projected onto the vampire as a beast within, enslaved to the undying, bloody past, serves as a national fetish underlying the repressed origins of Europe proper.

A small nation such as 'the serbs' is by definition led by a mysterious, degenerate leader who is ready to sacrifice others and commit bloodshed only to prolong his political power. During the 1990s, this vision of the other Europe reinforced an imaginary relationship that extended the vampire metaphor from the realm of the Gothic period's horror genre to the mundane practice of global politics, strategically deploying violence to advance civilization and the rule of law in the Wild East of Europe. The signifier that will forever sink into historical oblivion— Yugoslavia, the proper name of the country that was erased to deny the striving of culturally heterogeneous populations to live in a common state—has been assaulted by the differentialist logic of the "clash of civilizations" to enforce local insecurity by bringing about a collective return to the ideology of the vampire nation.

Stoker's *Dracula*, which founded the literary discourse of the Gothic imaginary, appears as the incarnation of those old centuries that refuse to fade away in the face of modernizing Europe. This imaginary, sparked by a belated Romantic mourning for the glory of the past that permeated most of the notions of the nation across the symbolic boundaries of Europe, uses violence with the automatism of the beast who has no other choice but to feed itself on the blood of others. This hungry being is always engendered in zones of intense cultural and linguistic hybridization and simultaneously is imbued with the pathos of a race submerged in the narratives of its own past and viewed as a herald of a cruel modernity at hand.

Many "national" histories written and taught in the Balkans and in the rest of "Oriental" Europe are saturated with a celebration of violence that is monumentalized as just revenge and sacrifice offered to the glory of cultural life and survival. Small nationalisms contain this imaginary economy; they appear colorful but ostensibly irrational, steeped in gore despite enlightened intentions and dominated by discourses of masculine injury that claim the victim's right to feed on the blood of others as the only way to sustain survival.

This being is symptomatic of a phantasm that has haunted the imagination and reality of both sides of Europe ever since 1897, when it emerged as cultural documentation of the demonic rebirth of the timeless and unreflecting void of violence. This was the age when England saw the replacement of traditional gaslight with new and improved electric lights; simultaneously, the Gothic vampire was exiled to the urban shadows through Stoker's narrative evocation of the "Oriental" location of past European traumas. Lurking in the shadows, the vampire appeared as a specter of an ancient and forgotten power juxtaposed with imperial Victorian rationality and acting as its repressed underside. The creature was willing to quench its thirst for ever more blood by consuming the life essence of close and distant others, revealing a particular form of literary interpellation of the imperial past reaching into the present by covert and devious means.

The sadistic propensities of Vlad Dracul Tsepesh, which the Saxon chroniclers recorded as gargantuan feasts accompanied by torture and suffering and which served as Stoker's "historical" model, gradually transformed into blood drinking by the decadent aristocrat, a figure Europe had been trying to erase from its enlightened history. The figure haunted Europe by conjuring up its own criminal past that, ostensibly, had been conquered by modern civilization and the light of reason. The fear of light is symptomatic of vampires as creatures who hide in the shadow of the law that is responsible for establishing the enlightened rationality of the modern state. The vampire unambiguously embodies ambiguities of the empire as the obverse of being that was imagined by philosophers at the inception of the Age of Reason in the eighteenth century. This was also the period in which the state representatives of the Habsburg administration filed their first official reports about vampire plagues ravaging the Balkan regions of the Holy Roman Empire. The vampire is the true being of Western metaphysics as it grew into modernity by getting to know its borders.

The famous case of Petar Plugojević, reported in the *Wiener Diarium* in 1725 as the first scientific investigation of vampirism among 'the serbs' who had been exiled from Kosovo in the wake of Austro–Turkish wars, so stirred the European popular imagination that in 1763 a newspaper columnist in London used it as an allegory for the bloodthirsty nature of the tax law in an article titled "Political Vampirism." The emergent administrative structures of the modern state were imbued with metaphoric signification that transformed the ancient creature into a flexible construct that was available for a variety of discursive uses across cultures. Although the legacy of the vampire nowadays is claimed almost exclusively by Romania as a marketing tool (embodied in failed plans to build the Draculaland theme park near the Bucharest airport), 'the serbs' have been affected by this type of cultural profiling most recently, both as the dominant perpetrators of Balkan violence during the 1990s and as the military target of NATO in its desperate search for raison d'être since the end of the Cold War.

The historical Vlad Dracul Tsepesh allegedly had learned the art of torture from the Ottomans after spending his youth as a hostage to the Turks. Stoker's imaginary Transylvania was the borderland between

Europe proper and the Ottoman Orient, memorialized in literature as a space of the imperial arbitrariness of violence tied to alien power. This vision of violence was assimilated into the narratives of most Balkan nations after the process of "liberation" was initiated during uprisings against their imperial masters in the nineteenth century. The gradual impalement of Vlad Dracul's victims is represented as a practice rooted in an unenlightened, Oriental Europe imagined as a periphery immersed in a perverse enjoyment caused by the perpetual replaying of past tortures and massacres. The phallic character of the stake as a torture weapon, and as the ultimate palliative for the vampire's unholy existence, points to violence as an omnipresent and productive force of European identity. Europe's cultural imaginary is constituted as an ongoing performance that invokes a monumental memory invested with forms of identity born through this violent becoming. The border position of Transylvania as a site of conflict between Christianity and Islam is emblematic of the impossible locality the Balkans have represented for the Western imagination ever since the vampire plagues of the eighteenth century.

Translating Balkan Violence

The current division of previously monolithic, communist Eastern Europe into the "angelic" nations of the new-member European states (the Czech Republic, Hungary, Poland, Slovenia, etc.) and the "demonic" nationalisms of 'the serbs' and most of their Balkan enemies betrays the inconstancy inherent in the "innocent" gaze of the Western media consumer. Those who do not reside "there" (in the blood-soaked territories) are allowed to indulge in a media vision born of this intentional moralistic myopia, a discourse that features violent excesses and the incommensurable alterity of those small and bloodthirsty nations that exist in a realm far away from "here." Despite the addition of Bulgaria and Romania to the European Union and NATO, the global media would have us believe that the Balkans are inhabited by 'the serbs,' who personify the criminal remnants of Dracula's blood clan, while the inheritors of *Mitteleuropa* are cast as diligent descendents of Roman Catholic civilization and therefore more than willing to service the strategic and military needs of the U.S.-led West. It is symptomatic that the *Mittel Land* Stoker invoked in *Dracula* clearly belongs both to the worlds of the Balkans and to the world of Central Europe. What all these small nations share is their relationship to discourses of history, which are constructed as a narrative dominated by the burdensome memories of ancient but alive repression and spiced by stories of blood and sacrifice to sustain the spectral existence of the vampire as a shared narrative of national unconscious.

The Polish-born Nobel laureate Czeslaw Milosz imagined Central Europe as a margin of Europe proper, an ethnoscape stretching from the Baltic to the Adriatic, a transitional zone between proper Western civilization and the unfathomable identity of imperial Russia. Writing before the fall of the Berlin Wall, Milosz, unlike Milan Kundera and many other dissident writers and intellectuals, included the Balkans in his vision of Central Europe. Although Milosz himself identified with Polish Lithuania, he imagined that homeland as extending into the entire border zone that he saw as sharing a common destiny of victimization by its imperial neighbors. The main trauma of Central Europe, he wrote, was that "the division of Europe has been a palpable reality," not a historical fact confined to archives and textbooks.[1]

The division Milosz invokes was implemented by the drawing of Winston Churchill's Iron Curtain and the struggle that broke out between the "barbarian purity" of the Soviet communist project and the technologically superior lifestyles of the U.S.-led West, rooted in forms of structural hunger inherent in the ideology of free consumerism. This hunger, shared with the vampire, features the actions of the sole global superpower after 1989 in its almost automated search for strategic dominance of the planet's remaining resources. The absence of the capitalist–communist binary has taken "Eastern Europe" from its previous "Oriental" status into a zone closer to the economic North–South division, instituted by the binary between the noble Central Europe and the bloodthirsty Balkans, which, in turn, are emblematic of the vampire nation of 'the serbs.'

With the notable exception of the former Yugoslavia, most of the Central Europe nations in Milosz's conception were subjected to the patronage of the Soviet Union during the Cold War, suffering the consequences of their geopolitical smallness when confronted with the embrace of "Mother Russia." This sense of palpable subjection of weak and small peoples to powerful nations engendered a cultural phenomenon that Milosz calls the historical imagination. The collective awareness of the people who used to live behind the Iron Curtain has been shaped by their political destiny, which often has been determined by forces that opposed their own striving for sovereignty and is based in remembering past injustices. Milosz speculates that "the historical imagination is probably trained by a memory of collective suffering," thus forming the context for great works of culture to emerge from these small nations.[2]

Apart from the submissive "Christ of Nations" complex nurtured by the Polish national imaginary, Milosz projects a unique vision of a subaltern cultural production rooted in the suffering of the weak who were forced to endure the infectious bite of larger historical predators personified for Poland by the Russians and the Germans. The destiny of small peoples is a symptom of the masochistic imaginary, and it is no accident that Leopold von Sacher-Masoch was the product of life in Habsburg Bukowina. The hypertrophy of collective memory leads to guilt in periodic repetition of punishment, since only pain can be experienced as the real foundation of identity. In accordance with this cultural mechanism, Sacher-Masoch, who was also known as the "Ukrainian Turgenev," proposed a pan-Slavic state ruled by the cold and cruel beauty of an empress similar to Catherine the Great, who would play the role of national dominatrix for the united Slav(e)dom.

Inferiority and passivity were also qualities dear to another Polish maverick, Witold Gombrowicz, who glorified the undersized status of literature that would run away from projects based on memory of historical victimization. This entrenched kernel of the unhealed injury disturbs the victim in search of domination, who is eager to revisit the pain and free the subject from his or her own unfulfilled strivings. Violence repositions stories of one's greatness through the work of love as pain and initiates the perpetual circulation of the cultural imaginary to normalize aggression and laugh at violence. The literary and cinematic incarnations of the vampire situate their narratives amid small and oppressed peoples who are ruled by the revenant powers of ancient times that originated in the mist-enveloped sources of its bloody being.

National leaders often take up this narrative to defend against the violence of others and deploy it wisely, as they must calculate blood loss and gain for their own vampire nations. The genesis of ethnic others, subjects who do not fit the dominant vision of the national time–space continuum, is bound to territorial traumas of submission and domination. The symbolic value of "national territory" is always calculated against the threat of erasure by both large and small others, just as the collective identity of a small nation seems dependent on the will of those larger and more powerful imperial others. The less-than-civilized behavior of warriors in end-of-the-millennium Yugoslavia stemmed from the same feelings of dispossession, past and present, almost always rooted in images of stolen blood and hunger for lost territory. For 'the serbs,' a combined influence of local post-communist violence (Slobodan Milošević as a national messiah) and a global hunger for domination (the U.S. led-West) formed a contested media vision of postmodern vampire identity.

In the Balkans, the small nation is often armed and supported by a powerful ally, who, as Maria Todorova has suggested, often nurtures its "pet nation" to fulfill its geopolitical aims.[3] Exploiting the sense of weakness felt by a well-trained ally, the great power uses its pet's smallness and suffering for strategic gains in its relations to rival great powers competing for influence over a region. The pain and suffering of the pet nation, both real and imaginary, are transformed into a cultural imaginary that is always on the edge of the rational, anticipating the explosion of genocidal rage to free the guilt and perform its justified punishment operation. The fact that responsibility for the ethnic other is nonexistent turns the perpetrator, who usually was a victim in a previous historical cycle, into a creature reduced to basic instincts, less and more human at the same time.

The temptation to yield to old centuries of suffering for one's puniness and enact pre-emptive violence to avenge age-old injustices often turns memory into a source for the cultural imaginary of nations caught in a sadomasochistic economy of submission and domination. For Milosz, the imaginary of his nation had been haunted by the Molotov–Ribbentrop Pact of 1939, which once again partitioned Poland. Torn between Russia and Germany, Poland was again dismembered, providing an example of how the nationalist narrative of the small nation develops to compensate for historical losses. Those nations that find themselves being used as bargaining chips in the strategic gambling of their predatory neighbors develop this type of imaginary as cultural compensation for their weakness. Milosz claims that the basic difference between the East and the West in Europe has been that between "memory and a lack of memory," since those who have the power do not need to remember past injuries.[4]

Memory of the past is constructed as a burden necessary for the development of modernity, as the effects of violence are inscribed into the very core of national narratives to simplify collective choices when deploying retaliation. For the West, especially in the realm in which the direct object *us* stands in homographic relationship with the name of the last remaining superpower, memory is something of a curiosity, a subject confined to academic departments, history textbooks, and quite a few vampire flicks. The temporality of both the self and the other exist in the vanishing public sphere as "a vague recollection of a misty past."[5] This Gothic vision of memory allows the masters of the universe to act with only their own present strategic interest in mind, practicing the art of domination over the shrinking reservoir of planetary resources. The past and its certainties are assumed to be a menace, especially when they belong to others living in those pathetically small nations, seeking identification with power that they do not possess.

Danilo Kiš reminds us that political "reality" is constructed by the so-called great powers, who inhabit imperial space within which smaller ethnic communities are easily trained and sacrificed for the sake of someone else's strategic desires. In a chapter titled "The Magic Card Dealing,"[6] criminals in Stalin's gulag play a card game similar to Marseilles Tarot. The stakes in the game, called Devil or the Mother, are the lives of Stalin's political victims from around Eastern Europe as chance begins to rule life's outcome. Like those who belong to the small nations, these revolutionary idealists are caught in a larger web of signification that determines their fatal destinies. In the former Yugoslavia, both the quest for racial purity (embodied in the Ustaše installed by the German Nazis in Croatia) and the Titoist form of communism (fighting alongside the Soviet Russians until 1945, then opposing them after 1948) led to massive interethnic violence during and after the Second World War. Strategies developed by politicians to deploy memories of this violence, like a vampire's gaze into the unreflecting mirror of history, are what stir the cultural imaginary for both 'the serbs' and their numerous others.

Milosz remarks, with bitter irony, that the more sophisticated West is paying the price of its advanced technological development by regressing into historical and cultural amnesia. This tendency to forget what is not in the "vital self-interest" is the dominant discourse of the current global culture of oblivion in regard to the remote and less well-known parts of the ethnic spectrum. "Vagueness of any notions related to history" is what characterizes this U.S.-enforced vision of identity, which sees everything in terms of its present and future use value.[7] Milosz juxtaposes the sense of "proper place and time" that shapes the small nation's historical imagination to this politics of forgetfulness, which is often enforced through the educational policies of great powers.

It seems that the last remaining superpower needs no memory, because its fantasy resides in the perpetual present driven by faith in economic expansion at home and military operations abroad, the required ideal guided by pre-emptive strikes to stop injustice in its tracks with stunning displays of techno-praetorian force. The vision of Balkan ethnoscapes during the 1990s is an effect of this global oblivion about the other's past and about how the present has been misused by the protagonists of any ongoing ethnic conflict. Instead, most of these "Oriental" Europeans are seen as suffering from a mnemonic hypertrophy brought about by "too much history." The media ran off into the Gothic spin to frame 'the serbs' as the vampire nation rooted in excesses of violence that far exceeded the scope of real war crimes committed in the name of that nation.

Milosz's poetics of memory claim for Eastern Europe a cultural imaginary written down and erased by the imperial logic of the ever larger conquerors, those who are simply unable to empathize with the victim's sense of history as an effect of traumatic memory. In other words, the small nations suffer and imagine while the large ones rule by pushing the question of historical imagination into the background of purely academic consideration and expertise. In *Vampire Lectures* (1999), Laurence Rickels uses the psychoanalytic mechanism of projection to account for the schizoid split at the very roots of the cultural imaginary haunted by violence. The force of perpetual mutual devouring caused by the hunger of this unrecognized underside of being is at the bottom of European identity:

> Even as I attack Eastern Europe, it is the East that threatens to attack the West; it is not we who are actively colonizing (and in effect cannibalizing) the East: it is the East that is packed with animals and subhumans whose

drive Westward we must stop in our tracks back East. The threat, embodied, for example, as vampirism, always comes from the East (from Eastern Europe, for example), even when at all times it is the West that is doubling over with hunger.[8]

The oral fantasy of devouring and incorporation present in the blood-sucking of the vampire is not limited to the post-human nation of 'the serbs,' but represents the violent origin repressed by any imagined community within the symbolic extensions of Europe. Both imperial and "Eastern" others provide an ideal cultural screen for the projection of the eternal hunger of the vampire dormant within the West itself, spreading from its European roots into the colonial domains. According to Rickels, others are often imagined as agents of that eternal being intent on robbing us of the precious life force that defines our individual and group identity. If we do not act first and pre-empt our own loss by consuming the other, his otherness threatens to lodge itself deeply within US and taint our blood and race with the illicit desires of the vampire. During the 1990s, the global power of the U.S.-led West was forged through military intervention as a result of culturally profiling 'the serbs' as post-communist vampires. Acting out the repressed origins of national unconscious, a locus where the secrets of violence and sexuality are openly displayed as the traumatic effect of those old centuries, this type of cultural imaginary itself enacted a form of violence justified by the invocation of human rights.

The cultural imaginary of "other" European nations in the modern period resulted from the longing by the emergent middle classes for the days of their own imperial glory, a past imagined as a full presence of their own national being and belonging. The fall of smaller nations under the imperial rule of great powers was reinterpreted during the course of the very long nineteenth century in the agonistic key of liberation at any cost. Before the moments of national emergence, those marginal peoples were not well established in the West; they served more as the invisible reflection of the vampire in the Gothic literary mirror. However different the specific conditions of imperial enslavement have been for each particular nation of "other" Europe, the reinvention of the nation and its culture during the modern emergence took place in the context of multiple revolutionary legacies that strove against this global invisibility.

As Larry Wolff and Maria Todorova have already established in their influential works on the topic of "othering" Eastern Europe and the Balkans, the West tends to construct these localities as imaginary assemblages that display a "less civilized" version of identity for the gaze of Europe proper. Starting in the eighteenth century, these perceptions have been enforced by enlightened travelers who ventured into the proverbial "lands in-between" to discover the superiority of their own, Western civilizations. It is not surprising that the narrative of *Dracula* begins with Jonathan Harker's eastward journey, where he encounters the being of eternal and timeless void. The contradictions of European identity and its cross-cultural exchanges are embodied in the figure of the vampire as the subterranean divinity of violence lingering in the cultural zone populated by the minor Balkan nations.

This type of cultural imaginary simplifies the complexities of past events, creating an uncanny relationship to the present that is lived and understood as an extension of ancient traumas that constitute the actually existing memory of the nation. This type of relationship to the past has nothing to do with historical understanding as an accurate chronology and description of the past; rather, it infuses the realm of the national with fantasies that obliterate any desire for understanding in the present. This phantasm of the present lacks fullness when compared with the overwhelming power Stoker's hero imputes to the heroic legacy of old centuries. The emptiness of the present is characteristic of the emerging national cultures revealed by Jonathan Harker's seeing "no sign of a man" in the mirror when he encounters the apparition of the eternal count. "The whole room behind me was displayed; but there was no sign of a man in it, except myself."[9]

The void of identity devouring those other Europeans is manifested in the perceived inability to reflect and be reflected, since the magic mirror of history can only account for the imperial gaze proper to the Ottoman Turkish, Austro-German, or Russian political and military entities. At the same time, the narratives of imperial domination dovetail with local narratives of blood and belonging to establish a symbolic link to Europe, imagined as a cultural ideal that is out of reach for the peripheral and minor Europeans. Yet these lesser national assemblages remain invisible to the world at large, hidden and doomed to isolation they seek to avoid at any price. Therefore, their nature is constructed as the apparition that is exemplary of the violence the imperial centers have been keen on rendering invisible rather than recognizing as constitutive of their own "civilized" identity.

The return of the vampire as the metaphor for old centuries ruling the violent world of small Balkan nations is part of the imaginary economy based on visions of past glory that mimic the desire hidden within the imperial centers of power and domination. The codification of "national" tongues and the creation of literary canons that capture the people's voice reflect the folkloric version of the "glorious" past naturalized to account for the agonistic vision of a particular cultural identity as first beheld by the imperial European other. While invisible to the inhabitants of Europe proper in the present, these other Europeans strive to close the temporal gap at any price and reach the elusive world of modernity they envision in the imperial centers. Assuming an identity apart from the agonistic phantasm to which they are subjected by the gaze of the imperial center becomes increasingly impossible as they reproduce the violence of old centuries that "cannot be killed by mere modernity," refusing to even acknowledge the existence of the present. The words imputed to the notorious Transylvanian count resurrect a temporality symptomatic of this imaginary bias that constitutes 'the serbs' as the most recent phantasm of violence produced by the global media culture as a fantasy of return to the most ancient of its "historical" territories (i.e., Kosovo).

The vampire figures in Stoker's imaginary as a channel for the Gothic narratives of blood that stain a proper European understanding of the past while simultaneously framing the temporal context for understanding the otherness of Oriental Europe. The remark about the old centuries is recorded in a diary written by Harker, the protagonist-narrator of *Dracula*. The European Orient is visualized through this discursive lens, placing it in an imaginary region with a temporal delay of a few centuries, featuring violent desires that appear alien yet also vaguely familiar to the Western traveler. Within the context of British imperial discourse, the cultural imaginary is also colored by the encounter with colonial subjects in Africa and Asia as the phantasm of cultural otherness is transferred onto the figures visualized on the periphery of one's European identity.

Earlier accounts of travelers confirm these uncanny perceptual equiv-

alencies between 'the serbs' as a phantasm deriving from imperial encounters with colonized peoples elsewhere. Lady Mary Montague was
quick to notice that Orthodox priests "let their beards and hair grow just
like the Indian Brahmins" during her travels through Serbia.[10] 'The
serbs' are visualized as transitional people between Europe and Asia, at
once alien and exotic because of the unclear and hybrid identity they
have acquired through violent encounter with the Ottoman Empire.
'The serbs' function as an extended metaphor for the entire symbolic
region of the Balkans by virtue of this intermediary status, since the
West imagines the Balkans "not as other, but as an incomplete self."[11]
Positioning themselves as innovators, the intellectuals of other Europe
were always torn between the imaginary mirror of the West in which
they remained invisible and "nativist" rhetoric that tended to demonize
the West while favoring the local. The nativist drives of the nineteenth-
century national elites featured displays of songs and dance as the core
of communal identity, forgetting that this domestic *Volksmuseum* came
about as an effect of the imperial gaze that transformed them into
ethnic subjects in the first place.

The native imagination of so-called Oriental Europeans was formed
by feeble bourgeois longing for the days of freedom before they fell into
the hands of the Ottomans, the Habsburgs, or the Romanovs. This dy-
nastic triangle was constructed as the opposite of native cultures in
terms of natural purity, and foreign domination could never fully erase
—in fact, succeeded in multiplying—the local sense of victimization.
This contributed to the longevity of the cultural performance that led to
the emergence of the vampire nation. For Balkan nationalists, the continuing presence of Islamic populations among the Christians was a sign
of their own shameful backwardness, which had been brought about by
slavery and subjugation. The former master was constructed simultaneously as the hated oppressor and, inevitably, as the closest model for
cultural mimesis. After the collapse of the Ottoman Empire, Slavic
Christians' emergence from submission to Islam was followed by virtual
identification with the imperial values of the former masters, inverting
Muslim scorn for "dogs and infidels" who did not know the true faith
and applying it to those who betrayed the faith of the forefathers by
converting to Islam. The cultural imaginary born of past traumas sustained the long-gone days of imperial glory while simultaneously assimilating the worst features of the former master's political behavior.

In the realm of the cultural imaginary, both the eastern and western parts of Europe share this fascination with old centuries, with the archaic register that continues to haunt the national imagination with a secret vampire who refuses to die the natural death of everyday humans. The "mere modernity" that is clearly characteristic of more powerful European nations is entrusted with the task of keeping past violence secret and invisible by supplementing narratives of the nation through the emergence of the vampire as a dominant image in popular culture. Stoker's Gothic response to the vampire plagues of the eighteenth century invokes the impossible killing of the new temporality by the old one, in which Europe is featured as the agent of a superior force of civilization that nevertheless imagines the return of the living dead on its Oriental peripheries.

The Dracula Connection

Is it a coincidence that the name "Dracula" is derived from the Vlax bastardization of the Order of the Drakon, the name of the order Vlad's father received from Holy Roman Emperor Sigismund for resisting the incursions of the Ottoman armies into its Eastern territories? Once again, Central Europe and the Balkans are joined in the figure of the historical count through the symbolic value of the cross, as both regions are poised to defend Europe proper from Islamic conquest and domination. Dracula's own aristocratic heritage is supplemented by the nationalist rhetoric of Stoker's day, as well.

The question of the eastern boundary of Europe is posed again and again as the ultimate question lingers: Can this imaginary delimitation of Europe be drawn before Islam or not? Just like a fixation with the symbolic value of Kosovo appropriated by 'the serbs,' Dracula discovers his familial origin in the struggle against Islamic domination. When Jonathan Harker asks the mysterious count about his racial pedigree, the vampire, who is supposed to be terrified by the cross, identifies himself as a Voivoda, a noble duke ready to avenge "the shame of Kosovo":

> When was redeemed that great shame of Kosovo, when the flags of the Vlax and the Magyar went down beneath the Crescent; who was it but one of my own race who as Voivoda crossed the Danube and beat the Turk on his own ground! This was a Dracula indeed.[12]

Dracula's age transcends the bounds of a single human life and projects itself back into a past that provides him with sustenance to avenge "the shame of Kosovo," an imaginary location still quite memorable at the end of the nineteenth century, not just for 'the serbs' but for the literary imaginary of the West. Stoker's Gothic imaginary posits Kosovo as a sign of a pan-European struggle against "Turkey in Europe" in the name of the Balkan Christians who lived in subjection to their Islamic masters for centuries. The "humanitarian intervention" of the U.S.-led West ostensibly to rescue the Kosovar Albanians from 'the serbs' in 1999 reverses the civilizational pattern established at the end of the nineteenth century by intervening in the name of a predominantly Islamic minority. The phantom of 'the serbs' as figurative vampires of the new world order is reinforced by this reversal, allowing the West to show itself off as the impartial arbiter of ethnic tolerance while in reality destroying the last remnants of a South Slavic communist state.

The cultural imaginary functions here as a time-delayed mirror image of past traumas that are proper to multiple European collectivities, which are projected onto 'the serbs' through visual narratives of global news networks as they disseminate the real-time history of the Balkans. Dracula's speech about the need to avenge "the shame of Kosovo" functioned as a source of ventriloquism in the speeches of Western leaders during NATO's bombing of the former Yugoslavia. Bill Clinton even called on literature when he wrote, during the bombing, that in his vision of the world, "The Balkans are not fated to be the heart of darkness."[13] Although it is done through negation, the Balkans here are invoked as a location with Gothic undertones that make it comparable to Joseph Conrad's imaginary Africa.

The Gothic imaginary had been especially vivid in the figure of the Serbian leader, Slobodan Milošević, whose Kurtz-like persona provided the U.S.-led West with a perfect alibi for embarking on yet another civilizing mission to pacify the reawakened rage of 'the serbs.' Clinton's invocation of darkness, in the wake of NATO's intervention, provided a new frame for the leader of the vampire nation. The name of Milošević, the last communist president in Europe, has often been invoked to justify interventions against 'the serbs,' especially because of his willingness to sacrifice innocent civilians for the sake of his own bloodthirsty race. The distance between Clinton's and Stoker's Gothic vision of the Balkans as a European heart of darkness grew narrower every day, as 'the serbs' ended the twentieth century on the punishing end of Western civilization. The use of televisual images to disseminate narratives about the Yugoslav wars contributed to the awakening of global fear and hatred by displaying the effects of ethnic passions rooted in stories about a bloody yet glorious past that is not compatible with the present, post–Cold War global order.

The vision of 'the serbs' as the most violent of Balkan national assemblages became emblematic of the entire ethnoscape in speeches justifying Western intervention. Contaminated by the closeness of 'the serbs,' their neighbors were imagined as dominoes that would keep collapsing, spreading disorder from the Balkans into the heart of Europe itself. Those subjects who posses the heart of darkness, which marks their culture as temporally lagging and socially inferior, are portrayed as unable to understand what they are doing to one another. The peasants Harker encounters on the way to Dracula's castle are perceived in the same manner—as autistic creatures that "have neither eyes [n]or ears for the outer world."[14] This coding of the irrational peasant is symptomatic of the cultural imaginary that Jonathan Harker reads into this subterranean Europe, which is unaffected by the "mere modernity." As the narrator of *Dracula*, Harker suggests that the civilizing power of human technology cannot overcome the ancient creature of old centuries nurtured in archaic blindness to progress and enlightenment. The bounds of proper European identity are constantly caught up in this game of downward gazing at the next irrational threat of violence by the bloodthirsty neighbor to the south or east who is prone to ignorance of the conditions that exist in the world at large.

The political and military conflicts that erupted within the former Yugoslav federation were interpreted by the global media complex in accordance with this type of imaginary—as events that were motivated by ancient and irrational ethnic hatreds confined to the undesirable legacy of old centuries. This type of external gaze required an expedient military intervention that would bring to people who were unable to rule themselves some guidance and protection from the U.S.-led West. Needless to say, the colonially motivated genocide in which those same democracies have been engaged for centuries hardly provided an adequate moral justification to mediate the Balkan conflicts.

The cultural imaginary of the Gothic period, constituted at the end of the nineteenth century in English-language literature, has been transformed into a discursive lens for understanding the Balkans and its apparently endless violent confrontations. The last decade of the twentieth century added one more collective phantasm visualized through the lens of the Gothic imaginary: the bloodthirsty specter of 'the serbs' as the vampires of the post-communist period.

Established in media representations from the U.S.-led West as the postmodern incarnation of violence as such, the specter of 'the serbs' continued to haunt the global imaginary with apparent excesses until Milošević was overthrown in October 2000. The swift return to the world of Serbs as "regular humans" after that magical moment places a large shadow of doubt over previous representations of the collective assemblage in the global media universe. The producers of our world of daily information have been working extremely hard to resurrect the vampire nation in its Balkan home by promoting the representation of this small but predatory race as the main political challenge to the values and humanist legacy of Europe. This epistemic regime established the Balkans as a territory ruled by excessive force and violent sexuality whose temporal regression to the old centuries brought to life a new nation of violent communists-turned-nationalists. The sacrificial mechanism underlying this type of violent cultural imaginary was made visible by featuring Kosovo, a locality that 'the serbs' guarded as a precious wound that served as a reminder of their subjugation to the Islamic master. This was the bloody altar of their collective identity, where loss could be transformed into victory through imaginary cultural displacement: military defeat by the Oriental empire was imagined as a starting point for making death the centerpiece of the reborn vampire nation.

The mirage of "Greater Serbia" often invoked in the 1990s to justify intervention against 'the serbs' was also conceived in history by the Habsburgs to justify invading Serbia in the First World War. In fact, this imaginary mechanism served as a perfect cover for continuing NATO in the post–Cold war period, when it started to become clear that NATO was fast becoming a military organization without a clear mission.

Another important landmark was achieved during the war against 'the serbs' in 1999 when the precedent of bypassing the framework of the United Nations and the sovereignty of a nation-state was set. This was the first step in the US-led West's open identification with the role it imputed to 'the serbs' in the Balkan context—that is, the excessive aggressiveness the West brought to bear on the "vampiric" collective became part of its strategy in the global realm, as issues of security and "regime change" dominated political discourse during the reign of George Bush Jr.

Huntington's theory of the inevitable clash between the bearers of different civilizations takes for granted the supreme position of the U.S.-led West as the bearer of manifest destiny. Hidden from view is the predatory projection of the last remaining superpower as the vampire of vampires. The *chupacabra*, the mysterious blue-eyed goat sucker with a pale face and sharp teeth of Hispanic popular culture, became emblematic of the emergence of the United States as the vampire nation after the Cold War. A reverse racist imagery pops up in this representation, although the "politically correct" discourse goes to great lengths to disguise it and translate it into a non-genetic construct by redefining belonging to a community as part of religious and cultural heritage. Since the Latin American countries were the first to experience the violent hunger of their northern neighbor, the haunting of *chupacabras* made manifest the horror of domination that later would spread to other regions of the world that the last remaining superpower targeted because of their strategic value. The Balkans have emerged yet again as transitional territory linking the historical heritage of vampirism with its current global incarnation: the global empire as a vampire, thirsty for oil and labor of the cheapest kind and unwittingly usurping the problematic and violent heritage of the Gothic vampires.

The exemplarity with which the global media have endowed 'the serbs' for their ethnic crimes has created a climate in which notions of collective responsibility and punishment have been resurrected to justify military intervention that bypasses existing international law. Native intolerance was imputed to 'the serbs' while their neighbors were represented almost exclusively as victims of forced ethnic displacement, mass rape, torture, and massacre inside and outside concentration camps. The vampire metaphor was also used as a media shield behind which U.S. client nations (Israel, Turkey) could continue to brutalize their ethnic minorities (Palestinians, Kurds) on a scale that is at least comparable to the suffering of victims of ethnic violence in the Balkans. The enemies of 'the serbs' were therefore welcomed with understanding by the U.S.-led West, since the crimes committed against the vampire nation seemed fully justified by media coverage in the wake of the violence and other horrors that occurred during the wars in Croatia and Bosnia-Herzegovina.

The transformation of ethnic pride into a tool of neo-nationalism by Slobodan Milošević in the 1980s, coupled with an undecided strategic status, has resulted in political, economic, and cultural exclusion from the global community, transforming 'the serbs' into a spectral population in a shrinking common state. 'The serbs' were not the dominant nation in the former Yugoslavia; rather, they played the role of "ethnic glue" by being dispersed around the territory of that nonexistent country. This cultural adhesive was subjected to corrosive solutions by the United States, because undoing communist forms of political association was paramount in imposing the new world order espoused by George Bush Sr. and Ronald Reagan. The grotesque disproportion between the military puniness and the swollen national pride of 'the serbs' has made them a perfect surrogate victim to place on the altar of the newfound NATO unity, during the bombing of the former Yugoslavia in 1999, that was celebrated with a grand ball in Washington. Their struggle for a common state was read as a return of the old centuries that deserves only one, decisively powerful response from what former U.S. Secretary of State Madeline Albright called "our splendid military" at the time of the intervention. While all of the other ethnic groups in the former Yugoslavia have been granted the rights of nation-states, 'the serbs' have been looked on with suspicion when they have acted on the same desire.

The Skull Tower

What motivates 'the serbs' to cling to their "historic territories" with such violent passion? The cultural imaginary that originated in the anti-Islamic worldview that is deeply rooted in the heritage of Eurocentric visions of identity has been a major dimension of their national emergence since the nineteenth century. The destiny of Balkan Christians under the Ottoman yoke was a favorite topic of learned discussion among the Romantics and their heirs in the West, as well. Let us not forget Lord Byron and the location of his vampiric Lord Ruthven in a Muslim graveyard somewhere in Greece, connecting the spectral heritage of Europe to its undying Balkan roots. With the notable exception of England, Europe's politicians supported the Islamic withdrawal and dissolution of the Ottoman Empire in the Balkans during the nineteenth century; this was no doubt an attempt by "mere modernity" to come to terms with the injustices of the half-millennium of bondage endured by Balkan Christians. 'The serbs' were invented as an ethnic entity exactly as vampire plagues emerged in the Habsburg Empire; as modern ideas of nationalism were grafted onto the heritage of old centuries through the enforcement of a "not-quite-like-us" vision of identity of the emergent political subjects of the crumbling Ottoman Empire.

The continent responded to the English fascination with Balkan hauntings not only through Goethe's and Herder's Romantic longing for old centuries visualized among singing and dancing Slavs, but also through the French versions of the vampire legends by Charles Nodier and Alexandre Dumas père. Nodier was a government official in Ljubljana, where he encouraged the collection of Slavic oral tradition before writing down his own version of the *conte fantastique* (fantastic story) in "Le Vampire" in 1820. Nodier's stories establish a connection between violence and sexuality that would play an ever greater role in the development of the Gothic imaginary, especially in regard to sadomasochism. Dumas saw a play based on Nodier's story as a young man and produced a version of his own in 1851, borrowing liberally from Byron, especially in the title character of Lord Ruthven, whose revenant nature he expressed with the formula, "His love is death." The esthetic appreciation of the formerly decaying corpse of the Balkan oral tradition in the new fantastic literature of Europeans marked a definite shift in the representation of the vampire, establishing an imaginary relationship to this location that would spill over into the discourses of history and, ultimately, politics.

In 1849, Alexander W. Kinglake published the travelogue *Eothen* ("from the dawn," in ancient Greek) devoted to his journey to the Ottoman lands. Of all of the buildings he saw in "Servia," one captured his imagination much more than any other: The Ćele Kula, or Skull Tower, erected by the Ottoman authorities using the heads of Stevan

The Skull Tower: Gothic imaginary on the outskirts of Niš (Serbia). PHOTOGRAPH COURTESY B. GAJIĆ.

Sindjelić and his rebels as a warning to 'the serbs' who might contemplate any further uprising against the sultan. Kinglake was impressed by the "simple grandeur of the architect's conception" of a building for which about three hundred skulls were provided by 'the serbs' who blew themselves up in an ammunition storage area rather then surrender to impalement and other forms of torture. Kinglake was also struck by "the exquisite beauty of the fretwork" formed by the outlines of the human remains, giving voice to an emergent aesthetic appreciation of the violence that would come to dominate the vision of this part of the world in the next centuries.[15]

However, the first modern transformation of 'the serbs' into the other of Europe came on the eve of the Great War of 1914, the war to end all wars that was meant to be the ultimate proving ground of European masculinity. It was at that time that the menacing specter of 'the serbs' was invoked once again by Austria-Hungary, the last imperial power to die in *Mitteleuropa*, as a menace that threatened to invade its protectorate in Bosnia-Herzegovina. This was the first time that the specter of "Greater Serbia" was invoked by an imperial power to mask its own desire for conquest and domination. On the eve of the First World War, the proletarian feminist Clara Zetkin warned against identifying with the imperial narratives about the violence of small nations:

> The horrible specter before which the people of Europe tremble has become reality. The war is ready to crush human bodies, dwelling places and fields. Austria has used the senseless outrage of a twenty-year-old Serbian lad against the Successor to the Throne, as a pretext for a criminal outrage against the sovereignty and independence of the Serbian people and in the final analysis, against the peace of Europe.[16]

The lowly peasant race was accused of spreading its contagious nationalism into the Austro-Hungarian protectorate through the Black Hand secret organization, invoking once again the Gothic color of negativity. The assassination of Archduke Ferdinand in Sarajevo, the pretext for mounting an attack on Serbia, was interpreted in accordance with an already established imaginary relationship toward 'the serbs' as the vampire nation. The challenge to the last Central European empire was greeted by working-class writers such as Zetkin as an act of terrorist desperation to preserve imperial domination of the lands of the Southern Slavs.

Targeted by the Austro-Hungarian Empire for their vampiric propensities, 'the serbs' served as a spectral lure to involve all of Europe in that war to end all wars at the beginning of the twentieth century. This type of cultural imaginary was engendered as a response to being visualized and classified as an example of an endemically violent identity, whose thirst for blood and soil of others had no justification in reality. A curious fact about the Balkans is that its reputation as the "powder keg" of Europe originated during the First World War, when film was used for the first time ever to reproduce the violence of a war zone for Western viewers. According to Frank Stern, "Over twenty cameramen filmed the Balkan Wars of 1912–13. By 1913, most Balkan governments had banned filming by foreign correspondents, so the film companies resorted to staging the action—which soon became a media event or pseudo-event. In the Balkan Wars, a Danish cameraman and a British aristocrat who had failed to arrive in time for a deadly battle staged some battles on location."[17] This staging of violence haunts the region well into the present day, creating a vast imaginary repertoire that can be activated anytime a need arises to produce evidence of endemic Balkan violence.

Locating Violence

The racist implication of the political discourse about 'the serbs' has rarely been analyzed for fear that one may be equated with them and their bloodthirsty quest for ethnic purity. I am questioning this accepted truism with that risk in mind, hoping that I will be able to both deconstruct the effects of the intentional misreading of 'the serbs' by the media and the public relations industry and contribute to reorienting the local culture away from sacrificial narratives of blood and belonging. The most successful coup carried out by the information industry in the West has been the conflation of war crimes committed by 'the serbs' during the 1990s with those of the German Nazis during the 1930s and 1940s.

By invoking the Holocaust of the European Jews as a metaphor for reading violence in the Balkans, 'the serbs' have been represented as a genocidal nation intent on systematically annihilating their neighbors. However, this erroneous conflation not only falsifies the motivating force underlying the actual events in the Balkans; it also demeans the unique character of the Holocaust of European Jewry. In fact, these "other" Europeans, who are denied a sense of proper belonging to Europe, have been tainted with shades of cultural "blackness" that are most often tied to either their non-Western origins or their belonging to the religious cultures of Orthodox Christianity, Judaism, or Islam. The variability of cultural difference is in fact used as a marker of a lower standard of civilization, practically subsuming all of the people to the east and south of an imaginary center as subject to a set of practices that are tacitly incompatible with a proper European identity. This subtle form of racism has been operating throughout Europe since nationalism initially rose as the dominant ideology of the new middle classes, as Freud noted in his characterization of chauvinism as "narcissism of minor differences."[18] Therefore, an assemblage of vampire nations bare their bloody fangs once again, this time in the aftermath of the Cold War, invoking a terrifying sense of humor through the images disseminated by the global media.

The uneasy blending of laughter and horror in the dissemination of the Gothic imaginary testifies to the possibility of a simultaneous cultural representation of the parodic and non-parodic elements of the vampire figure. The past horror is supplemented by the uneasy laughter of the Western viewer when confronted with excessive violence and sexuality inherent in the representation of the Balkans. A completely non-parodic representation of Dracula is hardly possible, since Jonathan Harker's gaze at the East is imbued with the absurd bias nurtured by the cultural imaginary of the Gothic period. The simultaneous rising fame of the vampire in Hollywood movies throughout this century speaks of the fascination with violence and laughter that has marked the millennial temporality in the broader sense, as well. A good example is Roman Polanski's *Fearless Vampire Killers* (1968), which plays up the humorous aspect of vampirism by featuring an intentionally artificial Transylvania to emphasize the arbitrary nature of geopolitical imaginary.

The poetics of laughable violence have been resurrected in an emergent Hollywood movie form in parallel with the Wars of Yugoslav Succession (1991–95). Cynical laughter was the cinematic response to the "compassion fatigue" with which Western viewers suffered after perpetual displays of violence and bloodshed in media representations of Yugoslavia. The irony produced by a number of remakes of vampire films, including Francis Ford Coppola's *Bram Stoker's Dracula* (1992), as well as the success of Quentin Tarantino's *Pulp Fiction* (1994), which does not refer directly to vampires yet invokes the specter of funny violence, was symptomatic of the reception of real political tragedies within the popular-culture industry. While innocent civilians died at the hands of their post-communist masters in the former Yugoslavia, the global "dream factory" disseminated this type of violent imaginary, normalizing its reception by resurrecting the new and old cultural stereotypes about the Balkans.

Post-communist vEmpires

The mechanism of cross-cultural displacement of violent legacy between the centers of imperial power and the less than visible outlines of the cultural periphery is evident in the representations of post-communist realities in the former Yugoslavia during the 1990s.[19] After self-management by workers and the foreign policy of non-alignment failed, Yugoslavia became the synonym for, and symptom of, political practices whose violence was deemed emblematic of the entire Balkan region by a host of newly anointed experts clamoring for a determined military response from the centers of Western power.

Resurrecting past traumas became the favorite pastime of national-ist intellectuals within Yugoslavia to justify the conflict that began in 1991. The religious roots of each particular nation were suddenly re-discovered in the medieval legacy of old centuries, supplemented by the demands of the emerging consumer societies that already were in line with the global vision of the U.S.-led West. The modernizing social in-fluences achieved by Tito and his comrades were to be removed along-side communism as religion and its proponents gained unprecedented influence in outlining the shape of the mutually opposed national iden-tities of the post-Yugoslav states. These mutually exclusive visions of national identities caused the Yugoslav skeleton to fracture along lines that coincided with those of the former empires as the resurrection of ancient cultural imaginaries led to bloody confrontations between the former South Slavic brothers.

The secret of violence and its success in destroying working-class solidarity rests in the complex relationship between global and local forms of the cultural imaginary that have been used to motivate con-flict around the same fault lines that divided the former Ottoman and Habsburg empires more than a century ago, as well as the eastern and western Roman empires almost a millennium ago. At the same time, the terms set by the emergent nationalist elites differed: 'The serbs' were imagined as defenders of the ruined Yugoslav castle, enabling them to maintain the common time–space, while the rest of their separatist brothers favored imagining a new vision of identity for their emerging communities. The U.S.-led West could not help but favor this new vision of blood, since the enemies of 'the serbs' were also the enemies of a principal Cold War enemy, the Russian-led Soviet Union. The coarse filter of global cultural profiling missed the fact that Yugo-slavia was a homegrown workers' state whose skeleton was patched up after the horrors of two world wars and its mutual genocides and clas-sified 'the serbs' as the Orthodox Christian representatives who would possibly aid the strategic southward expansion of the newly national-ized Russia.

It is not hard to recognize the logic of Huntington's "clash of civiliza-tions" in applying this type of cultural imaginary to the complex web of intercommunal relationships in the Balkans and the rest of the global ethnoscape. This vision tacitly recognizes violence as inevitable in zones of insurmountable cultural differences, some of which can come in quite handy in defeating the chimera of communism as the principal ideological enemy of the global capital. A different ethical principle was clearly required to solve the ethnic puzzle presented by Yugoslavia—a politics based on Derrida's principle of infinite respon-sibility, which does not allow easy cultural profiling of the violence taking place "there" without taking into account what happens "here," closest to home. It is not possible to stop at the boundary of identity proper to our own community while judging the violence that happens in areas that seem remote and alien at first sight. The genocidal spec-ters resurrected during the Wars of Yugoslav Succession and tied to the names of Yugoslavia, Bosnia, or Kosovo cannot be properly compre-hended without taking into account the way in which the discourses about these locations as emblems of violence have been constituted within the core of identity that clearly belongs to European cultural heritage.

The national identities of most NATO nations that intervened in the Yugoslav conflict were formed by making invisible the violence they were so eager to visualize in the Balkans via the prosthetic aid of the global televisual media. In fact, by treating this type of violence as something alien to the common ancestry of Europe and its glorious civilization, they could justify the use of violence to put the stake through the heart of the post-communist revenant embodied by 'the serbs.' This ethnic phantasm represented a perfect spectral phenome-non, functioning as a scarecrow to intimidate those who were asking very rational questions about the existence of NATO after the end of the Cold War. During the 1990s, this phantasm had replaced both the specter of Marxism and the Soviet "Big Brother" as threatening appari-tions of humanity gone wrong. This emergence of 'the serbs' as vam-pires from the ruins of the Yugoslav castle during the 1990s set the stage for the replaying of the past European traumas of blood and belonging in a markedly Gothic manner.

The past struggles and traumas of the European nations gave shape to their current union through world wars and bloodshed that conveniently have been repressed and projected onto the former Yugoslavia. What Derrida calls "the secret of European responsibility" is the motivating factor behind various forms of "balkanization" executed during the last decade of the past millennium in the global ethnoscape. This secret is encoded as silence in the narratives that provide the nation with a story of its particular becoming, a silence born of violence that paradoxically guarantees its very being and becoming, like the biblical parable of Abraham and Isaac that Derrida analyzes in *The Gift of Death*. The bloody origin of each collective assemblage of meaning is repressed and kept silent, as the territory it inhabits becomes endowed with a sacred character. The oral traditions that are sung about Kosovo as a site of symbolic emergence of 'the serbs' after the tragic struggle and defeat at the hands of the Ottoman invaders elaborate this kind of narrative becoming that constitutes the national imaginary of minor Balkan nations. The call of blood to sacrifice others is at the root of this populist interpellation, manifested in the vampire.

The specter of 'the serbs' reinforces the Gothic vision of the Balkans as a site where "the old centuries had, and have powers of their own which mere modernity cannot kill," as established in chapter 3 of Bram Stoker's *Dracula*. Yugoslavia is the skeleton in Europe's closet, a place where civilizational and racial others are repressed, sanctioned, and eventually destroyed. Subjects who identify with the U.S.-led West have the luxury of conveniently forgetting that almost two centuries separate them from the various types of East (Eastern Europe, Near East, Middle East, Far East) in terms of this type of bloody "national becoming." Seeing itself as enlightened and endowed with "good conscience," the U.S.-led West casts itself in the role of a Balkan vampire slayer by applying its techno-supremacist logic of manifest destiny to rule the rest of the global domain.

The seventy-eight days of "humanitarian" bombing in 1999 were also marked by the power of the Gothic imaginary. The operation itself bore the name "Merciful Angel" to counter the violent performance of 'the serbs,' who were obviously cast in the demonic role of European vampires. At the same time, the U.S.-led West employed weapons whose names invoked the same sinister imaginary: Stealth, Phantom, Nighthawk. The link between 'the serbs' and their righteous slayers betrays a common origin of the desire for domination inherent in national narratives imagined as extending beyond life itself. The refusal of the U.S.-led West to see its own imperial image in the emergence of 'the serbs' reveals the cultural mechanism that is instrumental in imposing the rule of global superpower over the rest of the world. Local atrocities tied to 'the serbs' are always seen as exemplary and exceptional, requiring "peacekeeping" operations and media management to distance the unruly natives from the properly imperial desire that belongs to the United States. By transforming this part of Europe into a unique proving grounds of its military power, the emergent vEmpire extended the symbolic domain of the West through the range of its cruise missiles and the vision of the satellite and prepared the rest of the world for the conquests of strategic resources that were to come with its millennial adventures in the Middle East.

Vampires Like US

Contrary to the popular belief disseminated in the media, the notion of the nation as a pure entity is not what caused the excesses of genocide and war crimes in the former Yugoslavia. The phantasm of 'the serbs,' in fact, was formed in opposition to the role they had played as the ethnic glue that kept socialist Yugoslavia together, as their nationalism was portrayed as a cause for the policies of "ethnic cleansing."

In fact, their collective imaginary was constituted not by ideas of national separation and ethnic purity but by a striving for the assimilation of ethnic others and a common space that used to be represented by Yugoslavia. What drove 'the serbs' to war and crimes, at least initially, was a desire to preserve a common territory and confront the separatism and anticommunism of other nations within Yugoslavia. Ethnic cleansing or "humanitarian resettlement," the euphemism used in local public discourse, occurred in the ethnically heterogeneous regions of Croatia, Bosnia, and Kosovo, where 'the serbs' represented the most common ethnic denominator of the South Slavic socialist republic. They were dispersed throughout the former Yugoslav republic, with the notable exception of Slovenia, constituting almost half the population of the entire country. It was therefore necessary for the newly independent states to neutralize 'the serbs' and make them disappear from their new national territories to affirm their own sovereignty.

The reawakening of violence as the cultural imaginary to visualize the Balkans in the first half of the 1990s was tied to conceptions of time and identity that are seemingly out of joint with the West's hegemonic vision of human rights. It is perhaps understandable that the new imperial masters have intentionally overlooked the crimes of other Yugoslav nations to justify the breakup of the common state and of a solidarity based on communism. But it is odd that an otherwise sophisticated postcolonial theoretician such as Homi Bhabha has bought into this line of reasoning and felt obliged to write about 'the serbs' as the dark agents of nationalist fervor:

> The hideous extremity of Serbian nationalism proves that the very idea of a pure, "ethnically cleansed" national identity can only be achieved through the death, literal and figurative, of the complex interweavings of history, and the culturally contingent borderlines of modern nationhood. This side of the psychosis of patriotic fervor, I like to think, there is overwhelming evidence of a more transnational and translational sense of the hybridity of imagined communities.[20]

The logic and hegemony of the dominant cultural imaginary turns Bhabha's theoretical apparatus into the same hegemonic understanding of "Serbian nationalism" as the anomalous case of that modern narrative of the nation. Despite Bhabha's assurance that 'the serbs' are the exception and that subjects "this side of the psychosis of patriotic fervor" may be able to articulate a different vision of the nation, one is forced to ask a very difficult question concerning nationalism in general.

Could there really be "this side" that evades the grasp of desire for the imagined community to feed off the blood of its ethnic others? After a community has been plunged into violence to justify its survival, is there really a location outside the grasp of the desire for the blood of ethnic others? Doesn't the truth of the nation strike much closer to home—or, in Derrida's words, "What is happening *there* translates what happens *here*, always here, wherever one is and wherever one looks." If the ethics of infinite responsibility could be enacted globally, the specter of "vampires like us"—'the serbs'—needs its proper supplement in "vampires like US," the specter of global domination that, in teaching the world a lesson, subjected 'the serbs' to the ostensibly innocent gaze of its entire political spectrum: from the right-wing anti-communists to the human-rights activists and postcolonial theorists.

It is obvious that what Bhabha calls "the hideous extremity of Serbian nationalism" is not the only path of communal struggle for emancipation. Yet failing to recognize that hideousness is not an innate and essential quality that underlies the national character of 'the serbs,' but a projection of phantasms about national purity that emerged from the hegemonic media gaze of the West points up a major failure to understand the historical specificities involved in the imaginary genesis of the vampire nation. However "humanitarian" the motivations for the Western military interventions in the Balkans may have been, the outcome has been the destruction, impoverishment, and dependence of both 'the serbs' and their ethnic enemies in the global economic order.

In the pages that follow, I will outline the complexities of that becoming to show the intertwined emergence of the imaginary in both the imperial centers of power and the very visible cultural margins inhabited by the assemblages for which the phantasm of 'the serbs' is just the most emblematic one for my own understanding of the process of national invention. The concept of the cultural imaginary guiding my analysis is an adaptation of the Lacanian "register of experience" characteristic of the human misapprehension of reality in the earliest stages of development. I understand the cultural imaginary as a network of meanings articulated through the narratives of the nation imprinted before the possibility of rational choice exists for the subject. It is a realm of phantasms tied to one's collective being, inculcated through the remnants of ritualistic structures that still operate within the network of modern social institutions. Needless to say, 'the serbs' represent such a phantasm within the global cultural landscape, providing myriad mirroring structures both for the native self and the alien other.

Profiled in *The Vampire Encyclopedia* as the cradle of vampirism in Europe, Serbia again has been resurrected by the global media as a location tied to the violent specters of bloody massacres, death camps, and mass graves. As if the real horrors of war were not enough, the evil had to be amplified by activating narratives of violent lust and irrational hostility to mediate the representation of 'the serbs' for the rest of the globe. At the same time, NATO's violent measures were represented as a sterile, surgical display of superior technology and military power in the service of human rights.

Bhabha's perception of violence resulting in the "death, literal and figurative of the complex interweavings of history, and the culturally contingent borderlines of modern nationhood" was a mechanism inherent in the logic of separation that the U.S.-led West has applied in the former Yugoslavia since 1991—not in the practice of ethnic cleansing and conquests to reclaim Kosovo from Muslim Albanians or achieving the dream of "Greater Serbia." It is startling that this misreading of the foremost postcolonial critic reveals the same traits of the cultural imaginary responsible for framing 'the serbs' as the vampire nation.

As real human suffering was transformed into units of information, the anticipated televisual erasure of old centuries turned into their instant replay. The world watched a war unfold in Europe for the first time since the defeat of Nazism, accompanied by narratives that invoked death camps and the planned extermination of ethnic others. The evil of war crimes perpetrated against those who were perceived as a threat to the new world order caused the displacement, "both literal and figurative," both of the nomadic clones signified by 'the serbs' and of numerous others around the world who were tainted by a different, dark, secret mark from the immediate past—communism. The perpetual violence built into the notion of Western liberal subjectivity needed to be kept secret by displaying it elsewhere: in the Balkans of the 1990s and, more problematically, in the excesses of Abu-Ghraib in the first decade of the new millennium.[21]

2

BLOODY TALES
Figurations of Masculinity in the Post-Oriental Condition

Mourning is regularly the reaction to the loss of a loved person, or to the loss of some abstraction that has taken the place of one, such as one's country, liberty, an ideal, and so on. In some people the same influences produce melancholia instead of mourning and we consequently suspect them of a pathological disposition.
—Sigmund Freud, "Mourning and Melancholia"

And he didn't like girls, he thought they could never offer that kind of enchantment; it was only misery, despair and desire for what has been lost that brought on real ecstasy.
—Miloš Crnjanski, Masculine Stories

The epic world knows only a single and unified worldview, obligatory and indubitably true for heroes as well as for authors and audiences.
—Mikhail M. Bakhtin, "The Epic and the Novel"

For most Balkan nations, the process of writing down the nation as a permanent trace of collective imaginary is permeated by the ambiguous relationship to imperial rule by an alien power. As the new nations emerged in the course of the nineteenth century, the submission was culturally coded as part of a shameful legacy that had to be left behind, yet it was never relegated to complete forgetfulness. The memory of violence served as the imaginary fuel for the collective identity of the nation on its way to independence and statehood. The nineteenth-century transition to modernity was marked by a simultaneous emergence from the clerical control of literacy by the Orthodox church and the literary codification of the trauma connected to Islamic domination for the nations in the Ottoman domain of control.

This uncertain legacy installed the legendary forefathers of the nation as the essential model of masculine identity for generations to come. The collective memory was established through the image of a nation in a post-Oriental condition, constructing its identity from the violent legacy of Ottoman domination. Ivo Andrić noticed this tendency early in his career: "Both our traditional and written literature had turned Turks into a wrath of God, into a kind of scarecrow that could be painted only with dark and bloody colors, something that could not be quietly talked about or coolly thought about."[1] The "dark and bloody" hue of the national imaginary established a particular form of the Balkan Gothic, featuring violence as the dominant cultural force in constructing its sense of collective identity. The vampire nation emerged through the metonymy of blood and soil, extending its cultural network to include the symbolic wound caused by the Oriental predator.

The liminal geographic position of the Balkans offers a unique possibility for examining the effects of imperial control over 'the serbs' as an imaginary construct traversing Europe and the "Orient." The trajectory of national becoming is determined by the interaction of violent imaginary and the cult of heroic masculinity engendered in response to it. Exclusion from the symbolic domain of Europe proper for almost five centuries was to be surmounted by over-identification with Europe, imagined as a return to the community of nations that shared an ambiguous ethos inherited from local renderings of the Christian legacy. The reversal in the usual Orientalist discourse outlined by Edward Said (masculine West dominating the feminized Orient) created specific conditions for the emergence of the post-Oriental condition in the Balkans as Christian nations struggled to overcome Islamic domination.[2]

Each Balkan ethnic group imagined its own "scarecrow" to serve as a negative against which masculinity could erect its particular version of the nation's heroic greatness. Since religious affiliation became the crucial determinant of ethnic belonging in the Balkans, 'the serbs' turned to "heaven" for guidance in their discursive emergence and often sought mythic and theological justification for the excess of violence in the new national vision of race, class, and gender. The stock cultural portrait of the Islamic subject turned into a conglomerate of foreign conqueror and domestic traitor whose existence, for the emerging national subject, proved to be alienating, degrading, and aggressive. The bloody images related to Islam persisted long after the initial liberation struggles of the nineteenth century were over and the Ottoman Empire had lost its influence in the Balkans. It was through the educational system, and particularly through the study of national literature in elementary and middle schools, that this type of cultural imaginary was disseminated among the majority of emergent Balkan nations.[3]

The permanent trace of the post-Oriental condition remains dormant in the imaginary as a secret ingredient of the cultural identity of the emerging Balkan nation. The writing down of oral tradition simultaneously created the first secular monument of national literature as *guslars'* ritual mourning of a collective trauma of Kosovo was pushed to the margins of popular cultural practice. Before the age of literacy, violence could be mourned and worked through in songs about the loss of freedom, power, and glory to the Ottomans at Kosovo in 1389. With literacy, the monumental version of the cultural imaginary became lodged within the national body as an indivisible particle that served as a model of masculinity of future heroes. Bakhtin's characterization of the epic as a monolithic genre that does not allow for the intrusion of discourses of the "other" is crucial for understanding how masculinity was engendered among 'the serbs.'

The monumental and exclusive truths of the nation are archived in the heroic poems written down by Vuk Karadžić during the period of national becoming. Vuk was an autodidact who, through his work as a linguist, ethnographer, translator, and literary historian, almost single-handedly created the foundation of the South Slavs' national culture. By encoding the popular songs performed by the guslars, he also contributed to establishing the national imaginary for 'the serbs.' The bloody tales, mediating between the heroes, events, and sites of the past and the present recipient of the narrative, permeate the enormous temporal gap between past events narrated in the oral tales and the present situation of the performer and his audience—the proverbial epic distance. The sublimation of the national trauma thus achieved a written form and circulated through the national imaginary as its figurative blood, causing the constant return to the lives of the ancient heroes who emerged to resist imperial domination and subjection. The

Father and son:
gusle singing and
the transmission
of masculinity.
PHOTOGRAPH COURTESY
B. GAJIĆ.

very fact that the epic deals with the nation's collective memory gives
it an official air and turns it into a cultural expression of the dominant discourse of heroic masculinity articulating the unholy truths of
the nation.

The Domination–Submission Formula

The formulas present in the oral tradition researched by Milman Parry
and Albert Lord not only consist of the mnemonic techniques developed by the guslars but also represent a trace of the cultural imaginary
developed as the result of the domination by the imperial power emanating from the Porte. Constantly returning to their victimization by
the "Islamic hordes of Osman" provided 'the serbs' with cultural ammunition to resist imperial domination by identifying with the discourse of liberalism and nationalism of nineteenth-century Europe.

'The serbs' developed a specific cultural domination–submission formula that combined the emergent modernity assimilated from the
West, a cultural heritage of medieval Orthodox Christianity, and a historical trauma of "Orientalization" under the Islamic rule.

Christian Orthodoxy played a central role in forging the collective
identity of 'the serbs' in the eighteenth century. After they migrated to
regions under Habsburg rule in the wake of the Austro–Turkish wars of
1690, a multitude of familial and tribal configurations were united for
the first time under the name 'the serbs,' which was given to them by
Hapsburg census takers. Southern Hungary, the region to which they
migrated, was also the location where the first vampire plagues were
reported by Hapsburg officials, which was certainly tied to the arrival of
these Slavic newcomers in the empire. The uncanny coincidence of the
national naming and vampirism would continue to haunt the cultural
imaginary through the *topoi* of blood and soil. A sense of unity and
common destiny after their exile to the military frontier forced Rascians, Illyrians, Schiavonians, Frontiersmen, Morlacs, and others to
unite under the mantle of the Holy Roman Empire, whose borders they
would guard against Islamic incursions.[4] Christian Orthodoxy thus became the distinguishing mark of their low status within the Habsburg
context, as well as a common denominator from which the tribal configurations could be imagined as the single collectivity, 'the serbs.'

The fact that 'the serbs' gained their sense of proto-national collective identity as Orthodox Christians living in exile among Hungarian
and Austrian Catholics whom they were defending against Islam marks
their symbolic entry from "Asia" into "Europe" in the eighteenth century with a complexity that is often translated into reductive narratives
of "another slavery to the West" or "salvation from the Turk." Although
pressure from the Habsburgs to convert to Catholicism never ceased,
the military frontier represented the site of the birth of 'the serbs' as
products of Western European imagination. As Larry Wolff demonstrates in his reading of travel narratives by Lady Mary Wortley Montague, "She did not particularly associate them [i.e., 'the serbs'] with
Belgrade or even Serbia. She called them 'Rascians,' after the clan chief-
tancy of Rashka that antedated the medieval Serbian state."[5]

If we consider the Habsburg empire as a symbolic horizon of the
West for the Balkans during this period, it becomes obvious that 'the
serbs' as a nation were formed as a Western invention after their flight

from Ottoman retribution. It was only after the domestic agents of Enlightenment begin to respond to this collective vision of the West that 'the serbs' transformed themselves from Islamic slaves into Christian knights ready to avenge "the shame of Kosovo" with which Stoker's Dracula was so obsessed.

Vampire Times

While historical facts about the Battle of Kosovo are scarce and disputable, the accounts transcribed in the heroic epics collected by Vuk Karadžić during the nineteenth century offer a perfect example of how easily poetic practice can supplement and replace historiography as a source of the national imaginary and its relationship to the past. Jovan Deretić, in a chapter of his canonical history of Serbian literature, even goes as far as to call Vuk's collections of oral songs "a poetic history of the Serbian people."[6] This oxymoronic term, which joins the apparently incompatible realms of poetry and history, is symptomatic of a cultural milieu that is ready to blend fact and fiction to foster the imaginary version of its glorious and monumental past. The sublation of history and myth into a discourse of the nation is accompanied by the manipulation of the temporal plane, bringing the past into the present and reviving it through violent and bloody repetition of traumatic memories.

The heroic songs invoke the time of the nation not only as Bakhtin's absolute epic distance between the petrified and monumental past and the "flowing and transitory" present, but also as the past in the present, a perpetual trauma of defeat that is occasionally resurrected through cultural representations of the national greatness in suffering of 'the serbs.' Because of this, the Kosovo myth becomes ensconced in stories about the past as a site saturated with victimization, injustice, and suffering of national heroes who fight against impossible odds to preserve and further the righteous cause of 'the serbs.'

The Kosovo myth bridges the symbolic gap between the abstract ideals of the nation sacrificed (heaven) and the actual condition of the individuals who make up its body (earth). This rupture creates a space for all kinds of political and ideological manipulation of 'the serbs' by leaders who are willing to reopen the perpetually festering wound of masculinity engendered in the post-Oriental condition. The earthly death of 'the serbs' on the Kosovo Field and their ascent to the eternal realm is the performative aspect of this division that constitutes the nationalist discourse of "the heavenly people" whose needs abnegate rationality and reality.

Heaven emerges as the imaginary site where death becomes the guarantor of the ultimate masculinity of the national hero and his eternal life. The durability of memory projects this melancholic vision into literature, which no longer has the oral performance of the guslar to properly mourn the post-Oriental trauma. Literature is transformed into a crypt where the lost object invested with imaginary plenitude at Kosovo is buried alive and awaits its resurrection as if it were a vampire tied to the long-gone memory of "ancient times." The boundary between politics and esthetics is blurred to permanently transform the cultural imaginary into a weapon of war, as every male member of the national community is symbolically dead before birth, sacrificed on the altar of a nation that is unable to properly mourn its losses and therefore is constantly preparing to exact just revenge for its past traumas.

The Ancient Within

Often present in the folk imaginary as a wolf, the ancient animal ancestor of 'the serbs' is transformed into a variety of humanlike creatures challenging the boundary between the human and animal worlds. The vampire stands apart from the werewolf as a force that relies on insidious invasion of the body proper (as opposed to the openly predatory performance made globally visible in Bram Stoker's literary elaboration of Balkan folklore). Veselin Čajkanović, a leading Yugoslav interwar ethnographer, found that 'the serbs' continued to fear this invisible force, which could enter the body by using a moth or a bat as carrier of an "unclean" presence across the boundary between life and death. He identified this force with the ancient Slavic Černobog, the underground god whose elemental nature made him a violent but passionate counterpart to the supreme being of light and air. Functioning as the dark supplement to the Orthodox Christian god, Černobog was transformed into a fundamental part of national imaginary long after the uprising against the Islamic rule had ended. The pre-Christian subtext of the collective imaginary inhabits the underground territory of meaning submerged as the location marked by loss and melancholia. This violent counterpart would continue to haunt the cultural imaginary as it was being written down and territorialized during the struggle for independence from the Ottoman Empire.

Vuk's collection and transcription of heroic songs acted as a cultural weapon in expelling the Islamic master from territory claimed as "native" because of its many graves; the transcriptions articulated a local version of "human" rebirth as, and transformation into, a European nation. Guided by the revival of the Kosovo covenant, which will soon be discussed in detail, 'the serbs' were constructed by the national heroic tradition as just avengers whose ethnic formulas circulated through the oral performance of guslars. The potential for cultural and political mobilization inherent in the oral performance of the epic transformed the epic into a central narrative of the emerging nation of 'the serbs' who were expelled from Kosovo to inhabit the borderlands of the West in the Habsburg empire. The original subcultural diversity among 'the serbs' was much greater due to the effects of clashing cultural codes of a variety of civilizations contesting for control of the Balkans.

The narrativity of the singer's performance was an effect of that nomadic movement, as the "epic formulas" discovered by Parry and Lord began to serve as a preserver of an imaginary location for an itinerant nation that had become militarized to protect the West from Islamic invaders. The plurality of concurrent national narratives was scattered as much as the territory imagined by 'the serbs' as they moved along the fault line between the Ottoman and the Habsburg empires during the eighteenth century and nineteenth century. The Dinaric narrative of 'the serbs' outside Serbia gradually outlasted all of the other narratives because it offered an imaginary of the nation displaced and poised to raise itself from the underworld of nonbeing and by yielding to the national dream of the living dead. The de-territorialized existence of the imaginary in the songs of old men articulated the trauma of dehumanization inherent in the collective bondage to Islam that the nation had endured.

The paradox embodied in the oral tradition of 'the serbs' is that this sublime object of classical literary studies originated in a crypt where the ancient creature of memory rejuvenated itself through the blood and sacrifice of ever new generations of living subjects. The medieval tenets of Orthodox Christianity grafted onto ancient Slavic dualism persisted in promoting martyrdom for "honorable cross and golden freedom" as a supreme national value. Despite the noble ideals, the cultural marginality of 'the serbs' was greatly enhanced by the character of Ottoman governing practices, which included targeted conversion of young boys to Islam to serve in mercenary armies, as well as the steady supply of women for the imperial harems.

Decisive in the continual festering of the masculine cultural wound, the rage cultivated in the performance of the singers simmered underground, envisioning a space of increased humanity for 'the serbs' and a space of freedom to come. Singers often broke their *gusle* in fits of this post-Oriental rage, angry at the Ottoman culture as their arbitrary master. According to Lord, the oral performance was practiced as a remainder of classical literary heritage tied to the Homeric epic. On the other hand, the oral tradition became a repository of the ideology of just revenge by the subaltern awaiting the opportunity to turn the social order upside down.

Europe, Impaled

The posited ideal of 'the serbs' is represented as everlasting sacrifice embodied in the church that Prince Lazar built immediately after he chose the "heavenly kingdom" after the loss of Kosovo. Temporal returns to the location of national trauma are symptomatic of a subjugated culture, especially when ethnicity and religious affiliation are interchangeable. The community of faith is decisive in the subaltern's development of the cultural imaginary, since the Ottomans considered 'the serbs' recent converts to Orthodox Christianity at the time of the Islamic conquest of the Balkans. Their forced conversion to Islam was therefore legalized, since they could have theoretically heard the word of Mohammed, which was not the case with earlier members of Abrahamic religions. The retreat of 'the serbs' to the catacombs of faith to escape conversion in turn activated a host of ancient Slavic practices, which were revived and blended with ecclesiastical narratives, making the Christian nature of 'the serbs' extremely alluring to Western ethnographers in the nineteenth century as the embodiment of the most primitive origins of Europe. Belief in vampires was just one of the narrative *epistemes* dominant in this external vision of the ethnic collective.

The residual cultural ingredient of pagan identity was inscribed as a yet another, more primitive crypt, where belief in the Black God (Černobog) was supposedly on an equal footing with belief in a White God (Byelobog). It is especially the former realm of dark, underground cultural values that was activated during the struggle for recognition in the elusive mirror of modern European identity. The emergent national subject fought to return to Europe because its own phantasm of freedom was dominated by an ambiguous relationship to ancient cultural residues that festered in the collective memory of a nation impaled on the stake of its Islamic masters.

Prince Lazar sacrificed his people in Christ-like fashion while leading them simultaneously to eternal salvation and secular defeat. Biblical motifs from Christ's Last Supper are replicated almost exactly in the "Kneževa večera" (Prince's supper) poem of the Kosovo cycle, with Vuk Branković playing the role of the national Judas Iscariot and the role of Christ split between Prince Lazar and Miloš Obilić, the supreme embodiment of heroic masculinity in the national imaginary. It is worth noting that Obilić was a founding member of the secret Order of the Dragon, which united the Christian nobility against the common Islamic enemy, alongside Vlad Tsepesh's father, whose name—Dracula— was derived from *Drakon*, the German word for dragon.

This surprising link to the historical source of the Gothic imaginary engendered by Bram Stoker reflects the medieval origins of the post-Oriental condition, where the national hero's masculinity is tested against the invading Islamic other's violence. The mythic subtext of the loss and failure of heroism of 'the serbs' in the Kosovo cycle nurtures the cultural masochism of a small nation involved in glorifying its own just violence to come. The erection of a national community is always in doubt, because the symbolic masculine wound caused by submission to a more dominant identity requires periodic reopening to summon the forces of just revenge directed at its chosen surrogate victims. Being one with 'the serbs' requires one to accept this phantasm of power, which is based on a logic of perpetual impalement on the symbolic stake and endless mourning. This is also the origin of Četnik iconography in the Balkans, which features Orthodox guerrilla fighters allowing their beards to grow long as a sign of mourning for the dethroned national monarchy for which they are willing to sacrifice their lives.

To prevent an alien, "infidel" force from penetrating the core of his proper identity, the hero must embrace violence and nurture the collective wound inflicted by the Ottoman stake, whose imaginary power threatens at all times to become real. Giving in to conquest threatens the assimilation of "the faithful" through physical annihilation, territorial displacement, and gradual conversion to Islam. This cultural

Gothic politics: the cult of the Četnik warrior. PHOTOGRAPH COURTESY ZORAN PETROVIĆ.

mechanism is indicative of the Eurocentric cultural milieu within which the Kosovo myth was constructed and disseminated by the emergent cultural establishment in the course of the nineteenth century.

Even the disjunctive slogan of Patrick Henry is replicated by the Četniks, who display "Liberty or Death" on their skull-and-crossbones banners. The "honorable cross and golden freedom" glorified in heroic songs represent the two categorical formulas, reflecting the manner in which modern European ideas of nationalism and liberalism were hybridized once they were incorporated into the Balkan periphery ruled by the "Old Man of Europe." The historiography of 'the serbs' absorbed the messianic horizon preserved and transmitted by oral tradition, which is evident in the statement of a military pamphlet: "It was not only Serbia that fought with Ottomania on the Kosovo Field; it was also a fight between Christianity and Islam, between the cross and the crescent, between the tame Europe and fanatical Asia."[7]

This passage from the anonymously written introduction to the military-political treatise *Kosovska bitka* attempts to extrapolate the importance of the Battle of Kosovo within a larger clash-of-civilizations framework, lifting Serbia from its nineteenth-century position of tiny, agrarian Balkan state to that of a leading defender of European "tameness" and its Christian faith. The fight against the Oriental was the ultimate test of heroic masculinity that would guarantee inclusion in Europe, from which 'the serbs' had been excluded since the loss at Kosovo. Singing about the battle—mourning defeat at the hands of Islam to bridge the temporal gap and heal the wound inflicted by the Oriental other—played an invaluable part in this effort. In the case of 'the serbs' Benedict Anderson's statement, "It is the magic of nationalism to turn chance into destiny," could also be understood as the magic of transforming the bite of a larger imperial predator into a sign of one's own undead existence to come.[8]

Male Bondage

Oral tradition fulfilled this kind of destiny-producing role in South Slavic cultures of the nineteenth century. While describing the clash between Marko Kraljević and Đemo Brđanin—an Orthodox vassal fighting an Islamic convert—the oral epic foregrounds the sadomasochist economy of the national imaginary. The narrative is structured along the lines of mutual bondage and torture, which serve as the violent foundation for the emergence of the imagined community. The effect of heroic endurance of agony is achieved by singing the tale as an action-oriented narrative that is not yet in a position to articulate the interiority of the subject:

> When Đemo Brđanin saw
> Marko Kraljević above him
> Đemo tried to jump up to his feet
> Cruel chains closed 'round his neck,
> As he strained against them
> His arms ripped at the shoulders
> His legs snapped at the knees
> As heavy metal engulfed his body.[9]

Marko Kraljević binds Đemo with chains after Đemo's drink had been spiked by Marko's blood sister, Janja the Barmaid (Krčmarica Janja). She acts as a conduit of passivity, as the Muslim convert is degraded both by intoxication and by bondage by the infidel hero. As Đemo gradually awakens from his stupor, Marko mockingly invites him to drink wine with him, which causes Đemo's body to fall apart after straining against the cold hard metal. This bondage scene reiterates the narrative of Balkan masculinity by acting out revenge for the initial trauma of Kosovo performed by Marko. The torture is a repetition in reverse of an earlier episode in the poem in which Đemo, eager to avenge the death of his blood brother Musa Kesedžija at Marko's hands, catches Marko off-guard during his *slava* (a patron saint celebration).

Đemo chains Marko after a chase around Lake Ohrid and parades a bound Marko around the estates of Christian noblemen while asking for ransom. Đemo's betrayal of Christian values is reiterated, since no weapons can be carried during this kind of religious holiday, and Marko has no arms with which to defend himself. It is in fact Marko's mother who reminds him that he cannot bear arms, metaphorically taking away his masculine characteristics for the sake of a higher religious calling.

To further underline Đemo's disrespect of Orthodoxy, the epic bard turns him into a dark opposite of the patron saint, whose name is Đorđije (St. George, the dragon slayer). The revenge Marko perpetrates on Đemo as a surrogate victim for the generalized Islamic enemy is presented as an act of righteous torture that is justified by the previous transgressions of his opponent, until Marko hangs Đemo at the end of the poem. The domination–submission relationship of the two heroes of opposing faiths elaborates the sadomasochist dynamic of Balkan masculine identity, which serves as the model for all other types of communal identification to come.

The appearance of St. George as the piercer of the legendary nether-world reptile (the dragon that later will mark Dracula's name), as the righteous bearer of the lance that annihilates alterity, is the Orthodox Christian iteration of Michel Foucault's "counter-nature" bearing the gifts of death to any avatar of difference.[10] The act of piercing exists to make up for the antecedent violation by the threatening other, uprooting primal crimes at the very core of the imagined community through this act of initial violence.

The Lacanian imaginary construct becomes most visible in this performance in the joining of sexuality and violence through the use of phallic substitutes: the lance or the stake. One reaches for the phallic substitute when the other's evil attains proportions comparable to that of the vampire plague, which requires pre-emptive annihilation in acts of righteous vengeance. The origin of the law tied to the narratives of blood and soil becomes visible as the shimmer on the very tip of the protruding stake of the righteous bearer of phallic power that pierces the body of the threatening other who resides on the other side of one's communal *doxa*.

Breaking through the chains of bondage requires pain and sacrifice, the radical zeal of submitting to torture with a higher aim at heart. This underlies the pathetic bravery of Ðemo's pushing against heavy metal, only to encounter the corporeal limits set for him by 'the serbs,' the original ethnic community that is now punishing him for his treacherous conversion to Islam. The ethnic division of Slavic tribes produced by these imaginary interpellations of faith communities was extremely useful in mobilizing individuals to commit acts of violence among the former Yugoslavs, especially among 'the serbs' at Srebrenica in 1995.

Engendering Formulas

Bakhtin theorized the emergence of the novel as the irreducible narrative horizon born as a reaction against the constrictions of the dominant cultural codes presented in the "oldness" of the immutable world of medieval heroes. The modernity of the novel required a story of the nation that did not constrict the imaginary with the simplified binaries of epic struggles. The oral tradition reinforces this kind of rudimentary imaginary structure, especially for emergent national subjects who find themselves in submission to an imperial other. Among the Balkan Slavic tribes, national belonging had been formulated through either resistance or collaboration with the Islamic ruler. For 'the serbs' to imagine their collective identity, resistance to Islam as an agent of cultural domination had to be supplemented with the medieval models embodied in the figures of the Orthodox Christian priest and the blind singer of heroic tales.

However, the formulation of heroic narratives by the guslar would not follow Plato's demand to Homer never to show Achilles weeping and lamenting. Instead, South Slavic epic singing would be marked by the communal ritual of mourning for the injured masculinity of the Christian serfs. This oral tradition was so dominated by old men that Vuk Karadžic was able to locate it in opposition to "women's songs" without explicitly calling it "masculine," and in calling it "heroic" (*junačke*), he instituted an interesting cultural dichotomy in which "masculine" became synonymous with "heroic." The excess of the masculine in the national imaginary exemplifies Bakhtin's "single and unified world view" characteristic of premodern cultures, creating a very complex relationship to the modern notions of the nation.

For 'the serbs,' participation in oral performances about the epic world of knightly duels was complemented by rituals of declining Orthodox Christianity and the unwitting preservation of many forms of pagan Slavic culture. The Dinaric culture shared by these religiously divided populations, hardened by poverty, hardship, and exile, found common voice in the injured masculinity of its members, who got together to sing of shared pain and plot revenge for the injustices done to their community. Christian iconography of the divine, received through the process of conversion by Byzantine missionaries, assimilated an older conception of the divine among 'the serbs,' tied to an underground destiny they were forced to populate while living in their Islamic *millet*.

In his landmark study *The Singer of Tales*, Albert Lord posits the formulaic theory of Yugoslav oral verse making, tracing its origins back to Homeric roots in classical Greece. By stressing the formal side of particular formulas of oral composition, however, Lord overlooked the post-Oriental cultural context engendered during Islamic rule of the Balkans. Alongside his teacher Milman Parry, Lord conducted his research in the Dinaric region, where the tradition of gusle singing originated in obsessive repetition of past traumas, mourned in male company, to invoke at least two competing interpretations of Ottoman rule in the Balkans. However, whether Muslim or Christian, the singer of tales performed his heroic epic as a form of masculine lament, focused on the "loss of some abstraction" about which Freud speaks in his work on mourning and melancholia.[11] Both ethnicities are transformed into a narrative that focuses on accounting for the consequences of Islamic military domination, which split the population into the faithful subjects of Islam and the *rayah*, the Christian serfs whose faith marked them as inferior.

For the nationalist imaginary of 'the serbs,' the epic formula adumbrates the loss of sovereignty and submission to the Islamic other as the most archaic core of identity that transforms masculinity into a perpetual weapon of revenge. The scar tissue left after the glorious defeat at Kosovo functions as a messianic horizon of heroic masculinity that longs to regain the abstraction of a Europe lost but not forgotten. To be accepted as properly European, a nineteenth-century nation had to prove to its members and to its others that it was ancient, forged in blood and sacrifice, rooted in time older than time and disappearing into its own ancient and murky origins. The performance of memories of "old centuries" in the present found cultural expression in the Dinaric tradition of gusle singing stored and transmitted mainly by 'the serbs,' but also by their converted Islamic brethren, who sang for Parry and Lord in the 1930s in the interwar Yugoslav province of Sandžak/ Novi Pazar. Lord analyzed the heroic song as a purely formal concern, applying his research on classical Greece to the mechanisms of oral verse making. His encounter with Avdo Međedović and other native bards was mediated by this orientation toward the formal aspects of performance. The ability of those old singers to sit and spin the epic *deseterac* (decasyllabic line) for hours on end led Lord to posit his formulaic theory of oral verse making.

Yet the formulaic spinning of tales from the imaginary networks of the nation is inseparable from the effects of communal violence on the history of the performance. The poetic memory of the nation was formulated through a metaphoric linking of typical narrative features into a practically endless narrative about one's own imagined community. Lord, who was looking for the roots of the classical epic and the origin of Western literature, heard its echoes in the wailing of the guslars performing their rituals of mourning in the ruins of Oriental Europe. His modernist bias edified the oral tale about heroic men at the origin of the cultural foundation of the West had been lost and was now regained from its "primitive" Balkan roots. Finding in the Dinaric highlands of the former Yugoslavia what seemed to be a long-forgotten world of strong men living the ethos of blood and soil in accordance with a more ancient notion of masculinity allowed Lord to visualize the Homeric bard as the origin of all Occidental literature.

Lord's discovery, however, rendered invisible uncomfortable questions about the local, historical complexities that stemmed from the post-Oriental condition of the Yugoslav kingdom in the interwar period. Such arcane and vulgar affairs as Balkan politics, in his view, could not possibly have an effect on the study of oral tradition and its formal properties. Lord's logocentric bias posited the sung word of the bard as part of a classical paradise regained, where the word was unspoiled by the advent of literacy. He mourned the loss of fluidity and variation of the oral tradition while viewing writing as a toxic supplement that exterminated the vital force of the spoken word. To him, script became a crypt, a location where oral tradition was buried alive as the true nature of the nation was petrified in written form that kept all possible oral varieties from coming into being. He imagined the singers of tales to be incarnations of preliterate forms of memory coming to life as testimony to the extreme durability of the past and overlooked the bloody imaginary in favor of exploring the formal properties of verse making, in the same way that the bloodshed of *The Iliad* is often ignored to invoke the glorious origins of the West.

Hidden from the discerning gaze of their Christian brethren, the Southern Slavs performed and listened to heroic epics in this European backwater, barely touched by the "mere modernity" that would soon seek to kill off their old ways. Displaying the sophistry of the learned Western gentleman, Lord acted as a protector of this ancient form of memory, constructing a veritable *Volksmuseum* of the Dinaric highland subculture amid the continual war and turmoil of the Balkans. What he failed to notice was that the oral performance of the guslar interpellates violence from the start, affirming the agonistic worldview of a locality steeped in the endless repetition of suffering of a subjugated culture mourning the collective traumas of its failed masculinity.

The Stolen Blood

Marko Kraljević, a celebrated protagonist tied indirectly to the Kosovo myth, is said to have died only temporarily and will return when the time comes to avenge the defeat at Kosovo.[12] In the traditional songs, Marko, who lived under Ottoman suzerainty, usually acts out the transgression desired by the defeated collectivity of 'the serbs.' He is represented as a rebel who drinks wine during the Muslim holiday of Ramadan, plows up the roads built by the Turks, and overwhelms his opponents with his uncompromising devotion to freedom at any cost, which is usually embodied in the maiden or the mother of the nation to come.

One symptomatic episode takes place in the song "Marko Kraljević Abolishes the Marriage Tax," in which Marko confronts an Arab who has set up camp on the Kosovo Field and demands both gold and the right to sleep with all newlywed Christian maidens on the first night of marriage. The symbolic rape of the maidens by the Arab metonymically extends the female body into a signifier of the national territory and a site of the masculine power exercise. The significance of the

Kosovo covenant as rightful revenge is given its fullest expression, as women belonging to 'the serbs' are exposed and forced to compromise their purity during the prenuptial night with the Islamic master. As expected, Marko comes down as a vengeful sword and wipes this dark other off the face of the earth to avenge the injustice. Right before he makes the decision to challenge the usurper (who is never named) to a duel, he laments the destiny of the women who represent the entire nation in the making. While tears pour down the chiseled "face of the hero," Marko addresses the Kosovo Field directly:

Oh, alas, you flat Kosovo Field,
what sorrow have you lived to see,
after our honorable prince,
to see the Arabs acting as the law!
I cannot endure that shame,
nor bear the great sadness,
of letting Arabs commit such crimes
by kissing our brides and maidens.
Today I will avenge you, brothers,
either avenge you or die myself![13]

In the last two lines, Marko's intended addressee changes from the field itself to the "brothers" who will be avenged in the battle against the Islamic enemy. These brothers are all those who have been martyred at Kosovo, starting with the "honorable prince" (Lazar), who is explicitly mentioned and implicitly includes Miloš Obilić, the Jugović clan, and all of the other masculine models for 'the serbs' as transgressors of Ottoman imperial law.

The brothers, dead and alive, will unite to sacrifice themselves and repeat the sacrifice at Kosovo by defending the maidens' honor so they will not be defiled by infidel blood and forced to service the masculinity of their Islamic masters. Allowing the women to bear the enemy's children is the ultimate curse of subjugated masculinity, engendering both rage against external domination and a suspicion of women as a national contingency—prone to straying from the birth community and willing to join the more powerful enemy. An updated version of this cultural mechanism operated in the mass rapes in Bosnia during the recent Wars of Yugoslav Succession, in which women's bodies were transformed into a symbolic vessel that tied territory to a particular ethnic configuration. Violating the women of the enemy by planting alien seed to taint the other's blood acted out the fantasy of the single, homogenous territorial location.

The most prominent song elaborating the topic of unreliable women as a metaphor for stolen blood is found in the poem "Banović Strahinja," in which the hero named in the title tries to gain back his wife from Vlah-Alija, who had abducted her while the Christian hero was away visiting her family.[14] The two men fight for days, until they fall down, exhausted, before the woman in an apparent tie of masculine impotence. Banović Strahinja appeals to his abducted wife to take a piece of the broken sword and kill the man she does not want to be hers. The choice he offers the woman, who remains unnamed in the poem and therefore can be any woman, displays knightly respect for the lady. Allowing her to show her choice by killing the unwanted man opens up a space of mediation between genders and ethnicities, but only as long as she is ready to make the right choice in the eyes of her blood community. Acting as a form of lethal currency flowing between the two confronted versions of masculine power, the anonymous wife as a vessel carrying the blood of the community provides narrative motivation for the struggle over the territory between Islam and Christianity.

Vlah-Alija promises the woman thirty servants, gold, honey, and sugar in return for her favors, reminding her that she had spent many a night under his tent and that Strahinja would never consider her his true wife again. This moment is particularly interesting, since both the Islamic convert and the woman are on the wrong side of the law because they have been coerced into transgression, breaking the silent bond of blood to the community of 'the serbs.' Surprisingly, the woman turns against Strahinja, who is forced to call on his faithful hound, Karaman, to defend him. The woman, tainted by the alien touch, distrusts her real husband and sides with the Muslim. The dog has a greater moral value than a wife because of his animalistic sense of blind obedience to the master, while both the woman and Vlah-Alija are scorned for committing treason against their blood communities. Women and converts are suspect because they cannot "keep a word" and thus remain outside the imaginary boundary defined by the community of believers that, at minimum, saves it from religious and cultural assimilation.

Role models for women in the oral tradition are found in the figures of the Majka Jugovića (Jugovići Mother) and the Kosovka Devojka (Kosovo Maiden), who appear almost exclusively as lamenting the "earthly" dead after the Battle of Kosovo. The Majka Jugovića is represented as a symbol of the entire nation slain on the Kosovo Field, while the Kosovka Devojka represents all of the women with unfertilized wombs who have lost their potential husbands in the battle. Both oral narratives are structured around the process of lamentation that is repeated until the Majka Jugovića's heart is broken when a raven drops the cut-off hand of her youngest son in her lap. The Kosovka Devojka's sorrow is so great that her touch causes plant life to die. The metaphor of toxic femininity is again tied to the anxiety of 'the serbs' that the milk–blood dyad will be broken under the Islamic rule, because no men will be available to fertilize the "national" wombs of their women. During the nineteenth century, fear for the survival of an ethnic collective whose boundaries were delimited by belonging to Orthodox Christianity motivated 'the serbs' to develop the cultural imaginary based on blood and soil as a response to the constant threat of externally imposed genocide, conversion, and miscegenation.

Bloodthirsty Hearts

The most canonical literary reworking of the Kosovo imaginary of the nineteenth century is *Gorski vijenac* (The mountain wreath; 1846), by Petar Petrović Njegoš. *The Mountain Wreath* is regarded as the supreme embodiment of the masculine ethos and national philosophy based on the blend of new ideas of European Romanticism and the South Slavic oral tradition. In *History of Yugoslav Literature*, Antun Barac, a Croat of Yugoslav orientation, describes the importance of *The Mountain Wreath* this way:

> Derived from the people, from contemporary conditions prevailing in Montenegro and among all the Serbs, this work is at the same time the most comprehensive and the most humane of works in Serbian literature. During the period in which the foundations of the new Serbian literature were being laid in the struggle for a new language and new spirit upon the traditions of the older Serbian literature and upon the elements of the folk poetry, *Gorski vijenac* (The Mountain Wreath) is its perfect accomplishment. It is a blend of perfect simplicity, precision and profundity, with elements taken from the people; and it is also personal from beginning to end.[15]

A closer look at "the most human of works in Serbian literature" reveals that it is based on a historical event known as *istraga poturica*, or the extermination of Slavic converts to Islam that was ordered by Bishop Danilo at the end of the seventeenth century.[16] Because most of Montenegro had been under Islamic rule for centuries, religious conversion had managed to divide the country into those who accepted the conquering religion (*poturice*) and those who stayed loyal to Christian Orthodoxy. Njegoš, who was both the secular and the religious leader of Montenegro at the time, saw this process of cultural assimilation as the main obstacle to the liberation of all Christians living under Islamic domination in the Balkans.

Njegoš obviously identified with the problem Bishop Danilo had envisioned a century earlier, turning the actuality of the internally divided "blood" into a metaphysical problem of bondage to the forces of evil embodied in the Islamic feudal lords. The mountain wreath of the title is based on the classical symbol of victory devoted to the "dust of the father of Serbia"—Karađorđe—the man who gave his nation a "chest of steel" and awakened in it a "lion's heart" during the earliest uprising against the Ottoman rule in the Balkans, in 1804.[17] Njegoš represents Karađorđe as the incarnation of a new European masculinity and compares him to the likes of Napoleon and Wellington, portraying him as a man who was born in the bosom of a small nation to "baptize the land" and "break the barbarian chains." This invocation of the dead body of the symbolic father of Serbia establishes an imaginary link to "ancient centuries," starting with the martyr heroes of Kosovo and ending with Njegoš himself, who at the time was acting as a historical unifier of the otherwise unruly clans of Montenegro.

In his poem, "Svobodijada" (Libertiad; 1835), Njegoš begins to rework the Kosovo legend by depicting Islamization as the ultimate threat to 'the serbs':

> After the tearful Battle of Kosovo,
> the sons of Turkistan
> across the fallen Serbian state
> multiplied and dispersed
> quenching their tyrannical hearts
> with the Serbian blood
> like mad, insatiable

mountain wolves and tigers
entering a quiet herd
left without a shepherd,
confused and headless herd,
abandoned to wonder through the woods
until itself becoming a victim
of the insatiable beastly heart.[18]

Fear of contamination and miscegenation are prevalent in most of Njegoš's works that take up this subject matter. The ultimate defeat is perceived in the loss of blood as a metonymy for the community bequeathed by the forefathers through the oral transmission of the Kosovo covenant. The encounter between Christianity and Islam is represented from the point of view of subjugated men who fear the Oriental master as a predator that feeds on the blood of the weak. While 'the serbs' are imagined as the innocent flock left without aristocratic leaders, who were slain at Kosovo, the Islamic converts are portrayed as vampire-like beings nurtured by the "native blood" to multiply their "tyrannical" race. The ambiguous last two lines of the poem imply that 'the serbs' are now prone to becoming the victims of the "insatiable beastly heart," both through literal disappearance as a result of genocide and by appropriating the "insatiable beastly heart" for themselves. This ambiguity regarding violence is the symbolic underpinning of the collective identity of 'the serbs' as a national construct in the post-Oriental condition.

The Sweet Poison of Violence

Throughout *The Mountain Wreath*, the problems engendered after the trauma of Kosovo are elaborated within the post-Oriental condition of disjunctive temporalities. The eternal dimension of the nation cast in epic high relief was frozen after the loss of freedom and is plunged into the ethnic schisms of the elusive present. 'The serbs' as a spectral product of historical imagination are projected from the heavenly realm of the nation into the material world of conflict between collaborators with the Islamic master and those who uphold Christianity despite the oppression they are sworn to fight against. In a dispute between Vuk Mandušić and Captain Hamzo, retold at the assembly by Knez Janko for the benefit of other Montenegrin leaders, the issue of loyalty to the Kosovo covenant is taken up again. Captain Hamzo, a military commander in the Ottoman army, exalts his new faith over Christianity and shows pride in the wealthy lifestyle that conversion to Islam has provided to him in exchange for helping to spread its reach by the power of the sword. This enrages Mandušić, who harangues Captain Hamzo for treason against the blood community at Kosovo:

> Is a traitor better than a knight?
> Did you mention sword and Kosovo?
> Were we not together in that battle,
> and I fought then as I do now,
> while you betrayed us both then and now,
> dishonored us in front of the world
> spat on the faith of our forefathers,
> turned yourself into a slave alien?[19]

Kosovo is again represented as the ultimate gauge of masculine worthiness, with a sharp epic contrast drawn between "knights" and "traitors." The use of medieval knighthood to convey the essence of ethnic pride is symptomatic of the Romantic formulas borrowed earlier in the nineteenth century from European nation-building cultures. To imagine their national identity, 'the serbs' had to reach back to the age before Kosovo, which manifested the heavenly horizon before their fall into Ottoman suzerainty. The battle itself is reinterpreted as a trial of religious and national allegiances, where those who stay within the boundaries of Orthodox Christianity are worthy of their "knightly" calling, while those who betray 'the serbs' by converting to Islam are worthy only of scorn, expulsion, and, ultimately, extermination.[20] This communal identity envisioned by Vuk Mandušić, in accordance with the codes of heroic masculinity, continued to dominate the national imaginary of 'the serbs' long after the struggle for liberation from Islamic rule ended.

It is symptomatic that *The Mountain Wreath* simultaneously develops a negative vision of women, who are portrayed as creatures who have no firm faith, are prone to deception, and easily give themselves over to the enjoyment of material wealth. Knez Janko elaborates on the ways in which the manly hero is manipulated by various "non-masculine" creatures:

The merchant lies with a smile,
the woman lies as she sheds tears,
but the Turk is the most outrageous liar.[21]

The cultural imaginary of 'the serbs' demands the ordering of the community by distinguishing between those who are on the side of "truth" and those who are not, which, in the case of Njegoš, are merchants, women, and Turks. Merchants are targeted because of the traditional Orthodox Christian suspicion that wealth and material goods are inherently ungodly—the direct opposite of the Protestant concept of stewardship over wealth as a step closer to God. One of the main historical reasons for converting to Islam was economic, since the Ottoman feudalists controlled the land in the Balkan provinces of the Ottoman Empire. Many of 'the serbs' converted to improve their social position and avoid harsh lives either as serfs or as outlaws. Caving in to pressure from the Islamic master that results in changing one's blood identity is regarded as "feminine" within the symbolic order based on sacrifice and death. Any attempt to improve one's personal well-being by changing one's identity is contemptible, since it interferes with the laws of masculine pride established by the Kosovo covenant. Again, what matters is the community of men, a construct threatened by any sign of divergence that comes from different identities that make up the larger community.

Women and Turks are suspect because they are represented as prone to stepping outside the bounds of communal faith and custom, just as in the song "Banović Strahinja." A woman willing to betray her husband for the sake of wealth and social prestige belongs to the same non-human category as the unfaithful brother who betrays the community by converting to Islam. Njegoš's works are deeply embedded in a theocratic society that, due to the poverty and relative isolation of Montenegro, preserved the most rigid gender roles. Knez Rogan, commenting on an episode identical to the one in "Banović Strahinja" in which the convert Mujo Alić has abducted a Montenegrin girl to marry her, reveals the masculine mistrust of women in general:

A woman's nature is a funny business!
She does not care about this or that faith;
She would convert a hundred times
to please the longings of her heart.[22]

The direct comparison of women to religious converts works both ways within the masculine symbolic order: The women are regarded as latent traitors of the national cause, while the converts to Islam lose their status among "men" and are seen as feminized by the loss of access to the heroic masculinity of their righteous leaders. Masculinity is imagined as martial willingness to perform a selfless act of violence for the freedom of the people and the heavenly glory of their faith. Vuk Mićunović, the most heroic protagonist of Njegoš's epic, voices the dilemma of masculinity:

> Heroism is the lord of all evil,
> but also the sweetest spiritual potion
> intoxicating generations to come.
> Blessed is the one who lives forever,
> he was not born to die in vain![23]

The violence that engenders masculinity is a way to grant one life that never ends. Heroism is performed for the sake of the future, infecting the temporality to come with a sweet poison of violence. This identification with the animated monument shares its artificially perpetuated life with the Gothic vampire. The root of evil lies in this manly identification with blood and honor, as the mundane death is avoided by perpetual sacrifice of new blood on the altar of the people. The promise of eternity is alive if a man can accept violence as a special and secret mission entrusted to him as a categorical imperative within the post-Oriental condition.

Blood or Milk?

Ljubomir Nenadović (1826–95) quotes Njegoš as cursing one of the converts to Islam (Omer-paša) when he learns of his intent to attack Montenegro: "May God grant the Serbian milk that nurtured him give him leprosy! And may God grant that he meets Obilić eye to eye at the Last Judgment!"[24] It is Obilić, the self-sacrificing avenger of the impending defeat in Kosovo who slays Sultan Murad, who appears at the Last Judgment instead of Christ to reclaim the stolen milk—or, at least, to ensure that the curse of leprosy reaches those who abandon the communal bond of blood and lend milk to the enemy. This curse reflects the blood-for-milk substitution shared in the community to reinforce the imaginary of the vampire nation. Alan Dundes notes this type of substitution in "the efforts of the vampire to drink milk rather than blood" to replenish the dryness that results from extreme old age.[25] Since the pivotal role of the maternal in transforming milk into blood is usurped by the discourse of heroic masculinity, those who are ready to betray their own blood are worthy of an incurable disease.

The cursing of mother's milk that gives sustenance to the child who later decides to "cross the cross" is the best illustration of the divided identity of the Balkans during the struggles against Islamic domination. The internalized "heavenly" dimension of the communal past creates a masochistic horizon of collective identity that has the imaginary potential to invoke a violent revenge at any present or future moment. This masochistic positioning is paired with a sadistic desire to dominate surrogate victims who fit into the narrative of the Kosovo covenant as the treacherous other. Since they are perceived as illegitimate siblings, the Islamic converts are subjected to the unwritten code of revenge in accordance with the Kosovo covenant and exposed to bloodletting to avenge the milk of the nation whose being they have usurped by abandoning Christ. The ferocity of the war crimes committed during the Bosnian War (1992–95) is the performative rendering of this kind of discursive violence stored in the national imaginary and circulated through the heroic songs that eventually were transferred to the culture of war songs and turbo-folk during the wars of the 1990s in the former Yugoslavia.

Becoming Posthuman

The apartheid nature of Ottoman rule relegated 'the serbs' to *millets*, or religious ghettoes, created for the empire's non-Islamic populations. The execution of the last Bosnian king by Mohammed II in 1462 is a perfect metaphor for the Islamic invasion of the Balkans. The Ottoman ruler demonstrated a fascination with the Renaissance doctrines of human freedom as power and embraced them to repeat in reverse the military performance of Alexander the Great to conquer Western Europe. The issue of religious confession was crucial during this period, because those who did not belong to the chosen community of Islamic believers were treated as less than human. Although the last Bosnian king surrendered after receiving written assurances that Sultan Mohammad II would not harm him, the sultan considered the word given to an infidel the same as a word given to a dog and had the king decapitated.

Turks viewed non-Islamic subjects (*giaours* or *rayah*) as aliens to the true faith and therefore creatures of lesser humanity, while the Greek Orthodox head of the millet treated 'the serbs' as *serbos*, or slaves who had once dared to challenge the supremacy of Byzantium by proclaiming their own, autocephalous Serbian Orthodox church. Mourning this double domination, the epic formulas recycled the collective memory as a narrative that provided 'the serbs' with a sense of dehumanization that would motivate their struggles to eventually territorialize their communal identity after the Berlin Congress of 1878. Once literacy and sovereignty provided the cultural and political tools to transpose the previously analyzed ethnic formulas into a narrative of the state, the metaphoric leap from God to the nation as the ultimate reality became ensconced in written collections of oral songs and in the new language codified by Vuk Karadžić. The messianic horizon of the medieval worldview came to be dominated by the emergence of a nation born from the cultural conquest of the Oriental empire.

Thus, the imaginary of the nation naturalized heroic masculinity of the oral tradition as a categorical demand to which 'the serbs' had to subject themselves, regardless of their gender. The narratives produced by the guslars of the nineteenth century tell stories of desperate yet valiant resistance based on hope for the resurrection of the domestic imperial order. Yet nostalgia for the "native" was so hybridized by the post-Oriental condition that even Vuk Karadžić was able to imagine himself only as a Christian version of an Islamic bey on his plot of Serbia to come. His work as a founder of modern culture created a horizon for the new national location, marked simultaneously by unintended identification with the Oriental oppressor and a dream of Europe as the horizon of regained humanity and freedom.

Symptomatically, the popular literacy of 'the serbs' in the form of the new Cyrillic alphabet from its very inception carried within itself the ambivalent presence of both the Islamic and the Catholic adversaries. Orthodox church fathers who attacked Vuk for abandoning the linguistic purity of Old Church Slavic objected to the inclusion of both the "Turkish-sounding" *dž* and *đ* and the "Latin" *j*. These struggles in the nineteenth century over language and the alphabet reflect diverging models for imagining national identity among 'the serbs.' On the one hand, Vuk's reforms codified the dominant popular culture of the Dinaric mountaineers by writing down hundreds of thousands of texts from the guslars, as well as from other peasant men and women he had met on his travels throughout the Balkans. Linguistic purity was never part of Vuk's nationalism, since he was fully aware of the cultural variance of the Balkan region. Yet this cultural hybridity was assimilated into the overwhelming cult of blood and soil in the collective imaginary of the nation.

The civic cultural model, which had been initiated earlier by Dositej Obradović, was dominant among urban populations under Habsburg administration, but it proved unusable in the construction of the new Serbian identity. Weakened by its lack of the violent potential inherent in the populist imaginary, it remained isolated and limited to urban settings north of the Sava and Danube rivers. Vuk's model was based on the internalization of the Herderian *Volksgeist*: The common masculine wound encrypted in the oral tradition was enshrined as the essence of the national soul. The cultural complexity of the struggle for independence was embodied in the metaphor of Vuk's own transition from orality to literacy: He had taught himself how to write with "a pen dipped in gunpowder dissolved in water" during the uprising against Ottoman rule of 1804.[26] Using gunpowder to trace the signs of the new nation on discarded ammunition casings is a perfect symbol for the convergence of arms and letters in a struggle for recognition as part of the common European cultural space. The arming of the letter as popular literacy that emerged through rebellion is a symbol that has haunted the national imaginary of 'the serbs' since the idea of cultural identity based on the righteous use of violence was enforced during the struggle for freedom from bondage to the Islamic master.

Modern Melancholy

Danilo Kiš, the most internationally recognized author to emerge from the former Yugoslavia during the 1970s, mocked the predicament of minor cultures by imagining the figure of the national writer who is forced to constantly carry around a piano and a dead horse. "Every possible tune that was played on the piano is on his back, and all those who rode the horse in victory or defeat are on his back, too, all the meanings and allusions unknown to the world at large, all the wars, all the epics, all the epic heroes."[27] The haunting of old centuries presented in Stoker's *Dracula* as the necessary condition for the emergence of the vampire's hunger did not stop during the twentieth century; instead, it became lodged in the national imaginary as if it were the undead body of a revenant of memory. This burden is symptomatic of a traumatized culture that, with no proper way to mourn its many losses, perpetually reopens the masculine wound and seeks new blood to offer as a sacrifice on the altar of its seemingly endless melancholia. The return to life of the undead artifacts is a dominant metaphor in the realm of a culture whose meanings can be articulated only if the entire national imaginary is mobilized in the reliving of the original trauma and the compulsive reopening of the masculine wound, because the burden of the common blood is too hard to bear.

The "single and unified world view" Bakhtin ascribes to the epic world is also a world of men, naturalized in everyday life to function as the unreachable ideal for the entire collective imaginary of 'the serbs.' Literature was charged with the special task of shaping the nation's imaginary by casting its past into a mold that foregrounds the guts and glory of its heroes. The literary canon of 'the serbs' has been constructed through the invocation of this monumental dimension—a temporality posited at such a distance from the present that it causes awe and a sense of smallness among the contemporary inhabitants of the national time and space.

The unassimilated core of the premodern imaginary continued to inhabit the cultural underground as modernity tried to take hold after national independence was won from the Ottomans. The pervasive melancholia that inhabited the time and space of a minor culture fueled a permanent cycle of mourning, reinforcing the symbolic link between the crypt of oral tradition and the everyday life of the nation. This link between the aura of holiness surrounding both the icons of Orthodox Christian saints and the dark crypt of the oral epic reappeared in modern literature as an esthetic articulation of national martyrdom. There is no doubt that the historical catastrophes of the Balkan wars, the First World War, and the Second World War reinforced the cultural mechanism tied to the violent return of the being of blood and eternal hunger.

While writing his controversial collection *Priče o muškom* (Masculine Stories) at the dawn of the new Kingdom of Serbs, Croats, and Slovenes in 1918, Miloš Crnjanski chose to title one story "Adam and Eve," revisiting the origin of humanity for the collective of 'the serbs,' which had lost 40 percent of its male population during the First World War. A disheveled officer returning from the Great War represents the Adam of the new South Slavic world; he is no longer excited by the charms of the feminine, since "only misery, despair and desire for what has been lost" can bring "the real ecstasy" in his ruined life. A beautiful actress who desires to have his child plays the national Eve; although she wants to complete her desperate love for the officer, he can no longer feel any emotion but incurable melancholia for a life he feels he has already spent on the battlefields of Europe. Melancholia is thus violence turned inward, eroding the integrity of the subject by protecting the object of loss, which is granted eternal life inside the imaginary space of the nation. The new Adam commits suicide, unable to return his Eve's love, offering a stillbirth rather than a future to the new South Slavic nation. The peripheral modernity is impregnated with this type of melancholic timber as the literary imaginary of the modern writer became limited to fixing and repeating the violence initiated by the post-Oriental condition.

Before literacy and modernity, the guslar and his audience were immersed in a universe of oral tradition; the "heroes" of the ethnic collective, "molded in marble and bronze," were transferred from the imaginary world into the living present of the oral performance.[28] The "formulaic" constraint of the oral transmission of the national imaginary uses repetition to mobilize the nation and offers a cultural channel for collective mourning. Literary encryptions of the trauma such as that exemplified in Crnjanski's short story, by contrast, enshrine the masculine wound in its agonistic modern form, internalizing the violence through individualized silent reading and creating an imaginary predicated on violent returns of the hungry being of blood and belonging.

South Slavic Dreams

The culture that emerged among 'the serbs,' both before and after the breakup of Yugoslavia, was a hybrid engendered in the post-Oriental condition interpellated by this melancholic dimension tied to the perception of a traumatic past. The old centuries that survive in Dracula's castle are everywhere, placed in a dreamlike relationship with everyday life, which appears as less true and real when compared with the glorious suffering of the forefathers. The image circulated by the global media during the Wars of Yugoslav Succession (1991–95) invoked the specter of 'the serbs' as perpetrators of ethnic violence marked by excess and irrationality. In fact, this specter has been made visible as a projection in both psychological and visual terms. The obscene secret of European hunger and its temporally distant responsibility for the current state of global culture is revealed in the phantasm of 'the serbs.' The imaginary effect that is created in attempts to foreclose the undesirable past of violent wars and ethnic divisions that mark Europe and its colonial domains mirrors the imperial transgressions of empires that are displaced and articulated in the image of 'the serbs.' Is it an accident that the latest wave of the vampire's popularity as a literary and cinematic icon began with Francis Ford Coppola's film *Bram Stoker's Dracula* (1992), which was released after the media began projecting "Balkan violence" during the Yugoslav wars?

Images of the uncivil war that has transformed Yugoslavia from the most liberal socialist state in Eastern Europe into a series of new political entities dominated by nationalist governments have been projected by the global media as a return of the Gothic specters of blood and horror. Balkan territories that require remote-control bombing, humanitarian intervention, and "peacekeeping" are being visualized as an imaginary battlefield where ancient ethnic hatreds divide angelic and demonic forces. The West has viewed the political atomization of Yugoslavia through a bifocal political lens: as a legitimate struggle for ethnic self-determination by angelic "non-Serbs" and an illegitimate grab for territory by demonic and bloodthirsty adherents to the communist dream embodied by 'the serbs.' In that sense, the specter of 'the serbs' as the fiercest vampires of the new world order is a re-invocation of the most convenient, traditional inheritor of the vampire legend that screens a larger projection of desire for global domination that is inherent in America's triumphalism since the end of the Cold War.

'The serbs' are also a poor avatar for the specter of a new form of Nazism, due to the almost universal turn to the political discourses of ethnic exclusivism in the former Yugoslavia. Enforcing ethnicity as a guarantor of proper identity has acted as a perfect repellent for any form of solidarity, apart from the discourse of blood and "ancient centuries," to emerge among different communities. This was the vision of the U.S.-led West, striving to separate the combatants along ethnic fault lines imagined through the clash of civilizations. Since the end of the Cold War, it is not only in Balkan territories dehumanized by war and poverty that this type of ethnic-based terror has thrived. It is also reflected in the reality of ongoing "race wars" in the ghettos of urban metropolises around the planet, as well as in other religiously diverse cultural environments.

Since Marxism was dethroned as the official state ideology of Eastern and Central Europe, social and political modernization have been in retreat throughout the region. These nations reached the limits of their emancipatory potential in the past century, and the ethnos and its ancient confessional roots have turned into the dominant markers of belonging. Czeslaw Milosz's critique of postmodern Western culture juxtaposes what he calls the "historical imagination" present in the identity of small Central European nations. The individual cultural agent is able to "reconstruct the past and make us aware of its extreme durability" through a particular artistic medium to give shape to that which has been made absent by the global insistence on consumption in the present as the only possible desirable model of identity.[29]

The past owes its "extreme durability" to the fact that it imagines the origin of its collective identity in the Middle Ages. The temporal distance of the imagined ancestors causes the cultural imagination to free itself from the fetters of the present and soar toward mythic visions of past national glory. Literary texts that linked the nation's identity to a distant past were first imagined by writers who became "national voices" of particular cultures during the nineteenth-century struggles for political emancipation from various empires with overlapping influences in Eastern and Central Europe. At the same time, these discourses predicated on the historical dimension of collective identity acted as metaphoric blood in the emergence of volatile forms of nationalism in the region.

The most recent return of the past coincided with emancipation from the grip of communism, a favorite Cold War pejorative in the West for the military-party dictatorships that wore thin symbolic veils of legitimacy borrowed from Marx, Engels, Lenin, and even Stalin. Yugoslavia added Tito to this list of "revolutionary thinkers" in the form of obligatory glorification of "socialist self-management" in public discourse before 1989, which the Yugoslav version of apparatchiks touted as the ultimate form of emancipation from "socially alienated" labor. The descendants of Balkan serfs and indentured servants often saw the revolutionary promise as a transparent yet necessary lie, especially in social settings that tightly policed the industrial and cultural means of production. In Yugoslavia, a hybridized managerial class—the *rukovodioci*—took control of the country by using its communist legitimacy to promote family and tribal-network members into positions of power, allowing a fruitful coexistence of underground corruption and official "self-management" under Tito's soft version of the masculine cult of the partisan warrior.[30]

Half a century of institutionalized socialism built on the heroic imaginary of the epic world supplemented by the brave Tito and his partisans fighting the evil German Nazis and Italian Fascists while demonizing the so-called domestic traitors embodied by the Croatian Ustaše and the Serbian Četnici. Such overt ideological control over the founding narratives of the socialist nation exposed the Yugoslavs to continual celebration of the "national liberation struggle," which was cast in epic high relief contiguous with the earlier cultural imaginary formed by the oral tradition. With heroic codes from the folkloric traditions of the Dinaric highlanders grafted onto the emergent culture of the Yugoslav socialist state, the process of modernization engendered an uncanny hybrid of socialist realism, which was dominant in the literary life of the first decade after the end of the First World War. Like its outdated Soviet predecessor, posited by Ždanov in his famous address in 1934, Yugoslav "partisan realism" established its own unwritten esthetic rules, which resurrected the ancient heroic vision of the nation born out of blood, but this time under the close ideological scrutiny of the Communist Party.

The literature of the new socialist state was charged with reflecting the official policy of overcoming ethnic and cultural differences, which had been blamed for the inter-Yugoslav genocide of the Second World War. But the heroic masculinity of the communist warriors was modeled on the rural Dinaric cultures from which most of the victors emerged to invade the Yugoslav cities, the traditional fortresses of civic life based on tolerance and suspicion of any overtly imposed ideology. Therefore, the new literary and cultural regime ended up glorifying the righteous violence and re-creating many of the dominant gender roles contained in the epic exaggerations of the masculine war machines. Even though a large number of female partisan warriors were included in the new cultural canon of the socialist state, their image was infused with masculine characteristics associated with the warrior cult based on an earlier worldview.

The political manifestations of this type of cultural imaginary became increasingly volatile toward the end of the millennium, whose last and most violent century came to an end with an uncanny echo of political discourses that, in the wake of the failure of socialism, resurrected old European songs of blood and soil. Although the case of Yugoslavia may be regarded as an anomaly within the context of a unifying Europe and globalizing world, the bloody return of old centuries that the U.S.-led West visualized in the Balkans is a symptom related to a future that has been emerging throughout Eurasia since the bipolar world order was dismantled in 1989.

Needless to say, the political and military conflicts that erupted within the former communist federations were mediated by the Western information industry as driven by "ancient and irrational ethnic hatred," a code for the discourse in which only U.S. military intervention can provide the guidance and protection of "Western democracy" to peoples who cannot rule themselves. The racist implications of this political discourse rarely have been noticed in those "Oriental" countries whose "white" inhabitants are nevertheless regarded as "lesser" Europeans. The cultural standards of these other Europeans are tainted with shades of Gothic "darkness" most often tied to their Slavic origins or their belonging to the religious cultures of Orthodox Christianity and Islam.[31]

This disguised form of cultural racism has been particularly visible in countries that, until the late 1980s, lived behind the so-called Iron Curtain—that is, the now erased realm of the "Second World" of Soviet and East European communism. That other Europe played the role of ideological enemy of the West for the better part of a century while the military-party complexes that ruled "Oriental" Europe in the name of communism were portrayed as agents of an "Evil Empire." After Mikhail Gorbachev's reforms removed the ideological barriers between the two parts of Europe in the 1980s, the West reverted to models of control it had already tested in the so-called Third World: colonial and neocolonial practices of economic, political, and military domination.

The very logic that defines the nation-state as a territory bound by the blood of a single ethnic group is responsible for the emergence of modern Europe in the age of nationalism. The same sanguine logic of the nation-state was activated in the Balkan borderlands during the final decade of the twentieth century. The time delay of more then a century allowed enlightened Westerners to forget the bloody struggles that gave geopolitical shape to the continent and to their own national imaginaries. The attempt of the West to detach itself from the root causes of the Yugoslav wars is therefore a symptom of its unwillingness and inability to come to terms with the violent heritage that was responsible for the terrible wars and genocide of the past millennium that shaped the current political configuration of the European continent.

The discourse of post-Orientalism places 'the serbs' in the position of collective borderline subjects whose constant struggle with unresolved mourning for the glorious past and self-destructive melancholia cause ethical emptiness in the national subject. This subject has been transformed into a place-of-the-name of violence itself, the signifier filled with any content necessary to rouse to intoxicating violence and regain the moment of heroic evil. Therefore, 'the serbs' as a construct of historiography could be represented as an example of freedom and nobility in Leopold Ranke's *The Serbian Revolution* of 1829 but also as a menace to civilization that needs "to be eradicated" by Johann Georg Reissmüller, editor of the *Frankfurter Allgemeine Zeitung*, in 1993.[32]

This fluid quality of 'the serbs' as a collective representation questions the imaginary of the nation in both its "Western" and its "Eastern" articulations and places "native" intellectuals in a constant struggle to overcome the strictures of identity of their own ethnic collective. The East–West division of imaginary geography crumbles when confronted with the minoritarian conceptions of collectivity, scattered between the exigencies of masculine paranoia and a number of singular lines of flight from the bondage to the vision of compulsory heroism. However hard Europeans and Americans try to exclude the narratives that formed 'the serbs' as a phantasm to be expelled from the symbolic realm of the West, the nature of this specter's emerging on the margins of civilization points to the imaginary origin of the symptom tied to Eurocentric discourses of the nation. It is therefore paramount to recognize that the perpetual desire of 'the serbs' to emerge from the post-Oriental condition and return to the West is what fuels their cultural imaginary as violence, manifested in "uncivilized" practices during the Wars of Yugoslav Succession (1991–95).

3
SOUNDS OF BLOOD
Yugoslavism and Its Discontents

It was principally because of the war that I wanted to go to Serbia, into the country of the so-called aggressors. . . . I felt the need to travel into the Serbia that had become, with every article, every commentary, every analysis, less recognizable and more worthy of study, more worthy of, simply, being seen. And whoever is thinking now: Aha! Pro-Serbia! or Aha! Yugophile!—need read no further.
—Peter Handke, *A Journey to the Rivers*

As the tanks, airplanes, and missiles stood pointed at the external enemies of Tito's self-management socialism, the Yugoslav brothers found themselves caught up in the imaginary erected out of the blood sacrifice of the Second World War as a worker's paradise of "brotherhood and unity." Until the breakup of socialist Yugoslavia in 1991, the police had kept guns pointed inside, at those who would disturb this imaginary harmony of South Slavic nations, with different versions of ethnically based narratives of exclusion. The system of organized state violence grew out of the Second World War, designed by the victorious communists to ward off what was often referred to in political discourse as "*povampireni nacionalizam*" (reborn vampire nationalism).

Those ethnic groups that did not qualify as nations were given the official status of "national minorities," a term used to describe possible irredentist populations in the border areas. The greatest threat was seen in the fluidity of the Albanian "national minority," whose ethnic boundaries spill from Albania proper into Kosovo and western Macedonia. Other minorities included, among many others, Hungarians, Italians, Turks, Slovaks, Roma, and Rusyns. For almost half a century, the post–Second World War descendents of Serbs, Croats, Slovenes, Bosniaks, Macedonians, and Montenegrins were trained to ignore the genocidal past of that war and embrace each other as comrades in arms set on overcoming ethnic differences for the sake of universal working-class solidarity. Yet since 1991, the ethnically based discourses of exclusion have become the dominant political practice within each ethnic collective, leading to the violent destruction of the imaginary bond of brotherhood that kept the imagined community of Yugoslavs together. That is why Peter Handke, the Austrian writer who has been much maligned for his supposed pro-Serbian position during the Yugoslav wars, insisted on looking closely at the location singled out in the Western media for its exemplary bloodthirstiness.

In *Civilization and Its Discontents*, Sigmund Freud—another Austrian living in proximity to the South Slavs—observed that the "inclination to aggression" is a universal human phenomenon. For Freud, the regulatory cultural mechanisms of civilization often failed to contain or eradicate the desire of one human to dominate another by violent means.[1] If we consider the Yugoslav implosion as one of the cases in which the framework of the multiethnic state failed to contain this type of mutual aggression, then favoring one of the particular ethnic identities over another relies on violence as a productive source of national becoming that is pleasing to the observer in question. That is why the Russian media have justified violence imputed to 'the serbs,' while the American media have rooted for their enemies.

The struggle for the territorial division of Yugoslavia was fueled by conflicting cultural imaginaries based on separation and assimilation, whereby the ethnic territory re-emerged as a gendered metaphor of communal identity defended in the name of pseudo-religious differences between the Slavic and the non-Slavic brothers alike. Since the ideological framework of communism did not survive Tito's death, the remnants of the military-party complex that lingered in the wake of his rule anchored themselves within the imaginary discourse of ethnic particularity. This was the case in the rest of Eastern and Central Europe, as well: As the fear of bipolar nuclear confrontation faded, class interest was gradually replaced by ethnic pride as the main category of identification within the post-communist political universe.

The ideology of official Yugoslavism, symbolized by the slogan "Brotherhood and Unity," had been in decline since the 1974 Constitution transformed the country into a virtual confederation ruled by competing ethno-communist elites. Instead of following the Leninist model of "democratic centralism" present in other socialist countries, the 1974 Constitution decentralized federal power and handed control over every aspect of political and economic life to party elites in the six constitutive republics and two autonomous provinces. One of the results of this decentralization was a strengthening of the national claims of Albanian, Bosnian Muslim, and Hungarian ethnic entities. Edvard Kardelj, the spiritual father of the 1974 Constitution and Tito's right-hand man, was later accused by 'the serbs' of designing it with a future decomposition of Yugoslavia in mind. Tito's death in 1980 only accelerated this process of "balkanization," as no other name had the symbolic power and political authority to provide an adequate substitute for the power exerted by the paternal metaphor.

Nation after Modernity

Slavoj Žižek's *The Indivisible Remainder* opens with a statement of national belonging: "As a Slovene."[2] This identification with the national seems to be at odds with the writings of a philosopher whose Marxist–Lacanian meditations have earned him a reputation as one of the "hottest" postmodern thinkers in the West. It is especially unsettling to read this simple declaration of what is, without a doubt, a form of postmodern nationalism from a philosopher whose work until recently was part of a broader cultural space of the former Yugoslavia. The ease and speed with which Žižek was able to resurrect the Slovene in a "national" sense raises myriad issues related to the position of national cultures and their producers and receivers within the context of the so-called new world order promoted by George Bush Sr. at the time of the Yugoslav War. The shedding of the Yugoslav identity as a shroud imbued with falsity in favor of ethnically based identity that springs forth hungry for recognition that its blood is different is a symptom of the imaginary shared by all of the post-Yugoslav nations. The need of the global media to study the specter of violence that haunted the beginning of the last decade of the past millennium is acknowledged in Peter Handke's statement about his motivation for taking his wartime journey to the Danube, Sava, Morava, and Drina, rivers that traverse the

lands of the South Slavs. Refusing the call of national signifiers tied to
the names of peoples, he intentionally invokes the rivers' names to
bypass identification with any of the warring nations. Handke's skepti-
cism about the representation of the Yugoslav conflicts, coming from a
person of Austrian Slovenian background, stands in opposition to the
political certainty displayed by Žižek.

According to the Croatian weekly *Start*, Žižek's Slovenism was articulated when the Yugoslav People's Army tried to stop the secession of
its northwestern republic, to which he responded: "Today I have become a Slovene." Žižek constructs the embrace of his particular brand
of ethnic belonging as a direct result of aggression of the imploding
socialist state. His Slovenism is offered as an escape from the Balkans
toward the promise of *Mitteleuropa* and, perhaps in the not so distant
future, Europe itself. In the late 1980s, Slovenian hunger for Europe
was expressed in the slogan "Europa zdaj!" (Europe now!), as if Yugoslavia was not already a geographic part of Europe. However, a special
brand of symbolic geography was at work in this strategy of separating
the Slovenes and, later, the Croats as members of a different cultural
tradition from the "east" and the "south," which were associated with
yet another label in the emergent racist discourse of the former Yugoslavia: the Balkans. Of course, Slovenian nationalism was rewarded:
Slovenia today is the only country of the former Yugoslavia to hold
membership in the European Union.

Slovenia's escape from Yugoslavia was indeed a response to the rise
of 'the serbs' under the guidance of Slobodan Milošević, a collective
considered by their Slavic brothers to the west as belonging to an
inferior culture in two senses: as post-Oriental subjects of the Ottoman
Empire and as the bearers of an Orthodox Christian cultural heritage
tied to the legacy of Byzantium. 'The serbs' were a threat to the Slovenes' European identity because they had the power of numbers and
weapons, which could be used to coerce the Slovenes to remain part of
the abject cultural space of "the Balkans." The concrete political response to this threat was the adoption by Slovenia of a national flag
identical to the flag of the European Union. Belonging to Europe and
the West was defined by a Roman Catholic cultural heritage, a separate
Slovenian language, and nationalism based in civil society.

The racism of the Slovenian position was not immediately perceiv-
able by Western observers, because whiteness, technological superi-

ority, and universalist humanism have all been incorporated into the specter of Europe itself as the symbolic foundation of the West. The German push for political recognition by the European Union of Slovenia and Croatia was a symptom of this civilizational acceptance of the northwestern Yugoslav republics as belonging to Europe, while the rest were forced back to the south and east, into the realm of political immaturity, cultural inferiority, and social abjection. The byproduct of officially enforced Yugoslavism, an ideology based on a mixture of the Titoist version of Marxian "class interest" and the quasi-racial similarity of the South Slavs, was the long suppressed sense of belonging to the larger cultural spheres radiating their historical influences from the centuries past.

Tito's Clones

Milošević's attempt to insert himself into Tito's position with the help of the military-party complex while exploiting the injured masculine revolt of 'the serbs,' resulted in the cloning of the paternal metaphor within the boundaries of each particular Yugoslav ethnicity. While Milošević became a totalitarian surrogate for 'the serbs,' Franjo Tuđman performed the same role in Croatia; Milan Kučan, in Slovenia; Alija Izetbegović, in Bosnia-Herzegovina, etc. This authoritarian cloning created a political climate that de-legitimized Yugoslavism as an overarching ideological framework within which the common state of the South Slavs could function by resurrecting the narratives based on blood stolen by the former members of the fraternal community. The failure of Yugoslavism as a framework that brought together different ethnic groups represents a failure of culture as a space of mediation by giving birth to the rise of a new type of exclusivist discourse Etienne Balibar has called "the racism of cultural differences."[3]

This new form of exclusionary discourse is not as blatantly racist as the one promoted by the German Nazis or the American Ku Klux Klan. Instead, its exponents try to normalize their exclusivism by insisting on the incompatibility of different cultures and the impossibility of their mutual translation and interpenetration. According to this view, each ethnic group should stay within the boundaries of its own cultural framework, without attempting to bridge gaps and live in proximity to its "others." Any attempt to do so would repeat the pattern of "stolen blood" and increase perceptions of the ethnic and racial others as vampires bent on dispossessing the proper identity of the group's own national prerequisites—language, religion, and territory.

Since Yugoslavia had been founded at the intersection of a multitude of cultural currents instituted through the subjugation of its ethnic groups to different imperial powers, cultural differences were instituted as a part of the traumatic legacy of conquest and domination built into the imaginary extension of each of the particular ingredient ethnicities participating in the discourse of Yugoslavism.

Brothers No More

As the communist foundations of the state started to crumble with the demise of the League of Communists in 1988, the political destiny of the Yugoslavs was handed over to the leaders of their constituent ethnic collectives. The Communist Party had imagined the foundation of Yugoslavia to be the projection of the class interest of workers and peasants based on the post-imperial experience of common victimization. It saw the power of ethnic identifications during this period as less acute than the common memory of suffering through the world wars. But as the common South Slavic state gradually devolved into an array of new political entities based on different articulations of religiously based senses of cultural belonging, the call of blood became louder among its constituent nations.

Apart from the official "Brotherhood and Unity" sloganeering of the communists, the bond between different Yugoslav ethnicities had been forged as solidarity of labor, functioning as a social conduit for understanding and tolerance between different cultural traditions after the Second World War. Most of the Balkans kept trying to emerge from the perpetual struggle against the branding associated with the post-Oriental legacy, as the East and the South were figured as inferior cultural designations in the context of European imaginary geography, which, in turn, associated them with poverty and abjection. This social image was complemented by the cultural image tied to the legacy of the vampire: the excessive violence and unchecked sexuality of the Balkan post-Oriental subject.

In his novels *Na Drini ćuprija* (The bridge on the Drina; 1945) and *Travnička hronika* (The Bosnian chronicle; 1945), Ivo Andrić, a literary figure who is emblematic of the emergent culture of the Yugoslavs, imagined a community of co-sufferers as a cultural model for a common multiethnic entity of emergent post-imperial subjects. Published right after the end of the Second World War, these novels provided a literary imaginary for the newly created "second Yugoslavia" led by Tito and his communist guerrilla fighters. Andrić's ambivalent textualizations of his native Bosnia were rooted in narratives that stemmed from the situation of the post-Oriental subject. Using the metaphor of the great flood, Andrić posits the space and time created by natural disasters as the only channel for mutual understanding available to the Bosnians:

> After the interval of fifteen or twenty years in which they had once more restored their fortunes and their homes, the flood was recalled as something great and terrible, near and dear to them; it was an intimate bond between men of that generation who were still living, for nothing brings men closer than a common misfortune happily overcome. They felt themselves closely bound by the memory of that bygone disaster. They loved to recall memories of the hardest blow dealt them in their lives. Their recollections were inexhaustible, and they repeated them continually, amplified by memory and repetition; they looked into one another's eyes, sclerotic and with yellowing whites, seeing there what the younger men could not even suspect.[4]

The ancient creature of blood and memory works through repetition, binding old men together to endow them with knowledge accessible only to those who know the secrets of violent endings, human or natural. At the bottom of this negative commonality is a self-perception of victimization by forces outside the sphere of an individual's grasp or control. While socialist realist writers from the same period featured a positive Yugoslav identity through the triumph of Tito's partisans over the forces of fascism, Andrić found a context for unity in violence that the ethnic communities disguised because they needed to forget the origins of their division. This kind of culture is corrosive and insidious, giving voice to the ancient creature of memory whose call for blood rests on the secret gazes exchanged by the old men whose knowledge is beyond utterance.

The vampire of memory is born from the traumatic core of injured masculinity and marks the life of those who are not able to foresee the possibility that yet another cycle of violence is at hand. This paradox of unity in negativity again features the monumental aspect of collective and individual suffering rooted in the post-Oriental condition in which most Yugoslavs found themselves after their ostensible liberation from imperial masters. Anxious about their location east and south of the centers of European modernity, these imaginary subjects were bound to repeat the misfortune through narrative remembering of old men who do not speak but only look deeply into one another's eyes. Their disguised pain reinforces the fraternal bond between old men, invoking the secret of the victim that can never be fully worked through in the mere act of narrative iteration and displacement. Instead, the silence functions as the obverse of violence that can erupt any time the misalignment of external forces takes place, like a great flood that stands for the evil forces of history. This knowledge radiates from the glances exchanged between old men, because the power of horror defines the identity of subjects who are preparing for yet another bloody narrative without ending.

Beastly Bodies

Multiple wars, invasions, and occupations are imagined as part of an evil that is external to Bosnia, an effect of violence that arrives to render bloody the insides of post-Oriental subjects, causing tragic events that erode the bodies of its inhabitants as if they were caused by the great flood. While writing about the beginning of the First World War and the Habsburg drive to pacify and dominate 'the serbs' of Bosnia, Andrić invokes the boundary between the animal and human characteristic of the vampire's desire:

> The people were divided into the persecuted and the persecutors. That wild beast, which lives in man and does not dare show itself until the barriers of law and custom have been removed, is now set free. The signal is given, and boundaries [are] erased. As so often happens in the history of man, permission was tacitly granted for acts of violence and plunder, even for murder, if they were carried out in the name of higher interests, according to established rules, and against a limited number of men of a targeted breed and creed.[5]

The violence is naturalized by a fatalistic sense of the doomed course of the "history of man," which is constantly disturbed by the return of the animal ancestor who inhabits the secret interior of the subject. Driven by the destructive instinct given free rein through the tacit permission of the ruling authorities, the human being is reduced to its basic instinct for domination over targeted others. The beastly underside of the national imaginary supplements the infatuation with one's collective reflection as hatred and extermination of the simplified and reified cultural others challenges the fraternal bond between men who belong to different "breed and creed." The emergence of the "wild beast" is not imagined as incompatible with civilization, since murder, plunder, and other acts of violence are rationalized "according to established rules" and "in the name of higher interests," to excuse and even glorify the elimination of undesired cultural others. The violence is in effect a sine qua non of every communal becoming, requiring the sacrifice of the life essence of the other at the altar of that beastly vampire crouching in the depths of every national imaginary. Or, in the words of Walter Benjamin, "There is no cultural document that is not at the same time a record of barbarism."[6]

The failure of universal humanism is predicated on the ceaseless return of the desire for survival at the expense of the blood of the other. The beastly creature with a human exterior is seen as occupying a low rung in the scheme of evolutionary classification, yet it always gains the upper hand in times of war and conflict. Balibar's analysis of universal humanism leads him to conclude that "the problematic quality of *difference between humanity and animality* is re-utilized to interpret conflicts within society and history," reinforcing a kind of silent racism that dehumanizes religious and ethnic others by ascribing the beastly nature to them.[7] The Balkan vampire has been the popular symptom of this attitude toward one's neighbor who belongs to a different cultural tradition. The inability of civilization to see violence in its own foundations leads it to imagine the violent performance of humanity simultaneously as a metaphor for the bloody interior of one's own subjectivity and as a sacrificial position occupied by the object of one's insidious vampirism. Violence is civilization's imaginary other; the animal, a symptom of the insidious vampire involved in transferring the focus of violence from the subject to the object that underlies the foundation of high cultural values in the Balkans and beyond.

Tito as a Phallus

If Yugoslavism managed to sublimate the inner workings of its vampires, personified in the various ethnic identities locked within their

Freudian "narcissisms of minor differences," it did so by installing a sense of shared historical guilt among the major protagonists of the conflict. During the socialist period, both Serbs and Croats were constantly reminded that not all of them had fought alongside Tito and his partisans against Nazi occupation during the Second World War; some, instead, had been drafted into the ranks of Royalist Četniks or Nazi Ustaše. Anyone who diverged from the official ideology of the Communist Party could be accused of "nationalist deviation" and therefore cast in the role of the "domestic traitor" to Yugoslavia.

The figure of Tito functioned as a benevolent but strict paternal metaphor within the public sphere, preventing dissent by maintaining a constant level of collective guilt over the two most dominant ethnic groups. A communist Croat himself, Tito came to power by leading 'the serbs' from Croatia and Bosnia to establish the new order and liberate Serbia from the Nazi terror. Continuing to blur the macro-cultural boundaries of separation between the two groups, official communism reinforced a version of Yugoslavism based on Tito's personality cult. The communists' desperate attempt to hold onto power in the name of the father was expressed in the adoption of a slogan with vampiric overtones after his death in 1980: "I posle Tita—Tito" (After Tito—also Tito). The desire for perpetual life of the symbolic father of the Yugoslav nation was to guarantee the survival of his people beyond the grave, as well.

One of the cultural manifestations of love for the undead father was embodied in the attempt to continue with the celebration of the "Day of Youth." This holiday, which marked Tito's birthday, involved a relay race around Yugoslavia that culminated with a "baton of youth" being handed to the president-for-life at the central event in Belgrade on May 25. In the absence of the symbolic father, the baton was placed in the position where Tito used to stand, its shape symptomatic of the imaginary phallus he came to represent for the community of South Slavs. The structure of this performance was staged as if it was meant to parody the psychoanalytic theories of both Freud and Lacan, revealing the underside of phallic power that would soon crumble under the weight of the diverging ethnic imaginaries.

The belief that the undead father would continue to function as a metaphor of the survival of Yugoslavia was predicated on the same guilt that was supposed to keep the beast within from continuing its

Tito's shadow: Day of Youth rally. PHOTOGRAPHER UNKNOWN.

quest for blood. Cast in a role that apparently transcended ethnicity through power politics in the new Yugoslavia, Tito functioned as a screen onto which each ethnic group could project its own collective guilt. The enforcement of this guilt was tied to the inability ever to achieve the communist dream of fullness and wholeness embodied in the classless society. The absence of Tito signaled the moment that the burden of guilt could be transposed into its horrifying opposite—the bloody conflict between Yugoslav ethnic groups burdened with guilt tied to their tacit bond of belonging to a wider framework of quasi-religious civilization.

Nasal Racism

This sinister demonstration of loyalty to the supreme signifier of Yugo-slavism in the socialist period did more damage to the "Brotherhood and Unity" ideology in the early 1980s than did the uprising of the Kosovar Albanians in 1981 that started the unraveling of the common South Slavic country. The undead father was also invoked through another popular cultural practice initiated at the same time: street vendors began selling gold-colored aluminum pins in the shape of Tito's landmark signature. By wearing the signature on their bodies, the Yugoslavs demonstrated not only their loyalty to the afterlife with Tito;

they also tried to come to terms with collective guilt tied to crimes committed against one another. Unfortunately, the showdown would soon be re-enacted through the policies of ethnic exclusivity nurtured by Tito's authoritarian clones.

Ultimately, none of the cultural gestures that attempted to resurrect the dead father could preserve Yugoslavia as a political space, because implementing and justifying the simplistic appeal to the bond of common blood by Tito's clones did not require elaborate Marxist theories. Ethnic nationalism is an ideology that appeals to the lowest common denominator; it is obvious to the point of idiocy. It filled the emptiness left by the paternal signifier in the political space of Yugoslavia, turning it from a dream state of the socialist world into a nightmare ruled by vampire nations. Milošević's attempt to act as the sole substitute for Tito failed because the rhetoric of victimization and right of revenge he embraced in the late 1980s in the name of 'the serbs' prevented his appeal from extending beyond that group

The reaction of Slovenian leaders to Milošević's Serb-rousing rhetoric predictably was in tune with the age-old European practices of "nasal racism"—use of the thumb and the index finger to prevent the unpleasant odor of Balkan Orientals from reaching the refined nostrils of Central Europeans—that had been applied to those outside the magic circle of *Mitteleuropa*. Proximity to Europe was measured by the strength of that odor, with the unpleasantness increasing along the northwest-to-southeast axis. Bosnians, Albanians, and Macedonians ranked the poorest on that scale, but the Slovenes did not have to worry about them so much, because they had the Croats and the Serbs as territorial intermediaries—or, as Petar Tancig put it at the time, their own *cordon sanitaire*. This kind of political posturing brought Slovenia membership in the European Union before any of the other post-Yugoslav countries.

Slovenes' desire for independence, and for Europe, was intimately tied to this soft version of cultural racism, which is based on ideas about ethnic separation running along lines drawn by the former imperial masters. After communism lost its ideological validity, the former subjects of the Habsburg empire emerged as possessing a supposed cultural superiority that in Slovenia manifested itself in calls for a "civil society" that would, of course, exclude most of the rest of Yugoslavia. Other Yugoslavs figured in Slovenian nationalist discourse as "dirty Bosnians," transforming the desired civil society into a return to a claustrophobic vision of the ethnically homogenous nation-state.

Žižek recognizes the multiplicity of possible meanings inherent in the individual's relationship to the state, which, however, functions under the same name and constitution: "When the signifier 'our Nation' starts to function as the rallying point for a group of people, it *effectively* co-ordinates their activity, although each of them may have a different notion of what 'our Nation' means."[8] Žižek coordinates his intellectual activity with that of other Slovenes by symbolically descending into the Škocijan caves a century after Freud to claim the realm of unconscious exploration for himself and his nation. "As a Slovene," Žižek, the postmodern, Lacanian philosopher, finds himself confronted with the same figure Freud encountered in the depths of the caves: He analyzes Freud's encounter with Karl Lueger, the right-wing, anti-Semitic mayor of Vienna, as if Freud were recounting a dream and not a real event from his life. According to this interpretation, the mayor's last name is associated with the *Lüge*, a German word for "lie." Thus, "What we discover in the deepest kernel of our personality is a fundamental, constitutive, primordial *lie*."[9]

The Ethnoscapes of Hidden Horror

This underground lie supposedly constitutes "our personality" and lives at the expense of both the individual and collective identity envisioned by Žižek in the native ethnoscape of Slovenia, which before its union with other South Slavs belonged to the Habsburg empire. If collective identity is constituted by the primordial lie, then the ethical concerns of those psychoanalytic theorists who believe in the validity of this theory need not conform to anything but this fundamental lie. If the unbearable inconsistency of the symbolic order forces the subject to constantly falsify his own sense of irreducibly singular subjectivity, is the extrapolation of the lie to the "national" level not a logical next step? Therefore, the lie has been responsible not only for the successful operation of the institution of psychoanalysis, but also for the global information management of the Yugoslav implosion, which has been considerably influenced by the narratives manufactured by the Slovenian state as the self-appointed intermediary between the Balkans and the West.

Sylvia Poggioli, a reporter with National Public Radio, analyzed her experiences at the beginning of the Yugoslav wars, after the Slovenes seceded from the federation, this way:

> Starting with the 10-day war in Slovenia in June and July of 1991, one of the most difficult tasks for reporters has been to protect themselves from the propaganda offensive. The Slovenia Information Ministry organized a media center in a modern underground conference hall in Ljubljana. Here troops of young multilingual Slovenes constantly churned out reams of war bulletins. . . . We were supplied with excruciatingly detailed accounts of battles too far away to check personally before deadline. Often we learned the next day that the battles had never taken place.[10]

Freud's underground cave here is replaced by the underground media center for the dissemination of narratives whose mendacious nature has colored the perceptions of the Yugoslav wars ever since. The United States cast itself in the imperial role of protector of the unruly Balkans that was played by the Habsburg empire in the nineteenth century. Having provided a physical location for Freud's discovery of the "fundamental lie" at the bottom of the Škocijan caves, Žižek set out to impose narratives of cultural superiority on the less civilized peoples of the Balkan southeast. Identifying with "democracy and justice" of the Europe to come, Slovenes abandoned the common South Slavic state as a transitory step, fleeing the newly discovered old incarnation of the ancient underground god of blood displayed in the media phantasm of 'the serbs,' the ethnic group deemed irredeemable by the new post–Cold War global civilization in the making.

Bloody Songs

Music has been one of the key cultural components of the now defunct Yugoslav state, especially in its popular forms and manifestations. Because the Balkan Peninsula was inhabited for the most part by rural populations, the peasant song was regarded as the ultimate expression of the Yugoslav character. This notion, modeled on the mixture of Romantic conceptions of "folk" and a specific Balkan model of modernization, prompted Vladimir Dvorniković, the most significant Yugoslav ethno-psychologist, to posit the peasant song as the ultimate sounding of common South Slavic "blood and race."

Dvorniković's *Karakterologija Jugoslovena* (Characterology of the Yugoslavs) was published on the eve of the Second World War, in the same year the German Nazis and Russian Stalinists divided Poland, and Croatia gained autonomy from the Yugoslav kingdom under steady pressure by Adolf Hitler's government. Because external and internal projects to counter Yugoslav unity were so strong in 1939, Dvorniković's dream of a common South Slavic music was intellectually tragic. The scientific idea of race obsessed the enthusiastic Dvorniković, whose embrace of Bosniak and southern Serbian and Macedonian song came to represent the very embodiment of the South Slavic identity.

"Our folk song," which Dvorniković imagined as a collective voice of the South Slavic "blood and race," has been fragmented twice since he wrote the monumental *Karakterologija* in 1939. The final fragmentation of Yugoslavia initiated in 1991 through the formation of new state entities has been an effect of a process of political de-legitimization of the Yugoslav idea. This differentiation was followed by the sounds of new songs, whose specific ethnic flavor bears the marks of new incarnations of cultural racism given free rein during the latest inter-Yugoslav confrontations. It is especially tragic that Dvorniković imagined Bosnian songs as the "bottom of the soul" of all those Yugoslav peoples who suffered various forms of foreign occupation and domination.

Dvorniković quotes a singer he interviewed in Montenegro explaining singing not as an esthetic activity, but as a need to give expression to accumulated melancholy: "I don't sing because I know how; I sing to get rid of my soul's burden."[11] This cultural "burden" of the Yugoslav soul was imagined as the ultimate sounding of unity among different ethnicities. While trying to work out classifications of various cultural traditions, Dvorniković distinctly invoked folk music as the supreme embodiment of the Yugoslav national spirit: "The psychology of *melos* and music leads us in the most direct, experiential manner into the deepest emotional layers, into the rhythmic and dynamic structure of our national psyche."[12]

While tacitly reasserting Friederich von Schelling's theory of music as the most intuitive of all arts and therefore superior to them, Dvorniković also modernized Herder's Romantic conception of *Volksgeist* by invoking the notion of a common national psyche. It is also symptomatic that the identities of non-Slavic peoples, including, among others, the Albanians, Roma (Gypsies), and Jews, do not figure in the more than one thousand pages of the *Karakterologija Jugoslovena*, except as a negative against which the Slavic folk genius can be imagined. The tacit exclusion of non-Slavs turns into outright racism, especially when Dvorniković turns away in disgust from the singing of the Roma:

> The inner being and lyricism of the Slavic song is completely alien to Gypsies. Tenderness, nostalgia, pride, masculinity, heroism, subtlety, reticence, sacrifice for the loved one; all those elements of our real folk song do not come through in the Gypsy interpretation. . . . Let it be called Gypsy singing, but not the "Yugoslav folk song." . . . Our folk song should be protected from this kind of sacrilege.[13]

Thus, Dvorniković saw Roma singing as detrimental to the heroism and masculinity of the nation, which is based on his theory of "integral Yugoslavism" promoted by Serbia's Karađorđević dynasty before the Second World War. The war songs and turbo-folk that became the musical expression of particular ethnic nationalisms during and after the Wars of Yugoslav Succession (1991–95) were set against this kind of culturally based common identity and a community promoted by both the royalist and the communist Yugoslav states. The active suppression of any discussion of racially motivated genocide of the Second World War greatly damaged the Yugoslavism promoted during the socialist period, which could be characterized as proto-multicultural. While the Roma, Albanians, Jews, and other minorities received better treatment in Tito's Yugoslavia than in any of the neighboring states, the Slavic populations who shared a common language (Bosniaks, Croats, Montenegrins, Serbs) ended up nurturing mutual resentment based on unresolved issues involving collective crimes and punishments.

The literal and figurative displacements and erasures of cultural others during the latest Wars of Yugoslav Succession were accompanied by the sounds of war songs, repeating the same epic tunes of masculine pain and rage. The struggle for domination over the designated enemy of different blood and belonging was seen as righteous revenge over culturally inferior opponents.

Bacillus Bosniensis

While constructing the common Yugoslav cultural paradigm around the "Dinaric race" shared by the three major religious groups who inhabit the Dinaric Mountains, Dvorniković obviously felt uneasy about generalizing, because the cultural traditions adopted through foreign conversions and occupations pose great problems in forming the idea of a common "Yugoslav race." As a young man, he heard the essence of the newly imagined race in the sound of Bosnian urban ballads (*sevdalinke*). Songs of love, pain, and longing for one's youth defined the soul of the new nation, whose root soundings initially frightened Dvornikovič: "I have to admit that these songs were quite horrifying to me during my adolescent years. . . . Nasal, drawn out, with countless melismatic transitions."[14] Those songs were sung in the double voice of Oriental and proto-Slavic heritage. The Oriental was constructed as the underground, terrifying layer of the song, while the Slavic heritage was seen as rooted in the racial character of the brotherly tribes. Yet, he wrote:

> After transition to manhood, my relationship with this type of song and folk music in general changed fundamentally: after a long incubation, the infection broke out. *Bacillus bosniensis*, although my ancestors are not Bosnian, entered my blood, and from the bottom of my soul, somewhere from its most atavistic depths, a string emerged which vibrated upon hearing the most primitive song of the porters.[15]

Dvornikovič thus compares the development of his love of Bosnian song to being infected with a disease of masculinity, in his case contracted after initiation into love, sexuality, and the horrors of the First World War. Blood is infected with the eruption from the atavistic depths as boy becomes man, allowing the post-Oriental imaginary voiced in the urban ballads to take over. The contamination of the soul with this kind of masculine melancholy is his initiation into a community of men whose "blood" is infected by the pain and desire of the post-Oriental subject: centuries of racial segregation and gender oppression under the Islamic millet system nurtured a cultural tradition that eases both the singer's and the audience's "burden." Similar to the way Andrić imagined the secret knowledge of old men, this adherence to music as a source of cultural comfort shows Yugoslavs not only as the South Slavs but also as slaves from the European South. The continual contest between different civilizations to conquer and pacify the bloodthirsty Balkan tribes forged a desire for a community based on a common bond among subjects of different imperial masters, which often ended caught up in the obsessive search for revenge and redemption of its own stolen blood.

Dvornikovic's vision of modern Yugoslav identity is primarily a project based on the concept of common blood and language mobilized to counter the repetition of this unwanted historical destiny of submission. The narratives and songs symptomatic of differences assimilated from the former imperial rulers are overlooked in favor of the cultural narrative of South Slavic unity. Yet when Tito stopped acting as the ultimate figure of this type of common destiny, his political clones began to fashion new–old cultures of ethnic separation based on hatred of their former brothers by sounding those cultural differences in popular music. Songs were yet again used as a powerful tool in the formation of new collective memories, providing a return to the sense of isolation from the cultures of those who no longer belonged to the larger Slavic community.

The resurrection of particularized ethnicities marks a powerful return to an older conception of the people, outfitted in the 1990s with electronic media and a surplus of weapons accumulated during the Cold War paranoia that once pit Tito's Yugoslavia against both the Soviet East and the American West. When racial differences are imagined solely through a sense of cultural belonging, the distinction between "inferior" and "superior" ethnicity can be realized with a minimal level of political, social, and cultural performance of separation. This is indeed what occurred during the destruction of the latest Yugoslav incarnation, as ethnic subjects acted out their violence through a scenario interpellated by the call of cultural differences that marked their belonging to a larger framework of civilization. Whether Catholic, Orthodox, or Muslim, these primordial identities were activated to enact separation imagined as a common bond of blood based on culture bearing the name of religion.

Interestingly, Dvornikovic felt obliged to clamor against proponents of Nordic racial superiority as early as 1939, when Yugoslavia was about to be dismembered by the Nazis. Countering the racial theories of the German Ludvig Woltmann, Dvornikovic cast an ironic glance at the Nazi vision of Europe:

> We should not forget that Nietzsche's *blonde Bestie* was a man who introduced organized industry, electricity and radio-waves, but also caused a

great anxiety by authoring such grandiose cultural advancements under the rubric of "world war," "air war," "total war"; it is not unusual that the criterion of superiority turned against him within the soul of other races.[16]

The turn caused by the technological utopia of Nordic racial superiority in "the soul of other races" took the form of new fractures effected through the hygienic extermination of those below the racial divide, something that Dvorniković sensed was already taking place inside his "Yugoslav soul." Since the name "Slavs" already contains etymological echoes of these people's slave identity, their fantasies of superiority are imagined as a return to past days of medieval glory, before they descended into the status of the subjugated nations. The assimilation by imperial religions and cultures they currently consider their own is essential in imagining a new conception of race as an effect of specifically Slavic modernity. Therefore, Stoker's *Dracula* invokes old centuries as if they were *opposed* to modernity, while Dvorniković shows that popular music invokes the old as *part of* the modern emergence of the South Slavs. The conflicted heritage of subjects of peasant blood with the memory of kings emerged as a potent metaphor during the nineteenth century in the struggles for independence from foreign domination in the Balkan region.

One could reduce Dvorniković's invention of the Yugoslav race to a cultural apology for the centrist tendencies of the Karađorđević dynasty. But a closer look at his idea of common "blood and racial filiation" among the Balkan Slavs manifests a deeper internalization of the modern concept of the nation as a bond between blood and ancient temporality:

> However, blood and racial filiation (at least in the beginning), a common life through the centuries, a common struggle and historical destiny joins individuals and creates a common psychological type out of them, starting with daily life routines, from reactions in the most insignificant situations to those transpersonal and cross-generational leanings which bind all of those individuals into one collective, into one will, into one common way of thinking and feeling, in short, into one *spirit* of the nation.[17]

Modern South Slavic identity is imagined according this homogenizing model posited by the interiorization of the Herderian gaze that imagined the *Volk* as an amalgam of racial and cultural categories. The

Gothic imagination provided the literate intelligentsia among the Balkan Slav with a vision of identity rooted in the songs and dances of illiterate peasants with whom they identified as the ultimate voicing of the nation's blood.

The Vienna Agreement between the Croat Ljudevit Gaj and the Serb Vuk Karadžić in 1850 defined the project of South Slavic cultural unity as a choice of a common linguistic dialect (*štokavski*) that was supposed to be the root of the new Yugoslav identity. While searching for the spontaneous and the original in writing down the songs of the people, Vuk imagined the relationship of the Balkan Slavs as a project based on "folkloristic" unity of a peasantry whose motto was "One People of Three Faiths." The minute Balkan urban classes, steeped in racial and cultural hybridity, developed a peculiar habit of imagining the people to whom they belonged as imaginary peasants who had spent the entire nineteenth century singing songs and shedding blood for love and freedom. Balkan urban mentality emerged as a simultaneous embracing of and distancing from the "primitive" non-culture of rural populations, whose life was posited simultaneously as a national ideal that countered the artifice and degradation of urban life and a rustic existence that was to be avoided by all means.

Although blood is invoked as a basis for collectivity, the second part of Dvorniković's definition of the national spirit offers "historical destiny" as a source of the true *Volksgeist* that gives direction to the common identity. He strove desperately to imagine Yugoslav identity as a totality of "one will" and "one spirit of the nation," gradually slipping into the discourse of racial supremacy based on the primitive power and vitality of the Dinaric race. Dvorniković proceeded to define the Dinaric man as the organic basis of the "Yugoslav race" by setting the issue of superiority aside. Yet the "great anxiety" of the race slotted for extermination by Hitler lingered as he explored the depths of the "Yugoslav soul."

The turn "within the soul of other races" caused by preparation of the "total war" effort on the part of the Aryan race caused Dvorniković to cast a superior look from the margin at the center of Europe. He imagined the North as the seat of "technology"; as German ingenuity led astray by the stupidity of racism. This gaze from superior heights is assimilated and returned from the borderlines of Europe, where Dvorniković imagined the birth of genius from the bosom of the Dinaric mountains. Balkan's status as "not quite Europe" provided him with the lens of an unacknowledgedly post-Oriental subject: The technology that fueled the modernization of Europe, for him, was at the same time responsible for the return of its violent and aggressive barbarism through the practice of "total war." Although he set out to counter and criticize the very notion of racially based evaluation of cultures, he could not resist the temptation to challenge the natural right of the "blond beast" to rule the world. Once again, blood and beastliness were utilized as discursive devices to characterize relationships between struggling communal entities

Singing the Nation

Dvorniković internalized the Gothic gaze from the imperial center, providing his own people, deemed an inferior civilization by the European cultural core, with their own vision of cultural superiority. He scorned European musical notation systems as "a bloodless scheme of Western musical mathematics," since its signifiers were not able to contain the fullness of "our folk song."[18] The signs of an emerging superiority complex are rooted in the internalized gaze of the perceived aggressor found in the Germanic race, which historically imagined the folk heritage of the Balkans as the core of Europe's primal identity during the Romantic period. "Our folk song" is imagined as a being full of blood, just like a sated vampire, encompassing the passions tied to the imaginary body of the nation that the technologically superior West has repressed or forgotten. Blood figures as a metaphor for the inability of the Western musical-transcription system to grasp the vital power and melodic subtlety of Yugoslav folk songs while, at the same time, music figures as the sounding of passion tied to hot Balkan blood full of violence and sexuality as an effect of the post-Oriental condition.

Dvorniković located the most intense expression of such national passion in the territories where Ottoman domination had lasted the longest in Yugoslavia. He figured folk song as the dark side of collective imaginary, an abyss emanating from the pain of unfulfilled desire and repressed rage. Dvorniković heard the most acute expression of the Yugoslav soul in songs that invoked the sentiments of *dert* and *sevdah*. These two Ottoman Turkish words, which denote the *pain* of perpetual frustration and the *melancholy* caused by loss or distance of the desired object, were assimilated into the vocabulary of Bosnian, Serbian, and

Carousing: an outlet for guilt and pain. PHOTOGRAPH COURTESY G. STAJIĆ.

Macedonian populations as the supreme signifiers of collective suffering that bind men together into a community of carousers ready to vent the accumulated frustrations boiling in their blood. This homosocial bond is strengthened in communal settings as men drink, sing, and fight alongside one another.

Dvorniković imagined the *kafana*—the Balkan combination of café, restaurant, and bar—as a post-Oriental location were men gather to vent their individual and collective frustrations by drinking plum brandy, occasionally smashing glasses on the floor to relieve their "burden" while listening and participating in the performance of the song. The fact that women (invariably perceived as fallen) and "Gypsies" continue to be the main facilitators of this type of national sounding manifests a paradoxical cultural coding of race and gender. Men achieve the full-blooded status of their manhood only via the other, who mediates their desire for oblivion through singing and dancing.

The descendants of subjugated races revel in their injured masculinity while listening to songs that evoke the sweet pain of longing for loss. The folk song evokes *sevdah* (derived from the same Arabic root as the Portuguese *saudade*), the black bile of melancholy that lingers in the singing of Bosnians: "*Sevdah* languishes in the soul; a muffled pain which can erupt with mad and limitless intensity."[19] The eruption of violence was rooted in this lethal melancholy of the South Slavs as they fought to affirm their particular racial-cultural identities during the wars would delineate new spaces of collective identity after the implosion of the common state in 1991.

Blood and Song

Another complication in understanding the relationship between blood and song among the South Slavic nations is compounded by half a century of military-party dictatorship that imposed itself under the title "communism." After Tito and the Communist Party emerged as the leaders of socialist Yugoslavia, Dvorniković's "integralist" theory came to be seen as reactionary because it glossed over ethnic particularities. Yugoslavism no longer was defined as a concept founded on the project of a common "Dinaric race" shared by the Bosniaks, Croats, Montenegrins, and Serbs; rather, it became a project that emerged from common struggle against Nazi and Fascist occupation and the class interest of "workers and peasants" joined in a "national-liberation struggle" during the Second World War.

The troubled history of racism fueled by Hitler's doctrines transformed the Independent State of Croatia of 1941 into a mass-extermination site for Serbs, Jews, and Roma (Gypsies) as humans of lesser quality. This overlooked aspect of non-German Nazi practices is what determined the violence-prone identity of the populations that the West has termed "Croatian Serbs" and "Bosnian Serbs." These populations were "racialized" as victims of the Croatian Ustaše, who implemented their notorious solution of the "Serbian problem" by "thirds"— that is, one-third were exterminated; one-third converted to Roman Catholicism; one-third were expelled from the territories of Croatia, Bosnia, and Herzegovina. The borderline incarnations of 'the serbs,' who survived the genocide were brought up on communist ideology and hatred of "fascism," a term that originally lumped together Croatian Ustaše, Nazi Germans, and Fascist Italians but later, in the official communist discourse, came to include the entire world of "Western imperialism." Because they were directly exposed to genocide in the Second World War, these two populations of 'the serbs' contributed more than anyone to Tito's "national liberation struggle" against "foreign occupation and domestic traitors."

Communist propaganda after the Second World War never properly

addressed the problem of mutual slaughter, making collective grievances almost impossible to work through openly. Tito's soft totalitarianism imposed the official "Brotherhood and Unity" ideology, which
suppressed dissidence and discussion in any direction. This is why 'the
serbs' in Bosnia and Croatia saw any move to break up Yugoslavia as a
return of "fascism" and implemented their own pre-emptive version of
genocidal revenge on the Bosniak and Croat populations at the beginning of the latest war. Needless to say, the return of right-wing emi-
grants from around the world under the Ustaše banner after communism collapsed did not help to restore the confidence of 'the serbs'
in the second independence of Croatia. Therefore, even the ostensibly
innocent Slovenian call for Europe from Alpine heights resounded with
frightening clarity in the blood of those whose ancestors were sacrificed to Hitler's "new European order." For them, the vampire nation
was embodied in their former brothers' return to the ideologies of
blood and soil from which Yugoslavia was promising to absolve the
Balkan region.

Fraternal Folklore

Contrary to Dvorniković, communist cultural officials saw folk songs as
a separatist or chauvinist tool that could undermine political unity
precisely because folk music was rooted in the "blood and soil" of local,
regional identity. Instead of portraying them as "Yugoslav," the communists often took care to identify folk songs specifically as Serbian,
Croatian, Bosnian, Macedonian, or Slovene and created folkloric performances to display "cultural" particularities. To produce a common
"proletarian culture," the Yugoslav communist establishment often
masked differences by sponsoring folk music societies and professional
folk singing and dancing ensembles.

Yugoslavs who lived outside urban centers usually identified with the
local folkloric heritage as the essence of their being and belonging even
as the state tried to promote the concept of "Yugoslav" folklore through
cultural-artistic societies. They put on shows that usually began with
the performance of a "Yugoslav" number, which was supposed to accent
official "Brotherhood and Unity." Songs were chosen to represent each
of the constituent nations and dances were choreographed into medleys
with musical transitions, forming what came to be known as a "plait of
folk songs and dances." This musical version of the Communist Party

The knife dance: domination and submission in the folk imaginary. PHOTOGRAPH COURTESY B. GAJIĆ.

platform was supposed to promote interethnic confidence and understanding by blending the folk songs of various ethnic groups. After the
fall of communism, the musical plait was disentangled along fault lines
set by cultural differences borrowed from former occupiers, producing a
new staging in the late 1980s in which mass political rallies were accompanied by performances that highlighted racial and cultural pride. The
rise of the turbo-folk genre in Serbia under Slobodan Milošević was part
of this political current to counter Titoist versions of multicultural
communism in the name of ethnic awakening.

During the last decade of communist rule in Yugoslavia, belonging to
a different cultural framework became the central metaphor of a new
type of ethnic totalitarianism with racial undertones. Naturalized cultural differences that stood in Dvorniković's way when he tried to provide an inclusive definition of "our" song as a collective voice of the
Yugoslav race reappeared as the communists' control over public life
gradually weakened after Tito's death. In the realm of popular music,
cultural differentiation relied on claims that, for example, Slovenian
polkas and accordion music were part of the Germanic-dominated Central European heritage while Macedonian songs reflected five hundred
years of Ottoman Turkish influence. In contrasting the Slovenian north-

west with the Macedonian southeast, the pseudo-racialists claimed that no common link could exist between Europe and Asia, between the West and the East, between the North and the South.

Although all of the territory of the former Yugoslavia is situated geographically in Europe, the imaginary geography instituted by multiple invasions, occupations, and civilizing missions structured different identities for members of each particular Yugoslav ethnic group. For example, Bosniaks' horizon of identity could always be extended to include Istanbul as "one's own" site; Croats', to include Rome and Berlin; and Serbs', to include Athens and Moscow. This extension of Slavic identity made the possibility of Yugoslavia's breakup along "civilizational" fault lines realizable within a framework of "differentialist" racism.

Slaving Away

The internalized gaze of Western European Romantics who envisioned the Balkan population as "noble savages" striving for independence from empires gradually became the core of South Slavic modern identity. After the formation of the first Yugoslav state, an attempt was made to imagine a culture based on common Slavic blood that would "integrally" assimilate non-Slavic races into a Dinaric-based identity of shared historical destiny of subjugated peoples. Dvorniković's work crowned that effort but was published too late (as is often the case in the Balkans), as Yugoslavia had only two years of life left before it was dismembered as part of Hitler's new European order ruled by Nordic races. "The North" and "the West" reasserted themselves as superior terms within the imaginary geography that continues to structure Eurocentric conceptions of identity and alterity. Yugoslavs remain locked within this classification as "Yugoslaves"—as peoples whose songs and dances entertain and provoke nostalgia for an imaginary originality of being that belongs to the Orient even as their dreadful bloodshed awakens the need for the West to distance itself culturally and impose military order on unruly races of the South.

During the Second World War, "brotherly" blood was shed along "civilizational" lines, proving that Balibar's statement that *culture replaces nature* functions in ordinary racism, as well: During the Second World War, the Ustaše exterminated hundreds of thousands of Serbs, whom they perceived as people of low cultural quality who were con-taminating the purity of the Croatian *Lebensraum*. What defined 'the serbs' as racial others was their adherence to Orthodox Christianity and the use of Cyrillic script. In 1941–42, the national language was exclusively called Croatian; books in Cyrillic were burned; and Serbs converted to Catholicism (effectively becoming Croats), were expelled across the Drina into Serbia, or were exterminated at Jasenovac and other death camps.

Laibach: Postmodern Provocations

One of the most sinister manifestations of cultural racism in the early 1980s was the rise of the rock group Laibach within an emerging punk and new-wave scene in the former Yugoslavia. Performing in dark, Nazi-like uniforms with stern expressions on their faces and mechani-cal bodily movements, the members of Laibach evoked uneasy laughter from their audiences. Initial reactions from the official communist es-tablishment were usually couched in terms denouncing the use of the name Laibach, the German name for Slovenia's capital city, instead of Ljubljana. The group was part of a hierarchically organized artistic movement that called itself *Neue Slowenische Künst* (New Slovenian Art) and included theatrical, dance, and visual art components. The names of the individual artists were intentionally suppressed so the collective could be placed in the absolute foreground of the movement.

Although contemporary cultural critics received most of Laibach's performances as a parody of the totalitarian legacy of both the left and the right, the band expressed the widespread desire for the order, clean-liness, health, and beauty inherent in the tacit superiority of the newly emergent Euro-American culture that identified the "West" as the ulti-mate achievement of global civilization. Laibach's parody through post-punk performance of over-identification with the socialist state's inher-ent totalitarian logic was an early manifestation of Slovenes' desire to distance themselves from the object of their parody, fleeing the union with those other peoples who were regarded as belonging to a different cultural tradition. The formation of the artistic collective around Lai-bach was one of the first symptoms of the Yugoslav cultural dissolution that began in the 1980s. This is how Laibach's program was presented to the Japanese magazine *Takarajima*:

Laibach in Belgrade: Slovene Gothic irony. PHOTOGRAPH COURTESY CRPHO (CENTER FOR THE DEVELOPMENT AND PROMOTION OF HUMANE RELATIONSHIPS) ARCHIVE.

NSK (Neue Slowenische Künst) is an organized cultural and political move- ment and school established in 1984 . . . as an organization active in the area between ideology and art. NSK unites the total experience of Slovene art and politics. Our cultural and political groundwork is the Slovene nation and its history.[20]

This cynical blending of politics and art in the Yugoslav context, which had overcome its own version of socialist realism by the mid-1950s, achieves a double-edged effect: On the one hand, it exposes the trap- pings of Tito's soft totalitarianism and its effect on art and culture, not through critical distancing, but through parodic identification with its theoretical assumptions; on the other, Slovenian allegiance to and en- dorsement of the Germanic *Mitteleuropa* are present as tacit acknowl- edgment of the discourse of white, European supremacy.

Musical articulations of Slovenian cultural supremacy appeared in the pseudo-parodic performances by Laibach in the decade that preceded the latest Yugoslav war. The post-punk band used a variety of totalitarian images to promote its musical performances. With strong roots in conceptual art, Laibach's musical performances identified with political power in the form of military uniforms, as well as in calls for the abolition of individuality and submission to the will of the state. Laibach throve on the ambivalent reactions of the cultural and political establishment and grew into a hierarchically organized art movement.

By invoking the historical presence of Austria and Germany in Slovenia, the band stimulated an uncanny feeling among audiences: Most urban youth took the music as sarcastic retrofitting, while some officials threatened bans and legal action. The critical distance that rock culture nurtured in the 1960s and '70s was replaced by the erasure of distance and parodic identification with the aggressor. When asked about the Slovene character of its music, Laibach answered:

> The creative ability of the artist identifies with the national spirit. Every artist carries within him certain (ethnic) characteristics, which are the result of a common origin and kindred lifestyle of a group of people over a longer historical period. These characteristics are reflected in his work. It is impossible to imagine Cervantes or Leonardo as Russians, Voltaire and Verdi as Germans, Dostoyevski and Wagner as Italians or [Laibach] as Yugoslavs.[21]

By identifying themselves as protagonists of Slovenian, and not Yugoslav, art, Laibach offered the best articulation of a model for cultural separation in all parts of the country toward the end of the 1980s. Laibach's call became clear only after Slovenia demanded separation from the "eastern tide of chaos," as if the band was claiming they were part of white Europe and the West because their (Slovenian) music was more sophisticated than that of other, "primitive" Yugoslavs. Interestingly, Laibach's statement draws from the same theories of "national character" that Dvorniković invoked, except that the sense of "our" song is now applicable only to Slovenia and not all of Yugoslavia.

Žižek's analysis of Laibach's cultural mission is quite different. Žižek, who speaks from within the same Slovenian culture, presents his compatriots as psychoanalysts who manipulate the process of transference by performing the underside of the obscene superego of the socialist state. "By means of the elusive character of their desire, of the undecidability as to 'where they actually stand,'" Žižek writes, "Laibach compel us to take up our position and decide upon *our* desire."[22] To the contrary, Laibach's performances of totalitarian imagery were far from undecidable and elusive for those who stood on the eastern side of the symbolic boundary that began to divide Yugoslavia after Tito's death. Their parodic performance clearly articulated Slovenian supremacy within the disintegrating socialist state, provoking both laughter and pity. The confusion arose in the field of reception from the fact that many intellectuals could not directly confront their performance precisely because it was so blatantly totalitarian. And though they had a hard time "decid[ing] upon" their desire, it was not so hard for the political elites in the eastern part of Yugoslavia to decide on theirs, and on versions of ethnic violence, cultural superiority, and military means to achieve it.

Although the Laibach phenomenon played a tiny role in the context of the former Yugoslavia at that moment, it became one of the symptoms of the emergent blood-based culture that would come to dominate the country in the 1980s and lead to war in the early 1990s. Since the very name "Slovene" proclaims Slavic origin, the new nationalist leadership chose a new strategy that replaced "genetic" identity with a cultural one. Laibach's intentional or unintentional participation in this project was manifested in its choice of a German-derived name to claim allegiance with *Mitteleuropa*, thus playing into the Germanic dream of geopolitical domination of other Europe. According to this reading of the Balkans, Slovenes and Croats belong to the (superior) West because their culture is rooted in Roman Catholicism and they carry a post-imperial status as a former Habsburg territory, while the other Yugoslavs belong to the (inferior) East because of their former domination by the Ottoman Empire and culture rooted in Orthodox Christianity or Islam. South Slavic identity is consequently subdivided according to these new criteria of belonging into an agonistic common subjectivity doomed to division and failure.

Good Slavs, Bad Slavs

Petar Tancig, Slovenia's minister of science and technology when the Yugoslav war broke out in 1991, introduced a novel type of racist discourse based on cultural differences:

The basic reason for all the past/present mess is the incompatibility of two main frames of reference/civilization, unnaturally and forcibly joined in Yugoslavia. On one side you have a typical violent and crooked oriental-bizantine [sic] heritage, best exemplified by Serbia and Montenegro. . . . On the other side (Slovenia, Croatia) there is a more humble and diligent western-catholic tradition. . . . Trying to keep Yugoslavia afloat . . . is also very bad geostrategic thinking, as independent (and westernized) Slovenia (and Croatia) could and would act as a "cordon sanitaire" against the eastern tide of chaos.[23]

Is it so strange, then, that Žižek begins *The Indivisible Remainder* with a statement of national belonging—especially since that belonging is accompanied by Freud's discovery of his most vivid and influential metaphor for the unconscious after wandering through the Škocjan caves in Slovenia? If the father of psychoanalysis saw in the Slovenian landscape the concealed foundation of Western European civilization, is it strange that one of Slovenia's proudest sons would appropriate the "return to Freud" initiated by Jacques Lacan? Žižek's vision of Freud in the native landscape serves to authenticate and essentialize his position as a Slovenian philosopher in psychoanalytic theory by playing the double role of a Balkan tour guide for the curious Westerner and a civilized, "Westernized" Slav.

Žižek as a figure and a symptom of the Yugoslav implosion is certainly less visible to this type of uninformed Westerner than the Bosnian bloodshed and the vampire nation of 'the serbs' as the designated aggressors in the post-Yugoslav conflicts. The look at Žižek's "narcissism of minor differences" is *Unheimlich* exactly because it brings to the fore questions that the U.S.-led West has not been willing to confront in regard to the destruction of Yugoslavia.[24]

It is especially in regard to the phantasm of 'the serbs' that most media outlets have failed to recognize the enlarged and distorted projection of their own imperial past in atrocities committed in the name of a territorialized collective identity that calls itself "the nation." If the aggression by 'the serbs' caused Žižek's transformation into a Slovene, is that process of becoming as an effect of aggression not also part of a larger process that reveals all identifications, individual or collective? And inversely, aren't 'the serbs,' then, especially in the image constructed and disseminated by the global media, not manifesting behavior that forms the very core of dominant identity that the U.S.-led West is trying so hard to disavow? The vampire phantasm is a symptom of a mechanism centered on the topoi of blood and soil, displacing the cultural anxieties tied to violence inherent in modern European identity by visualizing it in its peripheral locations, such as the former Yugoslavia.

4

LOCATIONS OF HORROR
Bosnia in the Literary and Political Imaginary

But first, on earth as Vampire sent,
Thy corse shall from its tomb be rent;
Then ghastly haunt thy native place,
And suck the blood of all thy race.
—Lord Byron, "The Giaour"

There are two worlds, between which there cannot be any real contact
nor the possibility of agreement; two terrible worlds doomed to an
eternal war in thousand various forms.
—Ivo Andrić, The Damned Yard

A man should think neither that he is safe, nor that the past is dead.
—Meša Selimović, Death and the Dervish

The "native place" of Lord Byron is the imaginary Orient he came to encounter in the Balkans, a location haunted by the presence of the violent "living corpse" bent on draining the life fluid from "all thy race."[1]
The post-Oriental legacies of violence in the region were transposed by
the literary imaginary into a constant struggle between those who
crave the blood of others and those who are bent on preserving the
cultural integrity of their native realm by staving off intrusions by the
carriers of alien blood. Yet some cultural figures attempted to imagine
hybrid cultural locations within the Balkans as emblems of constant
struggle to overcome these blood-driven identities. One of the greatest
figures of Yugoslav cultural transnationalism was born in Bosnia, in the

location that has come to symbolize a type of violent zone stuck between the major cultures that mark the boundary between Europe and the Orient. The biography, literary opus, and posthumous destiny of Ivo Andrić are all symptomatic of the missed opportunities that could have made Bosnia a model of pan-European integration rather than the example of its failed civilizing efforts.

The internationalist claims of Titoist politics during the socialist period were compromised by his political clones' attempts to insert themselves as new national masters of the imaginary dearest to their particular ethnic corpus. The effects of the agonistic context created by the legacy of the Kosovo myth were predicated on confrontation between the two "terrible worlds" within the context of imploding Yugoslavia as politicians competed to resurrect a vision of identity based on victimization of their own ethnic collective and the necessary and preemptive sacrifice of ethnic and cultural others. The survival of one's own blood is thus predicated on the violent appropriation of the other's, whose world is seen as a very real source of domination.

Although Andrić devoted his literary and political work to the mutual understanding of those conflicting worlds within Bosnia in particular and Yugoslavia in general, his texts reveal the insidious presence of macabre memories that resurrect the sad and unrecognized realities of domination, occupation, and assimilation. He imagined the divisions and separations within Bosnia as the reason for its exclusion from the symbolic realm of Europe and its placement in the Orient as a legacy of military domination by the Islamic conquest of the peninsula. His literary imaginary codes the trauma of Bosnia's impossible identity as an effect of imperial violence responsible for the national becoming of its conflicted subjects. The perpetual confrontation between the cultural realms of Islam and the two types of Christianity (Eastern Orthodox and Roman Catholic) within imaginary Bosnia engendered the representation of a hybrid cultural site that was constantly threatened by the encroaching power of those larger forces of civilization arriving from the outside. Irreducible to the liberal rhetoric of good conscience underlying humanitarian interventions, the political chaos and genocidal violence initiated during the 1990s are symptomatic of unresolved traumas of identity tied to the nation as a homogenous imaginary location. This is the gap opened up by the division between the Orient and its European counterpart that requires modern national identities as narratives to go beyond the divisive logic caused by foreign domination.

The problem of identity as the origin of Bosnian conflicts was first broached in "The Development of Spiritual Life in Bosnia under the Influence of Turkish Rule," based on the doctoral dissertation Andrić defended in Graz, Austria, in 1924. He later elaborated on the similarly conflicted concept of the imaginary in his literary rendition of building as a form of sacrifice in his masterpiece *The Bridge on the Drina* (1945), for which he was awarded the Nobel Prize in Literature in 1961. Most of his narratives develop against the backdrop of desolate and unmerciful geography and climate, with protagonists struggling to survive the strangeness and divisiveness of history and politics into which they are forced. Andrić views the clash of the invading Islamic civilization with the two varieties of Christianity as a crucial factor that contributed to the confusion in answering the riddle of Bosnian cultural identity. In the dissertation, Andrić singled out Turkish rule as a conspicuous factor that introduced a set of cultural values that were incompatible with the European orientation of Bosnia's inhabitants:

The fact of decisive importance for Bosnia was that at the most critical stage of its spiritual development, when the fermentation of its spiritual forces had reached a culmination, it had been invaded by an Oriental warrior people whose social institutions and customs meant the negation of Christian culture and whose faith—created under different climatic and social conditions and unfit for any kind of adjustment—interrupted the spiritual life of a country, degenerated it and created something quite odd out of it.[2]

This statement, saturated with Eurocentric cultural determinism of the national as the effect of collective response to "different climactic and social conditions," is definitely echoed in what Edward W. Said termed "Orientalism," a prevalent tendency of Western cultures to construct "an idea that has a history and a tradition of thought, imagery and vocabulary that have given it [i.e., the Orient] reality and presence in and for the West."[3] This construct of the Orient and the Orientals in the Eurocentric worldview functions as a representation of an alien world of others who need to be restructured, dominated, and colonized for European culture to gain its sense of identity and strength "by setting itself off against the Orient as a sort of surrogate and even underground self."[4] The other within is envisioned as a subterranean entity whose return from the dead threatens the proper identity and community of Europe as a Christian legacy.

However, the Eurocentric dimension of Andrić's writing is quite different from this type of discourse, since the main historical and political condition of Said's Orientalism requires both political and epistemological domination by the West of the East. In Bosnia, the Ottoman military conquest of the Slavic population produced "something quite odd," indeed—a hybrid culture in which clear distinctions between Eastern and Western elements of identity gradually became indistinguishable. Although the two religions, which later defined national alliances, drifted apart, the two cultures were imperceptibly blended together, forming hybrid identities that were the first casualty of the Bosnian War (1992–95).

Andrić cites the anthropologically odd colored candles Bosnian Muslims use to celebrate Bairam, an Islamic holiday temporally close to Easter, to illustrate the processes of cultural translation that informed the everyday life of Bosnians.[5] The candles are made in colors that are not used in any other Islamic nation and presumably are a substitute for the eggs the Christian population colored for Easter before they converted to Islam. The two elements of religious practice were thus blended together, creating a specifically Bosnian cultural syncretism. But while different cultures were imperceptibly hybridized, Bosnians continued to live in geographic isolation brought about by the region's rugged terrain and a lack of roads to the outside world. This isolation caused opposing cultural traditions to end up steeped in mutual contempt, intolerance, and hatred fueled by differences of habit and custom. Religious adherence served as the foundation on which the national sense of identity was built, rationalizing and justifying a continuous struggle between "the two terrible worlds":

> It so happened that both the [Muslim] master and the [Christian] slave, as the antagonism between them grew stronger and stronger, sank deeper into the darkness of their deformed religious life. Indeed, only the heavens could provide the strength for such a struggle and such a life.[6]

The heavens, which Bosnian Muslims, Serbs, and Croats all imagined according to the teachings of their respective religious communities, were imagined as a source of divine justice that sanctioned human actions on earth, even if those actions included murder and other forms of violence and torture. Both the Islamic masters and their Christian subjects drew strength from this imagined source of divine justice— Muslims, in an attempt to assimilate and eradicate the Christians; and Christians, in an attempt to destroy "the underground self" by preserving the culture that tied them to Europe. The marginal geographic position of the Balkans offers an exceptional opportunity to study the effects of domination by an "Oriental" empire on the formation of cultural identity of small European nations in the Balkans.

The reversal of familiar colonial roles set up a condition specific to subjects placed in bondage to their Islamic masters. The portrait of the Ottoman Turk is transformed into the image of a ruthless conqueror whose culture and religion are the alien agents of the political and cultural power of Islam. This is the dominant narrative of the nation from which 'the serbs' emerged as a self-generated phantasm confronting the imminent return of a historically defeated Islamic master through its many imaginary surrogates. While the revolutionary youth of Bosnia (*Mlada Bosna*) set themselves against all foreign domination in the Balkans at the beginning of the twentieth century, regardless of the revolutionaries' faith and culture, the nationalist discourse of the most recent conflict, in 1992–95, thrived on resurrecting those imperial traces and identifying their incarnations in the subjects on the opposing side of the cultural divide.

Domination in any form, and particularly as a memory of Ottoman rule, was assimilated into the national identity of 'the serbs' as a negative influence that impeded the development of sovereign cultural and political identity. Zoran Konstantinović believes that Andrić's anti-Ottoman attitudes were part of the emergent Yugoslavism of the Serbian, Croatian, and Muslim students and intellectuals who gathered in this revolutionary youth movement, which was devoted to abolishing religious divisions as the only way for Bosnians to overcome their backwardness and isolation.[7] If we understand Andrić's Orientalism as a response to the Ottoman imperial legacy, the unification of the progressive elements of Muslim, Catholic, and Orthodox Bosnian youth to fight for the common Yugoslav idea becomes part of the historical context within which he wrote his doctoral dissertation. Andrić's opus articulates a deep frustration with the tripartite structure of Bosnian religious, political, and cultural life, which was instituted by foreign imperial influences radiating from Rome, Byzantium, and the Levant.

Andrić's own destiny reflects both the hybridity and the tragedy of the Yugoslav identity as it is engendered within Bosnia, and it is symptomatic of a wider tradition of negativity tied to the Oriental legacy as part of the foreign-domination narrative. That is why Andrić feels obliged in a footnote of his dissertation to provide the following disclaimer about his treatment of Islam and its cultural influence outside Europe: "This part, as well as any other part of this discussion that refers to the influence of Turkish rule should not be understood as a critique of Islamic culture as such, but only as a critique of the consequences of its transmission to a Christian, Slavic country."[8] In other words, Islamic culture has value and authenticity before it imposes itself on the values of the peoples it is trying to subjugate and dominate in its westward imperial drive.

As is evident from the previous chapters, this type of discourse reflects a longstanding trend in South Slavic literature. Andrić offers by far the most interesting literary articulation of the post-Oriental condition, which started with the heroic songs that served as cultural weapons by reviving the Kosovo myth during the rebellions against Ottoman imperial rule in the nineteenth century and continued through such canonical works as *Smrt Smail-age Čengića*, by the Croatian Ivan Mažuranić, and *Gorski vijenac*, by the Montenegrin Petar Petrović Njegoš. Both the Ottoman masters and the domestic Muslim populations were imagined as archenemies of Christianity, Slavdom, and Europe whose violence remained lodged in the cultural unconscious as a vampire-like predator that was destroying one's own race from the very interior of the nation. Njegoš's text is devoted to the extermination of Islamic converts (*istraga poturica*); Mažuranić's represents Smail-aga as a tyrant whose bloodthirsty behavior calls for revenge, which results in the annihilation of all Islamic subjects in the Balkans.

Andrić himself warned against the exaggerations the Turks and their domestic counterparts have been subjected to in South Slavic literary works: "Our traditional and written literature has transformed the Turks into a wrath of God, into a kind of scarecrow that could be painted only with dark and bloody colors, something that could not be quietly talked about or reasonably thought about."[9] The bloody palette of the artist steeped in the post-Oriental condition calls for a critical appraisal of national literary constructs, because the violence tied to the name "Bosnia" has its roots in identifying those cultural figures with values the locals consider quintessentially European.

Oriental Violence

Andrić scholars, from the early essay by Isidora Sekulić to the latest studies by Boguslav Zielinsky, have noted his preoccupation with representing the Oriental dimension of Bosnian cultural identity. While most critics rightfully point to Andrić's fascination with the Islamization of the Slavic cultural heritage, they reveal their own Orientalist biases in the process of interpretation. Sekulić, for example, generalizes that "the people in the Orient believe in the miraculous and have proofs for the existence of the supernatural."[10] In an essay analyzing Eastern elements in Ivo Andrić prose originally published in 1923, Sekulić claims that his stories were affected by the Orient mainly on the formal level. First, Andrić borrowed a mode of narration that resembles oral storytelling, which is episodic and rich in detail and often uses the travelogue narrative as its backdrop. "The Oriental story, even when it is a modernist one, is above all a silent weaving, an incantation, a fantastic and richly colored image; heaven or hell, wailing and bloodletting, or the whispering of deeply concealed secrets."[11] Sekulić treats the dominant Islamic heritage of Bosnia as an alien element that contributed to the degeneration of "purity" in the native culture and was responsible "for all of the primitive, cruel, terrifying, and above all mysterious and colorful types from that ancient, Turkish period of Bosnia."[12] Again, Islamic subjects here are represented as "types," not as singular narrative elaborations—violent yet colorful and ultimately bearing the responsibility for Bosnia's backwardness and isolation.

Sekulić attributes another Oriental characteristic to Andrić's fictional universe: the absence of representations of middle-class life. Because the interiors of Muslim houses are hidden from the reader's gaze by impenetrable walls, most of the stories are set in the streets, at *hans* (roadside guesthouses), and *mehanas* (Oriental cafés). The narrator, who has no access to a world that is deeply concealed behind tiny windows and tall walls, is forced to represent life as it occurs on the street, populated by bloodthirsty heroes, holy fools, cripples, and perverts who are then imagined as the norm of Bosnian Oriental reality. This fictional construct is bared to the bone and functions as the mirror image of interior life hidden from view, reflecting the excess of violence and sexuality of those who are left to fend for themselves as subjects deprived of family life; who are lonely or cast out of the mainstream of communal spaces.

Sekulić regards female characters as emblematic of the Oriental universe hidden behind the veil. They are never fully developed as literary images but act only as negative textual forces, saturated by the lack that motivates the male protagonists. She exposes some of the misogynist attitudes in Andrić's early work while, at the same time, obviously holding a conviction that she is contributing to the understanding of Oriental elements in his narratives: "Primitive, lustful, monotonous, the woman is there only to be chased, enticed, hunted down and possessed by the man; or to inflict some kind of suffering that will in turn awake the real or violent heroism, making the man 'glad that the time has come for the force to speak.'"[13]

She thus regards the passive and manipulative disposition of women as a symptom of Oriental culture that is complemented by the mad and destructive desire of Andrić's male protagonists, such as Đerzelez Alija and Mameledžija, to conquer and possess their elusive beauty. Bosnian Muslims and Turks are imagined as subjects who will become vicious whenever their passions are frustrated, because they live in anticipation of when the "time has come for the force to speak." In addition to embodying sexual lust and heroic masculinity, these men are prone to the *sevdah*, best described as the Bosnian variety of the blues, that Dvorniković analyzed.

Sevdah, a feeling of sweet yet painful sorrow, afflicts a man mourning the days of his youth, the one who endures the absence of a beloved who has gone to another man, or simply the man who wishes for a happier life that is impossible to achieve among the "borderline people" torn asunder by centuries of religious and ethnic strife. Not unlike the *dert* (pain) of Bora Stanković—another writer who reflected the vision of the Orient on the Serbian south—*sevdah* is most evident in the cafés where men smoke and drink plum brandy while female singers and dancers rouse their desires and comfort their blues. Andrić, according to Sekulić, is critical of this "Oriental" heritage: of its cheap sentimentalism and the effect that idleness and unfulfilled instinctual life has on the destruction of European cultural values in Bosnia.

The most important formal quality in Andrić's prose that Sekulić ascribes to the post-Oriental condition is his use of suggestion while developing a story, juxtaposed with rational power of Western analysis:

> No, no, that was a kind of life that does not know anything about consequences. And that is why it is impossible to think that kind of life. Instead of thought, there is imagination, the love of adventure, a concrete and suggestive expression. And something else, as well: the nameless and mysterious quality hidden inside every child of the Orient, and especially in the artist. The eastern quality is something one can possess or transmit to others only if he was born where the sun rises.[14]

Sekulić's exaltation of mystic thoughtlessness is influenced by her own neo-Romantic modernism, which treats the Orient as an exotic, supernatural and instinctual realm reserved for those on the other side of Europe. One only has to remember how analytic thought flourished in the East and was actually imported to the West through translations from Arabic in the Middle Ages to understand the Orientalist coloring of these observations.[15] There is also an imagined excess of meaning that resides in everything Eastern, an irreducible "quality that one can possess or transmit only if he was born where the sun rises." Sekulić qualifies this as an imaginary relationship to the universe prevalent in the Orient, as an attitude that "does not know anything about consequences" and is guided solely by emotion and passion.

That which Andrić considers a corrupting influence on the European legacy of Bosnia, Sekulić seems to exalt and estheticize by "Orientalizing" his own narrative techniques and styles of literary representation. By juxtaposing Andrić's suggestive style with the tradition of "Western analysis," she frames and restricts his literary capacity to a dimension that favors images and sentiments over thoughts and ideas. Other Andrić scholars point to the opposite tendency: Andrić was not only an incredibly acute observer of Bosnians and their cultural complexities but also, primarily, a diligent reader and student of the history and culture of the region.[16] His style is apparently the product of long and sustained literary contemplation of the hybridity inherent in the highly conflicted historical legacy of both Bosnia and the Balkans.

Blood, Divided

Andrić considers Muslim feudal rule over the Christian *rayah* (an Ottoman term used to denote non-Muslim serfs) as an effort to dominate the local territory through religious conversion, punitive taxes, compulsory bribes, and demographic practices known as *adžami-oglan* (blood tribute). This type of feudal tribute, depicted so agonistically in *The Bridge on the Drina*, is perhaps the best illustration of the manner in which the Ottoman administrators envisioned their domination over the Slavic community. Every seven years, the sultan's men would select and seize the strongest and brightest among 'the serbs' and make off with them to the administrative center of the Orient in Europe. The boys were circumcised and given new names and thus transformed into Muslims who were then trained to become janissaries and, later, even imperial administrators.

Andrić retells the story of Mehmed-paša Sokolović, one of those abducted Christian boys, who rose to the highest ranks within the empire and then returned to his native Bosnia to build the bridge over the Drina. The mournful call of his mother's voice as she screamed his Christian name and begged him never to forget who he is has been etched into the memory of the imperial subject. Later in life, the convert suffered from anxiety attacks, feeling the cut of a "dark blade" across his chest as he remembered the point where the road broke off and the abducted boys waited for the ferry to take them, as "blood tribute," to the center of the empire. This pain is in fact all he has retained from his origins in the village of Sokolovići, the original pain of separation from the birth community substituting for the memory of the event repressed as testimony to his post-Oriental condition. Andrić represents the pain of separation from the native blood community as a nostalgic cohesive linking of the old identity of the nameless Christian boy with his new identity as a powerful Ottoman statesman:

> Somewhere within himself he felt a sharp stabbing pain that suddenly cut his chest in two and hurt terribly from time to time as the memory of the place were the road broke off emerged, a place where desolation and despair were extinguished and remained on the stony banks of the river whose crossing was so difficult, so expensive, and so unsafe.[17]

Mehmed-paša's identity is fragmented by the pain of initial separation from the place of origin as the memory of his mother/land gradually fades and the only feeling that remains is the pain itself, paired with a desire to build a bridge across the cultural divide within and without. The "terrible worlds" of Bosnia's divided identity are projected onto Mehmed-paša's interior, where he continues to exist both as the imperial self and the subjugated other. The pain is a reminder of being tied to the stolen blood of his youth, the other struggling against himself as the Ottoman administrator. This underground identity is not able to detach itself and forget how the violently imposed domination engenders conditions for the abject becoming at the root of Bosnian identity. The responsibility to the other he used to be and the power of the subject he has become springs from this internal rift and transforms building into a reparative cultural practice embodied in his noble desire to build the bridge across the Drina, the river acting as a separator between the location of his origin and that of his destiny. Building is an attempt to bridge the rift between the two parts of his uniqueness, incarnating the clash of the two "terrible worlds" originating in the monocultural conceptions of cultural identity.

The Bosnian Contagion

Andrić's most significant political meditations on cultural identity can be found in *Travnička hronika* (The Bosnian chronicle), a work written from the point of view of two Western diplomats who arrive in Bosnia to promote the political influence of the two Western empires in the border areas of the Ottoman world. Jean Daville, the French consul, and Josef von Miterer, his Austrian counterpart, both write Bosnia off as a location whose people, customs, and events are completely alien to their European habits. Andrić skillfully exploits the perspective of the two newcomers to give literary shape to the corrupting influence of Bosnia on their enlightened sense of meaning and identity:

> The foreigner, thrown into that unfair and difficult battle, gets completely submerged by it and loses his real personality. He spends his entire life in the Orient but gets acquainted with it in a superficial and one-sided manner, able to see it only from the standpoint of either usefulness or harm of the struggle he is doomed to wage. Those foreigners, who like D'Avenat remain to live in the Orient, in most cases take on from the Turks only the bad, lower character traits, incapable of noticing and accepting their noble, higher characteristics and habits.[18]

The sense of erasure and loss of proper identity in the encounter with Bosnia is something that almost all Westerners experience in *Travnička hronika*. It appears as a cultural code that is illegible to the foreigner, who is exhausted by the perpetual failure to read its convoluted meanings. This failure of translation results in de-personalization and inability to notice the "noble, higher characteristics" of the local population.

D'Avenat, a French doctor who acts as an adviser and interpreter for Daville, gradually overcomes his "loss of real personality" and assimilates the "lower traits" of Oriental character: "Infinitely humble and servile in front of the powerful, influential and rich, he was arrogant, cruel and heartless to everyone who was weak, poor and imperfect."[19] Bosnia is imagined as a location that destroys one's ethical standards by imposing a master–slave dynamic in conduct with others in view of their perceived power and social position. The imperial subject of the French empire is uprooted from a familiar context, encountering Bosnian cultural particularities as the absence of reality, a violent vacuum filling up occasionally with negative emotional charges.

Andrić has both consuls in *Travnička hronika* developing the same ailment as their encounter with the Orient evolves during their years of diplomatic service:

> Both of them had to live in the same Oriental backwater, without any company or convenience, without comfort and often without bare necessities, they had to live among the rough mountains and crude people and constantly fight suspicion, negligence, disease, dirt, and trouble of every kind. In short, they had to live in an environment that spoils the Westerner and gradually makes him pathologically irritable, until finally, during the course of time, [it] completely transforms him, bends him, and finally kills him with silent indifference long before he actually dies.[20]

Death before death is the final result of the corrupting influence of the Orient, transforming foreigners into the living dead of the Bosnian hinterland. This location is coded not only as a zone of clash between cultures but also as an insidious sickness that infects Europe and gradually wears down its rational and enlightened identity, transforming its respectable citizens into creatures infected with the disease of the walking dead. The imponderable contagion that affects the European is a powerful symptom of the negative cultural coding of a location imagined as a source of "suspicion, negligence, disease, dirt, and trouble of every kind."

Andrić suggests that the cure for the Oriental disease can be achieved both by the oppressed domestic Christians and by the diplomatic representatives of France and Austria as part of the joint endeavor to "civilize" Bosnia by purging this ancient heritage. Von Miterer, the Austrian consul, gains the sympathies of Franciscan monks and the domestic Catholic population. The French diplomat, Daville, by contrast, does not have much local support because of the revolutionary sins his homeland committed against the church. The Orthodox Christians, hoping to emerge from their own lack of communal power, wish for the arrival of the Russian consul. The Islamic population of Bosnia is disunited, as well, since the local Ottoman administrators clash with domestic Muslim feudalists over the primacy of power in the province.

Silence of the Nation

Andrić invokes the experience of outsiders to reflect on silence as a literary zero-degree sounding of national space, the deathly silence shared by the divided communities. The internal divisions of Bosnia create a semblance of life rife with anxiety and uncertainty for a population hiding behind the façade of silence, anticipating with trembling the new cycle of violence to come, which arrives every time the balance between great powers is disturbed.

As the causes of suffering grow more intense throughout this early encounter between Europe and Bosnia, the question of Bosnia's cultural identity is asked through displays of fatalism and inertia as historical, political, and psychological differences emanate from the divided loyalties of its constituent communities. While describing the journey of a young French consular aide, Des Fossés, from Split to Travnik, Andrić uses the metaphor of silence to characterize Bosnia as a land of paralysis and tension. Des Fossés is immersed in the "unknown silence of a new world" and feels a foreboding about "Bosnia, the silent land," whose air is filled with "icy suffering without words and visible causes."[21]

In Andrić's most famous novel, *The Bridge on the Drina*, the response of the audience that watches as Abidaga's men impale Radisav is also silence: "The silence on both sides of the river was such that one could hear each blow and its echo somewhere on the steep bank."[22] This scene of torture forces the divided religious communities to withdraw even more deeply into fear and mistrust of each other, since each act of mutual violence increases levels of hatred and reinforces the positions of both the masters and the slaves. Andrić envisions the spectacle of impalement as the imaginary origin of this community, a space where victimization is transformed into a monument to reified cultural differences. If every member glimpses the origin of a particular community in the suffering of the body pierced by the imperial stake, this image of torture serves as the foundation of the imaginary shared by its members. The building of the bridge across the Drina sublimates this violent trauma into a transitory structure that could enable the exchange and transmission of the pain shared between the divided communities. Identification with the impaled victim is represented as a cultural process that allows the building of an architectural edifice that promises to rejoin the shards of the broken mirror that reflects the image of Bosnia.

National Sadomasochism

The building of the bridge is symbolic of imperial domination for the subjugated population, the violent force preventing the negotiation of cultural differences through the imposition of the Islamic millet system as a specifically constructed religious form of apartheid. The torture of the peasant ordered by the Islamic masters serves as an image that will feed hatred and produce 'the serbs' as the vampire nation that imagines collective revenge in the wake of loss and exile from the imaginary realm of Kosovo: "Straight and naked to the waist, hands and legs tied, with head thrown back against the stake, that figure no longer looked like a human body that grows and decays, but seemed more like an erect, hard and timeless statue that would remain there forever."[23]

This monumental erection of the dying body continues to haunt the imaginary of 'the serbs' to this day as a mask for a collective identity forced perpetually to resurrect its cultural values from violent takeover by a larger imperial force, when confronted with the image of one's own undead body, one's fear and rage as the victim overpowers any responsibility for the other. The nation is thus able to inscribe this type of violence as the origin of its cultural imaginary in constructing its own desire for the blood of others. The impalement of Radisav de-sublimates the narrative of the nation at its traumatic core, relating back to the theory about the aggressive undercurrent of the subject involved in the retention–elimination dilemma of the anal character in Freudian psychoanalysis.

Sadism has found myriad discursive masks to make itself visible in different gazes that narrate the identity of the Balkans. The most prominent is certainly the image of the Bulgarian built into "to bugger," a verbal expression for anal intercourse in English. Vesna Goldsworthy speculates, "Probably the most common words of Balkan origin in the English language—'bugger,' 'balkanization' and 'vampire'—all reflect, in a sense, the fear of the Other, the threat of possible invasion and corruption."[24] Wherever one stands on the issue of anal pain or pleasure, the Bulgarian is always already there as the etymological remainder that engenders the ethno-pornographic vision of the Balkans. At the same time, the cultural imaginary of the region bears the mark of the extreme orality of the vampire. Paired with the extreme anality of the bugger, this type of alterity reproduces a phantasm articulated in late-nineteenth-century Gothic writings in English. It is no coincidence that in Byron's England, the code word for a homosexual was "vampyre." And the term "balkanization" breaks down all notions of compact and homogenous unity enjoyed by the empire, providing a differential counterpart as the dominant lens for geostrategic visualization of the Balkans. This monstrous counterpart of Europe is enveloped in the dark where "the sun don't shine," the grotesque cavity of the body where the issue of control regulates the games of retention and elimination that characterize Freud's anal-sadistic stage.

Most of Freud's findings about anality are based on his analysis of Balkan folklore, where dreams of excrement signify money and treasure, pointing to parsimony and obstinacy as features of anal character. The other pole of the anal involves sadism, a dominant character feature required for muscle control, especially over the process of elimination, as the human first learns about death by observing the departure of the inanimate part of its body through the anus. Andrić reflects this type of regression of the subject by omitting the proper name of the peasant and narrating the impalement scene as something that has happened to "the body." The body becomes an allegorical site anally possessed in the name of the empire: a token sacrifice projected onto the time to come; a reminder of the tyranny "which would remain there forever." Projecting domination over the lower part of the body produces the timeless and the monumental: The stake moves along the spine toward its upper parts while slow and painful death consumes Radisav and erects "a timeless statue" in his place. The stake props up the dying body and transforms it into a monumental structure of the nation to come as silence envelops the community watching the enactment of this anal interpellation.

The sadism of the empire reproduces the bipolar nature of the anal dilemma, since its contradictory aim is to destroy and expel the inappropriate body (elimination) while simultaneously preserving the subject by mastering its death (retention). The stake as a torture weapon embodies the phallus of the empire that is ready to punish by reversing the process of elimination and invading the anal cavity to create a transgressive body as a sign of the nation to come. Yet the phallic signifier remains for the community of the oppressed, as the tortured body of the peasant rises above the crowd as a silent and monumental origin of its suffering. No longer subject to the laws of the empire, the impaled body of the peasant stands for a monument of the active–passive conundrum that inhabits the timeless space of subjugated nations, a masochistic plot stirring in the pleasures of just revenge to come. Those subjected to the empire develop what Czeslaw Milosz calls the "historical imagination," the epistemology focused on a sense of collective loss and pain that elaborates the story of submission for most of the nations whose feebleness defines their shared destiny.

A surprising twist in the narrative on masculinity has come from the latter-day psychoanalyst Julia Kristeva, who was not accidentally born in Bulgaria. She had defined the tragedy of the Balkan subject as "caught in an exquisite logic of submission and exaltation that offers him the joys and sorrows intrinsic to the master–slave dialectic and, on a more personal level, to male homosexuality."[25] The nature of *doxa* in its original Christian form, with the exclusion of the filial origination of the Holy Spirit in this early theological iteration, robs the next generation of its masculinity. Sons are forced into a passive familial role, offering their subjectivity gladly to the dominance of their generational and cultural elders and posing as submissives in overtly heroic masculine drag. Kristeva, herself a transnational subject in the process of assimilating into French Europe, gazes back on Foucault's "counter-nature," a form of discursive emergence she sees as tied to the prevalence of Orthodox cultural patri-dominion.[26]

The issue of counter-nature is tied here to the masochism rooted in the compulsive reopening of the wound as a mode of masculine mourning for the ethnic community and its lost moment of glorious and sovereign control over the body. It is also tied to masculine mourning's most significant prosthetic extension: the territory of its symbolic existence embroiled in the process of perpetual crumbling into impotence and loss. This balkanization of location features the appropriated realm of the maternal at the very root of its most ancient cultural layers, something that Kristeva in earlier works traced to the preverbal *chora*. Looking for the origin of all origins, springing from the desire for the ultimate prosthetic extension of being into its linguistic performances, this soft Balkan man becomes womanlike, ready to submit to the more ancient call of blood and belonging, rooted in appropriations of the maternal realm by the *doxa* of its exclusive religious submission to God the Father.

Manly Monuments

> And it still seems that,
> as my soul dreams on,
> the monument lives on,
> ready for eternity,
> reborn into new traditions,
> tempering young ambitions
> to erect the next monument.
> —Vladislav Petković Dis, "Spomenik"

These lines were written in anticipation of the First World War by Vladislav Petković Dis, one of the most original modern poets of the first Yugoslavia.[27] The poem is testimony from the periphery of Europe about modernity's dream of the monument born out of violence as a proving ground for the new, technologically advanced forms of national imaginary that would transcends a particular age and time. The image of the animated monument descending from the collective imaginary to "prepare our generation for the next monument" reiterates the structure of temporal repetition inherent in the logic of nationalism.

Appropriately titled "Spomenik" (The monument), the poem evokes the eve of the Great War, whose cause is often attributed to 'the serbs' of Bosnia. Dis's poetic imagination grasps the monumental image of heroic masculinity that has haunted 'the serbs' ever since their fall from the realm of imagined medieval glory into the abjection of the post-Oriental condition. "The new traditions" have been permeated with the ancient imaginary structures demanding that each of 'the serbs' sacrifices his blood in the name of the return of the arch-monument that requires new deaths, new martyrs, and new monuments.

Since 1389, the Kosovo narrative has been imbued with an intense mixture of calls to emancipate oneself from bondage to the foreign masters and paranoid suspicion of those groups who remind 'the serbs' of their historical miseries: Turks, Albanians, domestic converts to Islam, and, as has been shown, the women of one's nation. The burden of the Kosovo legacy provides local culture with a literary imaginary that is capable of uniting a nation of mourners behind a leader unscrupulous enough to tap into rage among 'the serbs,' who have been seeking revenge for the domination they were forced to endure under Islamic rule.

The hybrid ethnoscape of both Bosnia and the former Yugoslavia had been transformed into a battlefield of competing nationalist discourses descended from heavenly monuments to reopen old wounds and enable ruthless and irresponsible political leaders to manipulate their people. Half a century of Titoist rule left a legacy of power-hungry, destructive politicians accustomed to ruling by decree and manipulation and ready to latch on to the agonistic discourse of national martyrdom to gain and stay in power. Ethnic suffering was the discourse most readily available to 'the serbs,' because it operates on a level that bends below overt ideological control to set itself against the decades of one-party rule by the Titoist incarnation of communism and evokes knee-jerk responses to any perceived threat that foreign rule will be imposed once again.

Politics as Haunting

The reopening of old wounds after the disappearance of Tito as a paternal metaphor prompted the imaginary of 'the serbs' as specters that haunt the new global order to burst forth. Slobodan Milošević interpellated fear and violence among 'the serbs' by reviving a deeply embedded cultural memory within the decaying communist state at the tail end of the Cold War. Milošević conceived the collective identity as that of victims seeking justified revenge for past injustices, this time well armed and ready to implement pre-emptive strikes, and used the cover of the newly truncated Yugoslavia to mobilize 'the serbs' to implement the ultimate demand of the Kosovo covenant. During the

1980s, the discourse of anti-bureaucratic revolution was paired with that of 'the serbs' as "heavenly people" who drew power from the celestial realm to seek justice against their separatist Slavic and non-Slavic brothers.[28]

Again, heaven emerged as the sanctioning agent to absolve 'the serbs' of responsibility for their deceitful Yugoslav partners, who were now placed beyond human consideration and straight into the path of the violent justice of the nation. As Andrić noted, it was the "darkness of their deformed religious life" that provided motivation for "such a struggle and such a life" during the long medieval period.[29] The monumental return of this type of medieval performance was paired with political discourse, resurrected as a messianic vision, of a people who do not recognize the desire to separate among "others" who stand outside the proper boundaries of their ethnic identity. Literary tropes entered the nation's political discourse, issuing a call to blood stemming from the assimilatory nationalism that characterizes the imaginary assemblage of 'the serbs.'

On June 28, 1989, Milošević delivered a speech to more than a million people assembled to commemorate the six centuries that had passed since the mythic Battle of Kosovo. The speech, whose transcription the weekly *Nedeljne informativne novine* of Belgrade symptomatically titled "Kosovo and Unity," marked a turning point for Milošević's political career, for the destiny of the already unstable Socialist Federative Republic of Yugoslavia, and, ultimately, for yet another historical demise of 'the serbs' whom he was addressing on this solemn but nevertheless glorious occasion.[30] Thus, literary tropes of oral tradition found their way into direct political discourse. By creating volatile suspicion among the already restive South Slavic brothers, the speech transformed Milošević into an icon for a new emergence of 'the serbs.' The dream of Yugoslav "Brotherhood and Unity" was to be followed by a rude and bloody awakening as he called on 'the serbs' simultaneously to defend the Yugoslav state and act out their own conflicted cultural heritage. Capitalizing on the uncertainty caused by hyperinflation, decreased standards of living, and unemployment in the early 1980s—all of which began to plague the Yugoslav nations after the Tito era ended, Milošević tapped the imaginary trope of victimization to rouse 'the serbs' to struggle for separate entities inside Croatia and Bosnia.

Resurrecting the dead: Slobodan Milošević. PHOTOGRAPH COURTESY ZORAN PETROVIĆ.

This kind of populist politics fueled the devastating war in the former Yugoslavia that ended up resurrecting ethnic and cultural mon-
sters against whom 'the serbs' could affirm their newly rediscovered
"heavenly" position and once again basked in the imaginary realm of
freedom to come. The realities of military defeat and political isolation
were obscured by the *jouissance* of the nation as it rose from the bonds
of earthly existence. Milošević began his speech by fusing the past and
the present, eliminating the gap of six centuries by imagining a homogenous time of the nation. He thus created the impression of a seam-
less, uninterrupted collective national time for 'the serbs' as a specter
of the ancient centuries:

> On this spot in the heart of Serbia, on the field of Kosovo, six centuries
> ago, a full six hundred years ago, one of the greatest battles of those times
> took place. . . . Due to social circumstances, this great commemoration

comes in a year when after many years, after many decades, Serbia has regained its integrity as a state, as a nation and as a spiritual entity.[31]

By 1989, the population of Kosovo had already been transformed by demographic expansion of the Albanians, constant northward migration by Serbs and Montenegrins, and the ethnic policies of the League of Communists of Yugoslavia. Kosovo belonged to 'the serbs' only in national memory and cultural imagination; in reality, the province was becoming dominated by an increasingly assertive Albanian majority. The integrity that had been gained after "many years, after many decades" echoes Milošević's campaign to abolish the autonomous status of the Serbian provinces of Kosovo and Vojvodina, something he successfully engineered under the guise of "anti-bureaucratic revolution" at the end of the 1980s.

In fact, the popular imagination substituted the Albanians—as well as the Bosnian Muslims—for the Ottomans who defeated 'the serbs' at Kosovo in 1389. For the Kosovo myth to infuse the national imaginary, the collective identity needed an other to serve as a threat to the nation's dignity and integrity. With their predominantly Islamic religion and culture, the Albanians and, later, the Bosnian Muslims came to be defined as the main threat to 'the serbs' in their struggle for sovereign territory. A major contradiction lies in the fact that Milošević imagined 'the serbs' as the agents of European civilization fighting against "Oriental" others who threatened to separate from the common Yugoslav state.

The Occidental Part

Attempting to undo the binary vision inherent in the cultural confrontation between Europe and the Orient, Andrić's literary imaginary develops a borderline poetics that attempts to create an indeterminate image of Bosnia. The two civilizations end up so intermingled that it is extremely difficult for outside observers to distinguish their specific ingredients; at the same time, local differences become an indispensable part of local populations' ability to keep imagining their particular identities as part of two worlds "between which there cannot be any real contact nor the possibility of agreement."[32] His literary imaginary is perhaps best exemplified by the characters such as the doctor Cologna in *The Bosnian Chronicle*, a subject who is forced to live a borderline existence surrounded by a multitude of languages, religions, and civilizations:

> No one knows what it is like to be born and live on the border between two worlds, to know and understand them both and be unable to do anything to help them to come closer to understanding each other, to love and to hate both of those worlds, to doubt and hesitate all life long, to have two homelands and to have none, to be everywhere at home and remain forever a stranger; in short: to live as if one were crucified, as a victim and a torturer at the same time.[33]

This lament, delivered by Cologna to Des Fossés, reflects conspicuous preoccupations with the impossibility of a cultural encounter that are symptomatic of both the Yugoslav cultural identity in general and the Bosnian one in particular. Andrić's biography is informed by these borderline realities: His father was Catholic; his mother, Orthodox; and he grew up speaking the Ijekavski variant of Serbo-Croatian. His first poems were written in the same variant, but when he moved to Belgrade in the 1920s, he started writing prose in the Ekavski variant used in Serbia proper. Besides this early vacillation between Serb and Croat ethnicities, he devoted most of his writings to the lives of Bosnian Muslims, making himself into a quintessential Yugoslav figure.

His own literary imaginary articulates doubts and hesitations about the very nature of identity Cologna discusses in his monologue. The agonistic contexts of nationalism force a choice between the two worlds, as adherence to one community requires hatred of the other one, a choice a humanist such as Andrić could not make in good conscience. During the 1990s, the national identity of declared Yugoslavs marked them as a-national and subjected to abuse from particular ethnic communities. Andrić's legacy has suffered more than that of any other writer in the former Yugoslavia. His monument in Višegrad had been dynamited by Muslim extremists; his foundation in Belgrade was robbed of its assets by Serbian politicians; and nationalist Croats tried to purge his works from school programs. Locked up within the xenophobic universe of their emergent nationalist cultures and busy with inventing and reinventing vampire nations on the other side of the cultural divide, the guardians of nationalist culture were quick to forget and silence those who reminded them of their common Slavic origin and the fratricidal nature of the war they were waging.

The Unbearable Kitsch of History

Danilo Kiš, one of the writers from the former Yugoslavia who was least taken by the appeal of mass ideologies, once remarked: "Nationalism is the ideology of banality. Nationalism is a totalitarian ideology. Nationalism is kitsch."[34] Populist appeals to the bond of common blood spilled by the historical enemies-vampires invoked by nationalist rhetoric during the 1980s is the best testimony to this passing observation, which Kiš made in a treatise on the malignant small-mindedness of provincial intellectuals.

Resurrecting the ancient creature of memory from its underground crypt was the dominant feature of the Milošević's Kosovo speech in 1989. While paying lip service to the need for all ethnic groups to live in harmony both in Serbia and in Yugoslavia, he subtly underlined the theme of disunity that has always plagued 'the serbs': "Discord and treason at Kosovo will plague the Serbian people throughout their history. Even during the latest war, that discord and treason have caused suffering to the Serbian people and to Serbia whose historical and moral consequences far exceeded the fascist aggression."[35] Milošević thus implied that those who differ in either their religious or their ideological orientation were an immediate threat to the idea of national unity. His constant references to those who betrayed Serbdom in the Battle of Kosovo (both the mythic traitor Vuk Branković and the historical traitors who converted to Islam) gave a warning to those among 'the serbs' who might have wished to challenge the nationalist line he was towing. The unspoken message was: "If you don't unite behind me now, the Islamic fundamentalists will impale you as the Ottomans did six centuries ago and the fascists will slaughter you as they did in the Second World War."

He derived the reference to disunity in the Second World War from the division of the national ranks between the royalist Četniks, who supported Colonel Draža Mihajlović and the royal government in exile, and the communist partisans led by Josip Broz Tito. Milošević implied that the time had come for all of these ideological and historical differences to be abandoned in the name of the common national interest of a collective under attack. This type of political discourse not only weakened the communist regime of the time; it also encouraged those who had been exiled by Tito's regime to look at Milošević as the new national messiah. This new/old discourse was able to assimilate and transform stated differences inside the political establishment and the anticommunist diaspora. The closure of this ideological gap resulted in a popular return to the fundamental values of Orthodox Christianity, which were previously demonized by the communists as remnants of the Četnik (Royalist) legacy and mentality.

Within this new equation, the Yugoslavism of the Tito era was defined as inherently detrimental to 'the serbs,' because it divided the nation along ideological lines and denationalized it. Milošević continued with a list of grievances: "Even later, when the socialist Yugoslavia had been formed, the Serbian leadership remained divided in the new country, prone to compromises that only caused harm to our nation."[36] This statement challenged the very foundation of the so-called second Yugoslavia and expressed longing for the pre–Second World War era that had been dominated by 'the serbs' as its largest nation. The case of Milošević as a national icon demonstrates how the appeal of this type of imaginary discourse becomes powerful exactly because it transcends the common dichotomies of monarchist–republican or communist–capitalist and substitutes for them the violent imaginary of the ostensibly non-ideological category of the nation as a construct of ancient memory. In more ways than one, the building of the multicultural state that Yugoslavia was supposed to embody required an active endeavor to comprehend and bridge each ethnic group's "narcissism of minor differences."[37]

Milošević's nationalist message was also rooted in an intellectual and cultural climate of conservative Eurocentrism; in a perpetual return to the fundamental fantasy of historical imagination, interpellating the ethnos that has been ready-made by "centuries-old suffering" at the hands of the foreigner—that is, the Ottoman, Habsburg, Nazi, Fascist, and other invaders.

Tearing the Heart Out

Bosnia's geographic shape has often been likened to a human heart, a metaphor for the most vital cultural organ without which the transnational ideal of the common Yugoslav state could not survive. Yet the wars of the 1990s manifested the opposite, as well: Without the common framework of the South Slavic state and peace between its constituent ethnic communities, the heart of Yugoslavia was torn out by the emergent vampire nation, and its most vulnerable population—the Slavic Islamic community—was exposed to the vengeful practices of their Christian neighbors. The role of the global vampire, announced in Dracula's monologue about avenging "the shame of Kosovo," was confirmed for an international community informed by the global media complex. Milošević triggered the discourse of revenge and betrayal born as a violent counterpart to the Kosovo myth to stir up the ancient creature among 'the serbs.' Bosnian Muslims, perceived as direct remainders of Ottoman imperial rule, and Croats, figured exclusively as a return of the Ustaše set on either converting 'the serbs' to Catholicism or exterminating them, were presented as surrogate victims of the revenge that inheres in the Kosovo covenant.

In 1935, Andrić wrote an essay entitled "Njegoš as a Tragic Hero of the Kosovo Idea," in which he explored influences of the Kosovo covenant on Petar Petrović Njegoš, the previously mentioned Montenegrin prince, bishop, and poet. It is the tragic dimension of Njegoš's life and work that Andrić saw expressed in "the most horrible password" pronounced by Vladika Danilo in *The Mountain Wreath*: "Let there be what cannot be [*Neka bude što biti ne može*]."[38] Andrić called this verse the clearest expression of the "positive nihilism" of a population that stubbornly denied the reality of foreign domination to regain the lost fullness of the "national object" and give free rein to the desire for emancipation from the stranglehold of the imperial master. Using the example of Simon Bolivar's struggle for South American independence from Spain, Andrić saw every anti-imperial movement as a struggle carried out under this maxim, since most wars against foreign domination were fought and won against impossible odds. But at the same time, Andrić saw Njegoš as a figure who attempted to unify all of the South Slavs, which Andrić regarded as an implicit impossibility:

> The tragedy of that struggle was augmented and enhanced by the inevitable fratricidal conflicts that were frequently imposed by our [Yugoslav] history. The tragedy was that much greater for Njegoš, who from his heights, like all of the great and light-bearing spirits of our history, was always able to envision the totality of our nation, regardless of its religious or tribal affiliation.[39]

Thus, Andrić imagined "the serbs" as the prototype of a new anti-imperial identity of South Slavs, both as its main ingredient and as its "ethnic glue," a cohesive force that would keep the different yet similar peoples of southeastern Europe together by virtue of their destiny as historical victims and as the most willing rebels against anti-imperial subjugation.

Altering Islam

A similar concern underlies the works of Meša Selimović, another writer who has offered a powerful literary account of Bosnian complexities. Although he was the son of a wealthy Muslim landowner, Selimović considered himself part of the Serbian literary tradition. Like Andrić, he attempted to bridge the gap between the ethno-religious communities and developed a cultural and literary practice devoted to Yugoslavism, moving it beyond the political platform of the Communist Party with which he was disappointed. In an interview in 1972, he made an unusual appeal to the Bosnians:

> We ought to get rid of our inertia, of our mutual mistrust, of our dependence on everything that is indeed the thing of the past. We need to preserve *merhamet*, the humane dimension that has been with us even in the most difficult of times. This quality of our people looks to me like something most beautiful and most valuable.[40]

Selimović is arguably the most famous writer to have sprouted from the Bosnian Muslim culture in the twentieth century. His novel *Derviš i smrt* (Death and the Dervish) is devoted to the preservation of *merhamet*, a word that, according to its Arabic and Ottoman etymologies, signifies "mercy, compassion, tenderness of heart, or an act of forgiveness."[41] According to Selimović, *Death and the Dervish* was inspired by the loss of a brother who was executed by his communist comrades near the end of the Second World War. Selimović transposed the event, which haunted all his life, into a novel that examines the complexities of violence in a much larger sense, especially in the multiethnic environment of Bosnia.

The main protagonist of *Death and the Dervish*, Dervish Ahmed Nurudin, is forced to come to terms with the arbitrary power that suddenly imprisons and later executes his brother without a hearing or a trial. By placing the conflict between individual and institution in the context of medieval Bosnia, Selimović not only avoids directly attacking the socialist state for its past sins of arbitrary executions, but also gives his work a more universal appeal. He substitutes Ottoman officials for communist officials, and the dervish's struggle against violent and capricious power takes up the length of the novel. Ahmed Nurudin fights desperately to preserve his own vulnerable humanity, which is challenged not only by the powers that be but also by his own rich instinctual life.

The novel opens with a celebration tied to the dragon slayer, Saint George, that is saturated with the pre-monotheistic awakening of basic instincts; at the same time, Nurudin begins to feel oppressed by the lack of corporeal passion in his life. "I am forty years old—an ugly age: young enough to have desires and old enough not to do anything to make them a reality."[42] In the course of the novel, the reader realizes that it is both violence and sexuality that are part of his temptations. The main crisis revolves around violence: How can Nurudin be part of the same power structure that has murdered his brother without a hearing and without a trial? He is a cleric and finds temporary respite in studying of the Qu'ran, although his instinctual disquiet is combined with a spirit of rebellion that gradually overpowers the comfort he gets from the scripture. Nurudin rejects the corruption of the power structure and struggles to carve out an independent existential position for himself. He harbors Ishak, a semi-imaginary outlaw, who becomes identified with a disassociated part of his own self, a metaphor for his own doubt about the institutional order.

Nurudin rejects not only the arbitrariness of violence, but also the ability of power structures to appropriate his rejection of it. Toward the end of the novel, Nurudin becomes a local judge and is forced to sign the arrest warrant for his best friend Hasan to save his own life and reputation. Hasan, who according to Selimović, is based on his own father, represents the power of merhamet, the unselfish surrender of one's own heart to another.[43] But Nurudin's dependence on power is so fundamental that he is forced to renounce his friendship for Hasan, a man whom he loves more than himself. This act of conforming to the law of a power structure in which he has no trust is equal to signing his own death sentence as an ethical being. Therefore, the death in the title of the novel is not simply a physical absence from the world; it is the death of a life condemned to be lived within a community where violence can be used in such a random and arbitrary manner.

Selimović presents Nurudin's struggle against his own corporeal nature, as well as against the corrupt foundations of imperial power, as part of the unresolved identity of converts of any kind. Again, the oldness of time is invoked as a source of cultural malignancy: "The old alien times drag themselves behind us, stronger than us, erupting in the rebellion of the body that lasts a short while and is remembered until the next rebellion takes place."[44] The memory of the "old alien times" before the acceptance of Islam causes the converted population to retain their "right to sin" in the night commemorating the dragon slayer. Similar to Stoker's "ancient centuries," this temporality disguises the secrets of origin tied to the forbidden secrets of an identity that had to be renounced and forgotten. Although Nurudin tries to warn the local boys that St. George is an infidel saint, his own sinful awakening undermines his proper identity as an Islamic cleric.

"The rebellion of the body" is seen as a return not to Christianity but to an even more ancient cultural layer: that of Slavic paganism tied to the unholy specters of old, subterranean divinities. The awakening of this desire for the forbidden undermines the "dry and unattractive" law through the return to "ancient and juicy orgies" posited at the imaginary origin of those ancient times.[45] The narrator, who is cast into doubt by this awakening of the ancient desire, poses a question that haunts borderline cultures and locations: "Will the remote wild ancestors conquer us, will they bring us back to their ancient times?" Bosnia is imagined as a location of ongoing struggle between these conflicted temporalities: the new faith—Islam—and the remnants of the old heathen rites that survive under the guise of Christianity.

The Lost Identity

For Selimović, the tragedy of the Bosnian Muslim identity lies in the fact that Bosnian Muslims never became "real" Turks but, at the same time, were excommunicated from the community of 'the serbs,' to which they had belonged before the conversion. They were left in-between, in the existential vacuum created by the confrontation between the ancient past and the fleeting present, perpetually undermining Bosnia's possible futures. Selimović sets up a paradigm for imagining a national identity that would certainly prove unacceptable to most of the exclusivist cultures that have been resurrected on the territory of the former Yugoslavia since the latest wars. Hasan laments the cruel joke that has been played on the converts to Islam by the force of temporality fractured by the struggles against the ancient creature of memory:

> History has played an unprecedented joke on us. Until yesterday we were something we want to forget today. But we did not become something else, either. We stopped halfway, confused. There is nowhere else to go. We were uprooted, but we were not accepted. We are like a stream that has been separated from the main current by a flood and now lacks both its course and its goal—too small to be a lake, too big for the earth to absorb. With a vague feeling of shame because of our origin, and guilt because of our conversion, we don't want to look back and have nothing to look forward to, so we try to hold back time, fearing any kind of solution.[46]

The aquatic metaphor Selimović uses to depict the fate of Islamic converts reveals the borderline nature of their identity: Slavic Muslims were placed in between the dominant historical currents engendered by the Ottoman conquest of the Balkans and benefited from this at the expense of their former brothers. As collaborators with an empire, they came to be perceived as traitors by a native population that remained loyal to the ancient divinities disguised by the Christian faith. Hasan sees no future for his people, only a desperate desire to stop time and return to the age where he imagines a Bosnia that can no longer be. But the tragedy of identity does not stop with borderline subjects of this kind, since identity is shown to be differential, formed through a violent action that comes from a dominant imperial order that holds power over any subjectivity. The imaginary unity with the primal object of identification, embodied in the mythical Damp Mother Earth of Slavic mythology, is necessarily fragmented through historical development and often is perceived as traumatic.[47]

The Ottoman conquest of the Balkans, which interrupted the imaginary harmony of medieval silence, is posited as the external instance, providing Muslims with a provisory identity based on violence and domination. Therefore, Hasan's monologue implies that, in regard to the question of identity, nations share the fate of borderline subjects in that they are doomed to be separated from the harmony their nation both imagines and projects into the premodern era to validate its existence.

The ancient creature of memory is omnipresent, interpellating stories of blood and soil with differential outcomes. Selimović's literary imaginary is not confined to the difficult historical situation of Bosnia; it also activates existential insight into the horror immanent in each subject since the moment of birth within a communal narrative. The initial act of violent separation from the body of that first, maternal other, previously narrated as the blood tribute in Andrić's *Bridge on the Drina*, is given concrete literary shape in the divided subject of the post-Oriental condition by Selimović. He implies that suffering and un-fulfilled desires are the starting place of every identity that tends to treat life as a losing battle, unless one gathers strength to practice the art of merhamet, the unconditional opening of one's heart to another.

In fact, Selimović sees merhamet as a part of the Bosnian identity that often has been overshadowed by historically induced cruelties:

> During the centuries, all sorts of things accumulated in the Bosnians: the feeling of their own indeterminacy, of someone else's guilt, of a difficult history, of uncertain future, a fear of change, a desire for goodness and humanity which would be applied to all persons without any limitations (that is, the famous *merhamet*, a broad openness toward everyone, a striv-ing toward universal humanism, as a defense against one's own margin-ality), and frequent disappointments that engendered hatred.[48]

Striving toward universal humanism is a result of the acute aware-ness of "one's own marginality" that was born in the borderline zone between Islam and Christianity. The word *"izdvojenost,"* which I trans-late as "marginality," hides in its etymology the diverse nature of Bos-nian identity: it is derived from the verb *izdvojiti* (to separate, to iso-late), which literally means "to turn into an other." Bosnian marginality is imagined as a process of becoming that constantly turns one into an other. For Selimović, the embrace of humanist values, combined with Islamic merhamet, is a strategic move against the kind of abject partic-ularity that thrives in isolation, in the silence of the cultural zone that finds itself at the edge of two civilizations. Bosnia is imagined as a location simultaneously at the eastern end of Europe and at the west-ern edge of Asia, where the return of the ancient creature of memory is imminent.

Selimović's Hasan calls Bosnians *"najzamršeniji ljudi na svetu"* (the most complicated people in the world) before embarking on his mono-logue about the branch of the main stream that broke off and strayed into deadly ground. He equates Bosnia with *mrtvaja*, a dead body of water that has lost all contact with all other human rivers and seas and is therefore doomed to exist in the suspended state of the living dead. Hasan's behavior is a clear illustration of this point: Instead of trying to augment his father's wealth and establish himself as a respected member of his community, he is consumed by the desire for beauty and pleasure that ultimately ruins him. This *jouissance* is manifested in his infatuation for Marija, the mysterious married woman from Dubrovnik whom Hasan passionately desires. In a footnote to his memoir, Selimović analyzes this kind of behavior as a symptom of "Oriental sensuality" of Bosniaks, which is directly opposed to the Dinaric culture of the rest of Bosnian population, which glorifies "the struggle and revenge of Kosovo."[49] He argues that the orientation toward religion in the Muslim community created a culture in which "more passion was expressed in the personal, private sphere than in the public and national affairs, which were not directly tied to their national being."[50] Hasan's life is consumed by his obsession with Marija's beauty, and all of his energy is spent in attempting to get closer to her.

But when he gets the opportunity to get rid of Marija's husband, a merchant in Dubrovnik, after the husband is detained by the local police, Hasan instead helps him escape from Bosnia. He saves the husband even though this act directly conflicts with his desire for the merchant's attractive wife. Merhamet demands not only putting the other's life before one's own, but also the renunciation of everything one passionately desires. In this respect, Hasan's and Nurudin's characters merge through the upholding of the ethical principle of placing the well-being of the other before one's own. Examination of the bond between the two friends occupies the largest portion of the novel, until Nurudin betrays Hasan and signs the warrant for his arrest.

One of the most significant moments in their relationship is the moment when Hasan tells Nurudin about his meeting with Džemail. We learn that Džemail had crippled himself in a drunken frenzy by stabbing his own thighs with a sharp knife and can no longer walk. He is carted around by children and uses a pair of large sticks to move about while inside his shop. Džemail continues to drink and stab his disabled limbs when intoxicated, threatening to kill anyone who comes near to save him from self-inflicted violence. Everyone in his vicinity, fearing the enormous strength of his upper body, continues to watch as he mutilates himself. This kind of witnessing of violence by the passersby becomes emblematic of the entire national community:

> —Džemail is the real image of Bosnia, Hasan said.—Power on stumps. A man who is his own executioner [*Sam svoj krvnik.*]. An abundance without direction or meaning.
> —What are we then? Madmen? Unfortunates?
> —The most complicated people in the world.[51]

Cultural Disability

Hasan, himself a victim of "a naive faith in human honesty,"[52] imagines Bosnia as a disabled, well-meaning giant that is prone to self-imposed violence caused by outbursts of rage and frustration. Džemail's violence derives from his inability to resolve the unbearable tension between the demand of the cultural forces that foment fear, hatred, and revenge, on the one hand, and merhamet, on the other. It is as if Džemail hurts himself first so he will never be able to hurt anyone else. He is a victim of the predicament in which Bosnia finds itself in recurrent temporal cycles as a location that is culturally and politically peripheral to both Europe and Asia. "We live at the crossroads of the worlds, on the border between peoples, a target for everyone, always blamed by someone," Hasan says about his people while spending time in Istanbul. "The waves of history break over us, as if over a cliff."[53] Selimović imagines Bosnia as an entity that is never the subject of its own destiny; it is, rather, a passive and tragic victim of violent reverberations of the ancient creature of the past that originates in the invisible centers of political and administrative power. Every shift in the balance of forces is followed by a tragedy for those who reside at the end of the tectonic plates, between Orient and Europe, and who claim and reject Bosnians at the same time:

> For centuries we look for ourselves and recognize ourselves—soon we will no longer know who we are, we are already forgetting that we may even want something; the others honor us by letting us march under their flag since we don't have our own, they entice us when they need us and reject us when our services are no longer necessary, we are uprooted, yet not accepted, alien to everyone, both to those whose family we belong to and to those who won't accept us into their family.[54]

Selimović finds that the problematic character of the Bosnian identity lies in the fact that both the Orient and Europe deny Bosniaks' desire to belong to those two larger cultural formations because they bear the mark of monstrous indeterminacy caused by religious conversion. The Christians see them as traitors, while the Turks suspect that they might revert back to their old faith at any time. Hasan is so acutely aware of this impossible historical position that he loses all confidence in the established values of the community and finds solace in gambling, travel, and women. He refuses to get married and is completely uninterested in his father's large inheritance. This complete detachment from one's economic interest and family life, according to Selimović, results from the historical position of Muslims after the Berlin Congress in 1878, when Bosnia was awarded to Austria as a protectorate. While pondering the destiny of his father, Alija, a self-identified prototype for the character of Hasan, Selimović concludes that this "passive relationship towards one's own life after 1878" is the result of a "lack of collective direction and historical perspective," resulting in "national indeterminacy."[55] Selimović goes on to speculate that the socialist revolution of 1945 managed to liberate Muslims from their bondage to the private sphere that had become their only psychological and emotional refuge after 1878. In other words, Selimović saw the Muslims, as well as other Bosnians, as an inextricable part of the Yugoslav multinational and multicultural project after the Second World War. Socialism brought Muslims a sense of nationhood they were so sorely lacking in 1968, when the Bosniaks were recognized by the communist government as a separate nation.

The new cultural establishments of the Yugoslav successor states have been suppressing cultural figures such as Selimović ever since they declared national sovereignty. His complex identity as a Muslim humanist with communist leanings does not fit into any of the narratives of identity and origin currently enforced by the nation-states that have sprouted out of the ruins of the common South Slavic state. It is especially the vague memory of his family's origin in the maligned phantasm of 'the serbs' that presents an obstacle to his inclusion in the new revisions of Bosnian literature and history.[56] The narratives of blood and soil related to the newly forged origin of the people are not yet mature enough to contain the complexity of cultural figures who evade the simplified version of an imaginary economy that disguises the violent roots of its own origin.

5

QUIETING THE VAMPIRE
Voicing Violence in the Post-Human Age

The dividing line passes not between history and memory but between
punctual "history-memory" systems and diagonal and multilinear
assemblages, which are in no way eternal: they have to do with becoming; they are a bit of becoming in a pure state; they are transhistorical.
—Gilles Deleuze and Félix Guattari, *A Thousand Plateaus*

The function of the phallic signifier touches here on its most profound
relation: that by which the Ancients embodied therein the Nous and
the Logos.
—Jacques Lacan, *Écrits*

Later, of course, she no longer desired to return to that city, which at
one time I couldn't understand, and which now, when the vampires of
Nazism are raising their heads everywhere, I understand perfectly well.
—David Albahari, Bait

A multiplicity of intellectual figures appeared on the global scene to
denounce the violent rites and cure the nationalist hysteria from which
Slobodan Milošević emerged as the arch-vampire of the chimerical assemblage of 'the serbs' in the late 1980s. Resisting the figment of
collective imagination tied to common blood was extremely difficult for
those who were not willing to take part in the national imaginary and
its violent becomings tied to misappropriating the common past. As
the global gaze directed at Yugoslav political space performed a very
successful interpellation of the particular ethnic war machines hatched

out of the common South Slavic state, the image of the vampire began to function as a metaphor for the entire region as a zone of exceptional violence. This closely matched the imaginary economy projected onto the Balkans more than a century ago by the writers of the Gothic era. Those who voiced opposition from within the assemblage of 'the serbs' were confronted by an internal discourse from "national" Academics (with a capital "A") who treated the right of other nations to separate as a danger to the territoriality of the common South Slavic identity, and overlooked by those outside the national assemblage who were concerned with proving that the vampire within could be eliminated only through symbolic impalement by external vampire slayers.

On March 3, 2007, the anniversary of Slobodan Milošević's death in the international War Criminal Prison in The Hague, an unusual event took place at his gravesite: The photographer Miroslav Milošević (who is not related to the former president) visited after midnight armed with a hawthorn stake and performed the ritual of quieting the vampire. He also wrote in a memory book next to the grave: "Dark to dark, he's buried in the dark . . . It is midnight, the time of vampires." He called the police to warn them of his deed, but they responded with a symptomatic joke: "Be careful, or Sloba's [i.e., Milošević's] hand might get you from the grave."[1] This performance by the photographer, who belonged to the opposition group Otpor (Resistance) during the popular revolt against the Milošević government, was intended to ensure that the "history-memory" of the times enveloped in nationalist hatred did not return to haunt Serbia ever again.

Although Miroslav Milošević's performance contains definite elements of folkloric parody, it is symptomatic of the struggles those trying to defy and resist the spectral force of 'the serbs' had to wage. It was a struggle for a third narrative directed against both the internal violence of the cultural imaginary and the global cultural misunderstanding that classified 'the serbs' as modern-day vampires feeding on the blood of their ethnic others. A statement made by the distinguished actor, director, and writer Peter Ustinov while serving as a UNESCO ambassador is symptomatic of this type of labeling: "Animals use their resources in a much happier way than those evil creatures [i.e., the Serbs], whose membership in the human race is seriously overdue."[2] The subhuman dimension ascribed to the entire nation exemplifies the racist echoes that characterized the global hysteria of the 1990s, helping Milošević discredit any form of opposition as implicit collaboration with outsiders who held views similar to those of distinguished public intellectuals such as Ustinov.

Under those conditions, the vampire nation's cultural rebirth could be accomplished with relative ease, especially by returning the memory of recent and past sacrifices to public discourse, as analyzed in the previous chapters. The relentless performance of a new breed of intellectuals, whom I call the "neo-guslars," consisted of discursive mourning and wailing over the reopened masculine wound shared by 'the serbs.' During the crisis, the Academics emerged as the leading voices of the neo-guslars, spewing out masculine laments dedicated to the monumental national corpse that was arising from its ancient Kosovo crypt. Their voice resounded with echoes of Dracula's speech about the shame of Kosovo, bringing the corpse of the nation back from its medieval crypt to counter death and decomposition when communist Yugoslavia came to an end. The subterranean cultural force of memory engineered its demands for righteous violence in the name of the people by soldering the martial and the intellectual into a single discursive position. This positioning of the Academics made literal the anecdote related earlier in which Vuk Karadžić, considered the father of South Slavic literacy, taught himself to write during the uprising against the Ottoman Empire in 1804 by dipping his quill into gunpowder dissolved in water and scribbling letters on discarded ammunition paper. Metaphorically, he charged writing with the lethal substrate that has permeated modernizing culture from its outset. The Academics felt called on to respond to this call of gunpowder by conflating the codes of literary culture with martial values embodied by the guslars during the period when oral culture was dominant.

It is no surprise that literacy was perceived as a weapon in the struggle for global recognition of 'the serbs' within the European cultural domain of Vuk's age. His collections and transcriptions of oral epics were in fact a confirmation of values tied to an earlier period in European culture, when the martial codes of violence and dominant masculinity were in full force. Therefore, the first written monuments of 'the serbs' in the vernacular tongue were permeated by this agonistic relationship to the letter, which occasionally were challenged by the novelistic poetics of dissident writers in the penultimate days of the former Yugoslavia.

During the 1970s, a generation of writers who came of age during the Second World War began to develop their novelistic poetics by working through the legacy of fundamental violence reflected in the notion of the armed letter. In *Kako upokojiti vampira* (How to quiet a vampire) Borislav Pekić developed his narrative by showing how the European identity roots itself in the bloody practices of mutual extermination. Specifically, Pekić used an umbrella attached to the imaginary character of Adam Trpković, an accidental victim of the totalitarian dreams of Mussolini's Fascism and Hitler's National Socialism, as an omnipresent reminder of Europe's collective genocidal past. Thus, while Andrić used a stake as the dominant phallic signifier in his modernist elaboration of the violence that haunts the vampire nation, Pekić substituted a parodically tinged umbrella to underline his postmodern literary posture.

How to Quiet a Vampire is subtitled "A Sotie," a theatrical genre that was used to comment on important issues of the day, especially in everyday political disputes, in fifteenth-century and sixteenth-century France. In a typical *sotie*, actors wearing false noses and dunce caps played scenes based on daily events as opening acts for the featured morality or mystery play. The genre was eventually banned by the authorities; it gradually transformed into satire for the stage, and its informative function as a public arena for daily disputes was transferred to the emergent profession of journalism. Pekić picked up the clowning aspect of the genre to take up the heavy subject of the legacy of violence inherent in the totalitarian projects of twentieth-century Europe.

Published in 1977 and dedicated to Danilo Kiš, *How to Quiet a Vampire* is a fictional response to Kiš's political pamphlet *Grobnica za Borisa Davidoviča* (The tomb for Boris Davidovich), which had been published a year earlier. Kiš's book, which critiqued the Stalinism inherent in all communist-based impositions of revolutionary violence, no matter the price, caused the greatest literary scandal seen in the former Yugoslavia after the Second World War. Although Pekić focuses on Nazism rather than communism, the two authors use a similar pseudo-documentary narrative strategy to present their reflections on the nature and practice of totalitarian ideologies.

Pekić's *sotie* takes the epistolary form, featuring letters written by the fictional former Gestapo officer Konrad Rutkowski to his brother-in-law, Hilmar, a history professor in Germany. Writing from a city named "D." (apparently a fictionalized Dubrovnik) on the Adriatic's eastern coast in 1965, Konrad attempts to come to terms with the time he spent there after Germany replaced Italy as the occupation force in 1943. The interaction of these two temporalities provides the main narrative frame for Pekić's derisive literary performance as he sets up his own fictional undoing of the eternal violence that inheres in the desire for power of one human being over the other.

Konrad's twenty-six letters (and two postscripts) carry subtitles that cite major works in the canon of Western intellectual history, from Plato's *Phaedon* and Marcus Aurelius's *Matter and Memory* to Martin Heidegger's *Being and Time* and Albert Camus's *Rebel*. Yet Pekić leaves it radically unclear whether Hilmar ever received the letters, and every meaning enunciated in them ends up being suspended in the book's appendices, which present a series of contradictory psychiatric diagnoses of Konrad that either reinforce or undermine his sanity. This authorial gesture unambiguously connects the greatest achievements of the human "Nous and Logos" to the most egregious manifestation of violence, embodied in the political practice of genocide, in the twentieth century. Yet Pekić's artistic prose treads lightly when confronted with issues of human good and evil, as narrating genocide under the dunce cap could offend the victims who did not fit the identity molds of race, class, or gender of their more dominant opponents.

Phallic Fantasies

Indeed, the vampire announced in the novel's title is ostensibly Adam Trpković, a victim of the Mussolini–Hitler axis whose Adamic naming points to the new generation of socialist vampires born and bred in Tito's Yugoslavia. Just as Lacan pointed out that the ancients relied on the phallic function of the signifier as a mark of authority to give privileged meaning to their pronouncements, Pekić establishes a fictional relationship between the umbrella carried by Adam Trpković and the way the rest of his antiauthoritarian *sotie* is narrated. The umbrella, in fact, also represents "the new" in terms of the horizon of expectations intended for the reader: it is introduced to counter the expectations announced in the title by very clearly evoking the genre of vampire-hunting manuals originally published in the Serbian language.

The central element of these "how-to" manuals was the application of the hawthorn stake to the undead body of the suspected vampire, obviously setting up a zero-horizon of expectations for the crossing of narrative levels to occur within the text. While vampire-hunting manuals are boring and predictable, introducing the umbrella opens the horizon of the unexpected without compromising the relationship to the phallic function. Indeed, the piercing shape of both the hawthorn stake and the umbrella relate to the castration anxiety that drives Konrad's letters, which in the tradition of the sotie vacillate between intelligence and inanity.

The confusion of identity boundaries that Konrad experiences is paralleled by the shifting of narrative levels throughout the letters, whose undynamic plot development might otherwise make them rather uninteresting to read. Indeed, the reader is also confronted by a proliferation of other documents whose imaginative level does not rise above that of a police file or a hospital archive. While piecing together a narrative about the predicament of human subjectivity in the aftermath of differently justified mass exterminations of subjects who were unresponsive to the identity call of their totalitarian interpellations, Pekić ensures that the Nazi horrors are shadowed by the anti-human transgressions of the socialist universe he grew up fighting. Therefore, Adam Trpković, the "undead" municipal file clerk, not only appears as an incarnation of the Nazi victim in search of justice; he also serves as a vehicle for exploring the vulgar legacy of socialist realism. One of Konrad's letters, subtitled "*Ecce Homo*," reveals this aspect of the phallic function by describing the erection of a monument to Adam as a national hero: "When they presented him to me, he was barely hundred and seventy centimeters tall, but now he's grown to a height of ten meters, not including the pedestal."[3] Of course, the unheroic umbrella is missing from the monument in which Adam now appears "grand and mysterious, like a legend."[4] If it is possible to falsify the monument's size by yielding to hyperbole, Pekić implies, then it is also possible that righteous antifascists nurture the same phallic fantasy of their exaggerated heroism in the service to the nation.

Pekić deploys the umbrella narratively as a counterpoint to such monumental seriousness, substituting this phallic object for the principle of the rational motivation of putting an end to the vampire announced in the title. The umbrella's apparently incidental appearance in the narrative also manifests its phallic function as an unannounced, and therefore omnipotent, source of authority and meaning for the rest of the sotie's narrative development. The phallus "can play its role only when veiled," says Lacan.[5] Its unrepresentability is the source of its signifying power, giving form and meaning to a whole range of unrelated objects and events while remaining immersed in secrecy and hidden from view.

The umbrella is a narrative prosthesis with a wide range of signifying functions. It is both the cause of Adam's incarceration by Mussolini's forces (he did not salute the Italian flag because he was holding up his umbrella) and the cause of Konrad's death in a car crash: "The investigation determined that he bled to death. His abdomen was pierced by a man's umbrella, which he was holding in his hands instead of a steering wheel."[6] The umbrella acts thus as the vampire slayer's hawthorn stake, applied to the body of a narrator who is haunted by the presence of his Nazi past in Adam, the ostensible vampire. By disguising its phallic function yet performing its central narrative role, the umbrella leads the reader away from the high expectations set up by the epistolary subtitles that invoke Wittgenstein's *Tractatus Logico-Philosophicus* or Marx's *The Poverty of Philosophy*.

Vampire Logic

Konrad's end comes at the end of Pekić's text, as well, as the phallic narrative device is bared in the form of the umbrella-stake acting out its poetic justice. Indeed, passing through the psychoanalytical Oedipal drama requires identifying with the masculine aggressor's sign of gender difference. This object of difference extends the paternal metaphor embodied not just in the father figure but also in a range of enforcement apparatuses of mass control at the disposal of the state, army, and police whose power is applied arbitrarily, giving it the appearance of a providential power guiding the contingency of events.

Lacan's declared return to the radical nature of Freud's talking cure emphasizes the phallic function of the signifier itself, rebelling against the ego psychologists who redefined the psychoanalytic movement in terms of object relations, internal objects, or part objects. Julia Kristeva came up with the term "thetic" to account for the effects of this kind of linguistic domination by certain privileged signifiers, such as the phallus in the Oedipal drama. By juxtaposing prelinguistic, "semiotic" drives that can tear through the syntax of power to escape the horrors of scientific rationality, the avant-garde artist fashions different trajectories of escape from this type of signifying dominance by inflicting violence on the ruling "Nous and Logos" in the linguistic realm. Pekić's fictional gesture marks a parodic escape from the discourses of logic and philosophy invoked in the letters' subtitles while transferring the signifying dominance to the umbrella as a guarantor of narrative cohesion.

At the same time, the connection established between contingency and setup, the narrative space opened between the temporal incidents (the umbrella's intrusions) and the intellectual design of policing technologies, provides an unpredictable supplement to the unfolding of narrative events. It is not a dialectical triangulation ordered by the teleology of the Hegelian *Zeitgeist* but an almost accidental montage of improbable occurrences that is reflected in Konrad's epistolary ravings. The recounting in the letters of Konrad's struggle with Heinrich Steinbrecher, his superior officer in the Gestapo, replays the drama of the German nation, with Konrad divided between obedient and the rebellious narrative focalizations to depict the occupation from the perspective of an unwilling aggressor. His shaky resolution to murder Steinbrecher mimics the wavering between identification and aggression typical of castration anxiety in the Oedipal drama.

Needless to say, the direct authorial voice is steeped in mock philosophical jargon, while the impetus for the forward narrative movement is made possible by crossing between the temporal planes of the 1940s and the 1960s, prompted by the umbrella's unpredictable movements and transformations. According to Lacan, the phallic signifier is characterized by its detachability from the body as it circulates from one person to another in the fantasy structures that characterize the early processes of identity formation. Adam's unfathomable umbrella occupies this position in the text as it moves across time and space to connect episodes in the development of the plot. The reader first encounters the umbrella when Adam, sitting on an empty tangerine crate, is a prisoner of the Italians, and it is employed as a device that enables his ascension to heaven from beneath the gallows.

The umbrella is featured prominently in the narrative buildup to the execution scene, which also replays Christ's final hours, with Adam and two bandits slated to hang: "Three men trudged slowly through the black cordon under the demonic umbrella."[7] Further, Konrad has decided to kill Steinbrecher and wants to carry out his own execution of the hated superior as they watch the prisoners being led to the gallows. As the two bandits are being executed, Steinbrecher launches a tirade about the science of death, expressing it in a mathematic formula that is not unlike Lacan's approach to the topology of the unconscious in the late 1970s: When inhalation is subtracted from exhalation and the result is zero (i.e., $E - I = 0$), it is certain that death had occurred.

Vampire Fetish

Steinbrecher's status as a superior officer instigates Konrad's Oedipal rage, but anxiety paralyzes his ability to act against the embodiment of scientific rationality and kill the hated ideal. It is especially significant that Steinbrecher touches Konrad with his leather-clad hand as he expounds on the physiology of killing and dying: "He gently touches my skin over the knot of life. With his black-gloved finger. With a black finger like a black kiss."[8] The fetishistic overtones and sadomasochistic staging of the scene underline Konrad's anxiety through the phallic signification of Steinbrecher's "kissing finger." His shaky resolution to murder the superior officer is ostensibly strengthened until the time comes to watch Adam's hanging.

In fact, it is in this moment that Konrad slips into manic psychosis, and Adam's execution turns into the ascension of the unremarkable file clerk:

> But then the umbrella in Adam's hand spread out like a black cherub's wing and, after rising him slowly up off the platform—from which his executioners were watching his miraculous ascension, and where the limp bodies of the bandits were still swaying—it lifted him with a fatherly motion, devoid of all pomp, into the sunlit nimbus clouds as if into some phosphorescent tunnel, and this motion, to the noisy applause of the people and a military salute from the German troops, carried him upward into the heavens.[9]

The ascension reiterates the fantastic nature of the phallic imaginary that underlies the text, as the winged umbrella performs a prosthetic function in furthering the development of the narrative beyond probable reality. In fact, it becomes the central device that propels the narrative movement and reinforces the ludic structuring of Pekić's textual performance. However, the legacy of unresolved cultural trauma continues to lurk in the shadows, waiting for an opportune moment. It is also indicative that the phallic signifier disguises its Oedipal roots through literary sublimation before the bursting forth of open ethnic conflict that would erupt during the return to the culture of ethnic particularity enacted during the Yugoslav wars of the 1990s.

Rearming the Letter

The return of the armed letter in neo-guslar visions of national identity quickly supplemented the already instrumentalized notions of writing present during the first decades of Tito's era. The cultural scene in the late 1980s was dominated by such figures as Dobrica Ćosić, the gentrified son of a peasant who was ejected by the communists after years of faithful service and charged with nationalism, and who invoked memories of past injustices and genocide committed against 'the serbs' in his novels, short stories, and essays. The Academics, a solid majority of intellectuals ready to shed the blood of their own youth in wars that could succeed only in increasing violence and poverty, provided background vocals to the political melodies of Slobodan Milošević.

I am deliberately borrowing the language of popular music to speak about the re-emergence of the vampire nation during the age of mass rallies devoted to the phantasm of 'the serbs' to interrogate the dominant view that the violence of the Yugoslav wars resulted from a programmed takeover by new political elites. Popular music's ability to mobilize certain emotional responses within mass audiences was at least equaled by the technologies of crowd control Milošević employed in his rise to power. In the 1980s, mass rallies displaced rock concerts as venues of youth gathering in Serbia, appropriating the political arena by filling it with a new sounding of the people. The national sounds of the late 1980s were characterized by a banality of evil that aimed to resurrect the violence of a masculine war machine that was fully aware that its numerical strength exceeded that of the other post-Yugoslav nations. A brand-new turbo-folk culture swept 'the serbs' into celebrating old national-greatness-in-suffering themes. Milošević and the Academics increased the suspicion and hatred among ethnic groups by sampling the old tunes that led their nation down its self-destructive path during the 1990s.

'The serbs' have suffered the explosion of eternal and punctual "history-memory" outlined by Deleuze, rooting their rise from the crypt in the agonistic narratives about ancient and endless bloodletting in most of the national tunes performed for 'the serbs' by Milošević and the Academics. They were the ultimate assemblage of post-communist political culture, perpetrating the life of the bloody being of common memory by feeding on the unsuspecting youth of the ailing Yugoslav collective. By resurrecting sacrifices of the past and displaying a willing-ness to use violence, Milošević and the Academics became solid favor-ites of 'the serbs,' offering a perfect excuse to transform the plurality of the Yugoslav nation into a chorus of uniform chants to preserve the territorial continuity of 'the serbs' after Yugoslavia came to an end. This political ensemble overwhelmed the national scene to uphold the crumbling edifice of the common state, transforming it symbolically into a vampire's castle that served as the last refuge of that ancient creature of memory incarnated and resurrected in Milošević's political performance.

The primary cultural task after the former political star was ousted, arrested, and tried in October 2000 was to work through this legacy of violence and confront the perpetrators of national infamy and state terror that had shrouded 'the serbs' in the cultural vampire's dark cloak during the long, Gothic 1990s. The new vision of national identity disputed the need to view the national memory as an expression of perpetual returns to violence and sought to make sense of the recent past in its local and global cultural incarnations. The global forces that united in the West to confront the crimes of ethnic passion committed in the former Yugoslavia never managed to hold the high moral ground, however, because they were preoccupied with their own version of the original Gothic response, sending Nighthawks, Stealths, and Phantoms to invade the heavens above 'the serbs' and de-territorialize Kosovo, the locus of the vampire nation's re-emergence. These neo-Gothic fly-ing machines marked the establishment of a single global empire that turned to the notion of human rights to affirm its own global military supremacy by the strategic application of violence in the service of human rights. The territory of Kosovo, the most ancient of symbolic habitats of national death-in-life and inhabited by the specters of vio-lence and vampires of memory, was lost forever to yet another heavenly force: the one that resolutely turned against the imaginary empire of 'the serbs.'

Human target: resting from the protest against NATO's bombing of Serbia in 1999. PHOTOGRAPH
COURTESY ZORAN PETROVIĆ.

By manipulating the endangered position of the majority Kosovar
Albanians, the U.S.-led West took yet another strategic step to control
the global ethnoscape. In classic neocolonial fashion, the global media
presented the Balkans as a region that was both unable to rule itself and
too volatile to approach as it waged a zero-casualty war from a safe
distance. After the specter of Gothic military technology employed by
NATO brought an end to their territorial connection to Kosovo, 'the
serbs' were confronted with yet another loss caused by their own aber-
rant display of excessive suspicion of the other: by playing up their
status as a nation that had sprung up from the ancient past to annihi-
late its present, living national subjects, they simultaneously lost the
right and a hope for a position within the rest of humanity during the
1990s. Because they replaced the old, underground god of the Kosovo
myth with their own version of global justice, 'the serbs' were forced to
confront the specter of "the West" in a high-tech display of imperial
power. The bombed civilians responded by painting targets on their
own bodies, identifying once again with the position of subjects who
are unafraid to offer their bodies on the altar of the nation.

The bombing by NATO in 1999 symbolically removed the hyphen
from the history-memory system, creating an insurmountable exterior

force for the national imaginary interpellated by the Kosovo myth within the phantasm of 'the serbs.' As mentioned earlier, the operation to punish the vampire nation also generated an equally pathetic display in which world leaders, full of righteous good conscience, celebrated NATO's unity at a ball in Washington. Sacrificing the phantasmic 'serbs' provided an ideal basis on which to justify creating a new mission for the military alliance, which had become obsolete when the Cold War ended.

Finding the Imaginary In-between

The long years of the last decade of the twentieth century produced a martial culture of bloated patriotism that was not easy to confront by those who sought to disarm the vampire nation. Those who engaged in both civic and nomadic flight from the oppressive and falsified burden of national memory intoned by Milošević and the Academics were left with the unenviable task of confronting the evil closest to home. Standing up to the specter of state power amid war for the spoils of the common Yugoslav territory was not a safe thing to do. Resistance to the banality of the Slobist imaginary was located in capillary movements of urban intellectuals and in a youth culture enraged by the isolationism and provincialism to which 'the serbs' were suddenly condemned as a spectral nation whose face had grown repulsive and guilt-inspiring under Milošević's leadership. Goran Marković, director of the nostalgic film parody *Tito and I*, encapsulated this sentiment in testimony he posted on the Internet during the last years of the Milošević regime: "National feelings were acted out as if we lived in a porn flick."[10] Marković also described watching a prominent Academic on a television talk show in which the apparent affection between the guest and the host (whom Marković referrs to as "Hot Lips") was consummated in expressing mutual admiration of 'the serbs.' The Academic postulated that 'the serbs' were the original Indo-European race descended metonymically from Serbon Makeridov, the most powerful conqueror of Eurasia before Alexander the Great. This, Marković testified, threw him into fits of laughter:

> Serbon, the father of all nations, was a Serb. In fact, all those originating from him, all the known nations, were of Serbian origin. Contemporary Serbs are, in fact, only one of the many Serbs who over time became

Greeks, Celts, etc. The lively old man waved his hands and rocked on: the Serbs are not a nation—they are a race. And why be modest: All Indo-European peoples originate from the Serbs.[11]

By extending the ancient being of 'the serbs' to all nations of the world, the Academic once again was invoking the ancient creature of memory; in giving a stigmatized assemblage with which the rest of the world wanted nothing to do such a perverse and self-destructive articulation, he and his passive listener joined in the discursive production of 'the serbs' as the alpha and omega of global civilization. For Marković, saving one's fallen nation is better performed in the name of those times when human decency was part of a better world, again imagined as having occurred before the ongoing traumas of communist/nationalist authoritarianism set in.

Thus, Marković recognized his own membership in the stigmatized assemblage 'the serbs' when the intellectual abuse of that collective name reached its most absurd proportions in the Academic's diatribe. He followed this paradox of embracing his own ethnicity in its worst moment by recounting that it was the memory of his grandmother, a "dignified, just, and warm person who loved people and did only good," that saved his national feelings during the abysmal 1990s.[12] As mentioned earlier, the Bulldozer Revolution of October 2000 evoked a similar transformation, turning an a-national segment of the population into defenders of the last remnants of humanity among 'the serbs.'

Masculine Failure

The return to heroic masculinity, in both its local and its global articulations during the Wars of Yugoslav Succession, further compromised the use of long-term memory as a tool to dominate others who threatened the territoriality of "our" blood and soil. In memories of such duration and power, the lie of one's perpetual greatness and glory is narrated against the reality of one's political and economic smallness and insignificance. This insignificance is compensated for by calling on an imaginary dominated by the past and by the violence of its sacrifices. Freud noted this psychological mechanism at work in the wolf man, another East European requiring inventions and fantasies to compensate for an inadequate present: "These fantasies, therefore, correspond exactly to the legends by which a nation that has become great and proud tries to conceal the insignificance and failure of its beginnings."[13]

The great and the proud tend to erase memories that paint them as shameful and weak, compensating for their inferiority through narratives to sustain the imaginary power they perceive as part of their communal identity. That which is suppressed, yet remains constantly active, is the original bite of the ancient creature of memory, infecting subjects confronted with the common specter of their national community. This phallic lie is at the root of modern masculine nationalism, and Marković succumbed to it reluctantly in the course of his testimony, alongside all of those silent Academics who believed their work would provide a voice of resistance recognized on its own merit.

The struggle for memory was a crucial component of the cultural developments that followed the Milošević era. The tendency of the new, post-authoritarian state was to focus on the present and the future, letting short-term memories of the bloody national being slip under the velvet cover of forgetfulness. The memory gap left by the self-destructive Age of Slobism was so enormous that most of 'the serbs' fled into struggles for daily survival as they attempted to repress guilt and ignore responsibility. To counter this tendency, B92 radio and television programs took a lead in the most popular of public spaces— television—by producing a series of short videos under the title *Da se ne zaboravi* (So it's not forgotten).

B92's documentary collages about the mendacious origin of the nation of 'the serbs' raised the specter of responsibility and charged citizens with the task of standing up to such manipulations and abuses in the future. Rebuilding the public sphere after a decade of wars, sanctions, and interventions is a task that requires approaching the memory of violence in a light of infinite responsibility for ethnic and cultural others. The demobilization of the armed letter, and the compensatory boost this provided to young generations, required frankly confronting recent memories of violence, in which locations such as that of the Srebrenica massacre in 1995 continue to haunt the national imaginary. To force the public to confront the politics of silence and forgetfulness, *So It's Not Forgotten* features extreme moments of nationalist hysteria among journalists, politicians, and combatants—for example, the infamous "flying train" of the Bosnian War that, it was imagined, would fly over all of the enemies of 'the serbs' and bring the glorious victory they were seeking. The celestial dimension of 'the serbs' embodied in this imaginary flight is a symptom of the science fiction-turned-reality that dominated the image of the greatness and strength of the nation in order to affirm the bloody being of the community.

Fiction as Meta-History

Such domestic imaginary excesses grew even more absurd as the martial context of global isolation set in during and after the latest Yugoslav wars. To examine the legacy of resistance and opposition in the realm of culture, it is necessary to examine the position of literature inside the broken casings and tenements of the once vibrant space of intercultural relations. Indeed, the continuity of memory related to the common space is often present in the literature of authors who decided to leave the disappearing universe of Yugoslavia and pursue their vocation in emigration or self-imposed exile. The commitment to a larger framework of global civilization was embraced by a significant number of post-Yugoslav literary figures, who eventually fled their native realm for new, transnational becomings.

The prose of David Albahari is one of the metaphors for the persistence of culture broader than the narrowly conceived national one, sharing the commitment to human rights with other voices of difference that have not rushed to sink their teeth into the succulent bait of blood and belonging offered by the emerging class of national intellectuals in the wake of the common South Slavic state. While Albahari's early meta-fictions centered on the family and its imponderable lives and secrets, the writing he did after moving abroad took up the issue of memory and its remnants. Away from the native realm, the new identity in exile works against the confusing tranquility of the North American refuge, breaking off with the pure literary becoming to tell the story of the past in a different key. The meta-fictional poetics that positioned Albahari as a leader of the entire generation of former Yugoslav writers in the 1980s required a narrative motion of constant return to its own becoming, to a place where the narrator seems closest to the paradoxical truth of writing as writing. This was the poetics that characterized an entire generation that gave in to the exhaustion of the ideological universe of the communist state, reflected in meta-fictional searches for yet another way to lay bare the process of narrative becoming.

This position of the writer as the interrogator of the literary process itself coincided with the implosion of the common South Slavic state. The collective memories of particular Yugoslav nations were not left to rest in peace the half-century after the Second World War; the ancient creature of memory was revamped by the majority of "nationally aware" politicians and writers to settle old debts related to spilled blood and the sense of belonging. Writing itself was rearmed and used to stake claims on old territories and new bodies, never posing the question about the violence necessary to realize such a martial vision of collective identity or attempting to comprehend the limit of humanity that would be reached in the wars that followed.

Within the context of such nationalist paranoia, Albahari's meta-fictional poetics culminated in *Kratka knjiga* (Short book), which was devoted entirely to the simple human inability to complete a task—in this case, the writing of a book. The book never mentions the war looming in the background, yet the unwillingness to commit to any political option is omnipresent through a narrative refusal for it to become a book about something. This rejection of historical eternities and confrontation with the burdens of the past arrived with the author's immigration to Canada. Although too singularly post-Yugoslav to be treated as a narrative of any particular emerging national configuration, the trajectories related to Albahari's Jewish and Serbian heritage intersect when he voices the unrepeatable moments of suffering and the repeatable moments of history present in his *Canadian Trilogy* (*Snežni čovek* [Snow man; 1995], *Mamac* [Bait; 1996], and *Mrak* [Dark; 1997]).

The 1990s provided the temporal scene for some of the worst horrors of fratricidal violence in recent European history, causing a shift in Albahari's narrative searches. His artistic quest for yet unnamed locations of the written word yielded to the horrors arising from the clear and present danger of warring memories revived in the burial grounds of old even as new monuments to human infamy were gradually erected. His departure from Zemun (and Yugoslavia) and arrival in Calgary (and North America) transformed his writing into a proliferation of meta-histories that haunt the reader with their insistence that storytelling skills are helpless in the face of horror. What remains of memory fades into the background of everyday life as time begins to be measured by the loss of calendars that were taken to the new world, only to be forgotten:

On the other continent, on the other side of the ocean, the wars in Croatia and Bosnia turned into a distant echo. Now, as I write this, war is just a calendar for measuring memories. For example, I arrived in Canada when the Croats proclaimed the independent Herzeg-Bosna. I traveled to Winnipeg when the Serbs blew up the Ferhadia and Arnaudia mosques in Banja Luka. When the grenades exploded in a Sarajevo marketplace, I was already traveling in the far north. . . . And while the bus was sliding between the gigantic rocks, passing from bright sunshine into the deepest of shades, I leafed through the pages slowly recognizing the specter conceived in the files I carried with me. I was permeated by a really strange sensation, as if I were reading a novel from which I had barely escaped. I really was just that: a character who escaped his creator and forced him to write the story in a way different from the one he originally imagined.[14]

Time is thus ordered by a calendar of horror projected from the imploding homeland that can now be real only as a narrative onto the new world landscape, echoing the effects of the secret that travels with the narrator of *Dark* in the form of the files he takes out of Yugoslavia. The content of the files is never fully revealed to the reader, yet a variety of hints point a finger at the ethical responsibility of the Academics who worked alongside security services to turn the violent national imaginary into a war no one could really win. The files, another meta-historical device used by Albahari, were purloined from secret-police archives by a character named Davor Miloš, a childhood friend of the narrator who insinuates that the documents contain a clear and convincing answer to the question: why did Yugoslavia fall apart?

Assembling Memories

The subjects that come into being after the mass ideologies of fascism and communism have run their course will be confronted with what Gilles Deleuze and Félix Guattari called "multilinear assemblages" that articulate memory as the obverse side of history. This is where the bleak side of culture emerges, posing challenges to established identities based on sublimation and compromise. Albahari's inscriptions constantly examine the conditions of their own narrative becoming, reaching beyond historiography to discover singular echoes of those gruesome events that mark the apocalyptic decomposition of Yugoslavia. The voices telling the stories about the past emanate from inscriptions and recording machines to supplement and rectify the impotence of its narrators, extending the temporal limit of narrative events through the tension between those two types of narrative emergence. Albahari's writings continue to foreground the spectral property of transhistorical becomings by exposing gaps and divisions inherent in the very process of storytelling.

It is with a flight from the unspeakable side of memory that Albahari approaches the evanescent substance used to render such histories—national and narrative—opaque to his own narrators, who are caught up in the struggle for a truth that cannot be told whole. The beings sacrificed and disappeared in the name of race, state, or nation are repressed into spaces of oblivion, denied the power to perform a singular voicing of the horror that inhabits the contested interior of the national imaginary.

What Albahari engages is a language of memory that constantly declares its failure as a clear and unambiguous voicing of the past. While official histories try to come to grips with a limited number of narratives that originate in a desire for "punctual history-memory" and provide stories that are to form emergent national identities, these assemblages assume a form of narrative becoming by transgressing the limit of writing as the unambiguous voicing of the historical truth. The unceasing rendering of that which has occurred and now defies a straightforward account is what Albahari's narrators grapple with while trying to delegate the task of discovering the truth to someone else. There are witnesses and there are machines that play back memory, since the effects of horror cannot be narrated in a language ordered by logic and reason. Yet the stories always arrive, although with a delay motivated by the ostensible impotence of the narrative procedure itself. The violence tied to the past is constantly emerging before writing can begin to work through the punctual systems of national history-memory. This type of narrative strategy haunts the national by exposing the desire to write as the appropriation of its claim to represent the truth and reality. Therefore, when Albahari's narrator recognizes the time of the Yugoslav wars as "now, when the vampires of Nazism are raising their heads everywhere," he also reclaims the strategy of the vampire on the narrative level as a way to undermine the compact logic of blood and soil appropriated by the nation.

Writing confronts the tragedy of its own constant passing into oblivion, as is evident in a lamentation by the narrator of *Dark*: "One does not write (I am now completely certain of this) to reminisce or remember, one writes to forget."[15] Oblivion is the ultimate aim of those who venture into narratives, the impossible feat of transferring the burden of guilt and responsibility onto the reader. Since remembering involves the settling of accounts with a traumatic past, the process of writing desublimates the hard core of the national to evolve as an act of literary anamnesis. The labyrinthine trajectory of writing that forgets through inscription enables a welcome departure from simplified forms of remembering within punctual history-memory systems that are characteristic of the nation as a repository of covert violence against its explicit and implicit others. Yet ostensible liberation from the burden of memory leaves its trace, paradoxically archiving yet another form of remembering in the cultural imaginary.

This desire to forget moves Albahari's narrators to chart a different type of narrative map in the present of the self-imposed exile. The location of the adopted culture offers the fantasy of empty semiotic spaces for new literary becomings through the cultural translation of memories carried from the past of the native location. The old location and temporality insinuate themselves into the narrative as afterthoughts that are never fully able to purge the debt to the burden of memory through writing. The desire to put behind the past traumas can never completely prevent the harrowing memories from breaking through the surface of oblivion demanded by officially sanctioned narratives of the nation. Writing is not a simple cathartic discharge of the unwanted, because the effects of memory always interrupt the story in ways that cannot be predicted by historiography as an ostensibly rational story about the way events unfolded in the currently inaccessible realm of the past.

Writing the Disaster

The faltering wonder of Albahari's narrators constantly threatens to dissolve the entire universe of memory into a silence that those narrators invoke through the creative act of forgetting as inscription. Just like the masculine wound that will not allow itself to be suppressed by the painful irruption of trauma, Albahari's writing arrives before the voice can tell the story, not as a mirror of the voice itself, but as a mode of translation that requires asymmetrical rendering of realities constructed by the forces that be. The singular act of memory is played back in fragments, delaying the final coming to terms with humanity and its horrors. Writing the disaster requires a literary performance that disturbs the punctual modes of historical telling enunciated by the self-appointed prophets of eternity. Albahari tells so he can distance himself, so he can stay away from those stories with an easy and predictable flow. The malignant effects on subjects whose particular forms of being have been annihilated by twentieth-century genocides requires writing that reaches for those multilinear assemblages of the linguistic universe to establish possibilities for reading agony and disaster beyond the exclusive reliance on the narration serviced by the poetics of the armed-letter characteristic of national narratives. Writing down the nation is turned away from language as a mode of presenting reality and its deceptive orders and toward flight from the ever receding shore of humanity's horrors.

Meta-narration in Albahari's prose serves as a poetic strategy that forces the truth of writing out of writing itself, positioning the voice of the narrator in a self-reflective verisimilitude that produces a paradoxical faith in reader who is ready to bite into the bait offered by the constant receding of the narrative horizon. Far away from any reverent notion of character, Albahari's narratives produce a specific kind of literary irony that draws on the realities of the specular deception formative of the subject itself. Faking reality through writing and poking fun at human desire for an identity beyond language, literary protagonists get caught up in their own chimerical existence. This surrogate other stands between the writer and the reader in the wake of the vampiric creature of volatile memory, voicing through the narrator its own inability to fully come to terms with the traumas and disasters of the past. Laughter is never far from the surface of Albahari's meta-histories inscribed in the New World, stories fraught with attempts to come to terms with the unholy essence of historical deceits.

In effect, the new subject of the narrative is no more than a trace of memory—its body had been shot, poisoned, or burned in the name of this or that nation. Charged with possessing blood-related secrets by their tormentors, these subjects will never stop running away from history, despite its dominant influence on their lines of flight. The secret they are hiding and possessing, their incommensurable otherness, is what they are forced to give up for the sake of this or that identity. The irreducible difference of a borderline subject found in Albahari is moving away from the sacred location that guarantees the death of the subject. The difference imputed to the borderline subject is generated through the narrative movement, as the ever new tormentors enforce their power with maps imprinted on the body as the territory claimed by this or that nation. To satisfy their orders, the tormentors always find ways to determine who now represents the other, the enemy that hides the secret of its blood beneath the veil of cultural difference.

Albahari's abandonment of paragraphs and sections in *Canadian Trilogy* and beyond creates the density effect that splices voices and bodies of protagonists into a tide of language that overwhelms the reader with its performative urgency. Reading on means responding to this urgency, continuing despite the obvious failure of both writing and memory. This urgency comes from a place that has not yet been written, although it yearns for recognition, and perhaps even incarnation, in the narrative form. Those who are no more by the will of their tormentors, the erased beings of non-history, live on in the density of imaginary movements as notes sent into the future to those willing to step in and accept the heavy burden of responsibility for the past. Those subjects who continue to walk this earth after their tortured and slain tribes respond to history as a story about erasure and flight from the horrors committed in their name imagine a future different from those able to identify with the cultural imaginary of their particular nations.

Chronotopes of Ruination

To escape stories of family members' being annihilated by racial and territorial regimes, one is called on to rely on the calmness of the voice that the narrator employs to condense the language of disguised mourning. The scenes of everyday life in the present of immigration are conflated with stories about the past that tell themselves despite the failure of the books' narrators. The meta-narrative formulas are now complemented by the chronotopic work of memory that occupies the fictional universe of the trilogy's three short novels, *Snow Man*, *Dark*, and *Bait*, which Albahari wrote after his departure from Yugoslavia. These narratives take the material of memory-time tied to a specific location and shape it into a literary becoming charged with the task of showing the obverse side of history. Acting as a particular version of the Borgesian "universal history of infamy," these stories do not search for a metaphysical principle that guides the vampires of history; instead, they insist on the emergence of the background, the artifice of fabled becomings that veil the violence that no subject is able to fully confront.

Albahari's inscriptions are like whispers in the dark, torn away from the silence of untold histories; always questioning their own conditions as utterances about truth and reality; ending up in a circular motion of writing about the inability to write; unveiling the paradoxical reality of the subject stuck with the horrific burden of undying forces radiating from the past occluded by the struggles and individual sacrifices of ancestors. The narrators tell more by admitting to their inability to tell anything explicitly or authentically and by refraining from preaching from the moral pedestal of "universal humanity" to affirm the truth of the subject in the unmaking.

The narrator of Snow Man experiences this inability in its most acute form: he is unable to heed the advice of Donald, his North American interlocutor, and complete a book of memories about his native land. His feigned literary impotence results from the burden of history as a force that requires a flight from reality through the writing of its effects on the existential trajectories of different memory-history assemblages involved in the game of transhistorical becomings. Literary characters are not only places where these provisory constructions come into being; they are also the movements of desire that are often internally ridiculed by the narrative voice—that special place from which Albahari's poetics engages the telling of the story of history. Comparing his own literary impotence with his mother's storytelling gifts, he lifts the burden from an extreme focalization on the narrator's point of view. In Bait, a book whose title makes an associative link between the words "mama" (mom) and "mamac" (bait), the narrator shifts the storytelling focus to the mother who is the real subject of the book: "Mother knew how to use the rhythms of speech, she could braid several folk narrative lines, she could string along adjectives, she could turn around the entire sentence structure, she could really tell a story."[16]

But like many of Albahari's characters, the mother here is only a memory trace until the magic of low-fidelity technology brings her voice back into the immigrant's desolate apartment somewhere in the frozen borderlands of North America. The voice is captured on an old-fashioned magnetic tape, whose static and other noise interfere with the clear transmission of her story. The Magnetophone is outdated, and no one in Canada seems to be able to find the right one: "For days I went to shops asking for that particular kind of machine, regardless of its brand name. The sales people smiled and kindly shrugged their shoulders, showing me the latest models of tape recorders."[17] The Magnetophone is needed to play back the voice of the mother, to bring her memory back through the metaphor of writing as a voice recording of the past. Writing itself can never hope to achieve such high technical reproducibility, although it insinuates itself as a voice recorded on a magnetic tape to reach for the fleeting totality of memory as a clear and transparent voicing of the narrator's mother. The book's title *Mamac*, then, is not just an associative link to "mama" but also narrative bait extended from the past in the form of a writing machine able to play back the voice of memory long after mother is no longer able to interrupt or change the course of her own testimony.

Those who have been disappeared by the wrath of other tribes have no story to tell. Others, like Albahari, flee the battlefields to tell the stories that cannot be told. The otherness of emigration and exile, the hiding of one's particularity while holding on to a different set of stories and names, characterize the everyday life of exilic subjects. While maintaining the distance and alterity by the foreign flavor of their speech, those who have fled their native realm nurse a need to narrate the tales of past horrors with unusual and soothing calm. The wandering has begun once again, because the displacement of identity into a rupture opened between languages and cultures ceases to offer any guarantee of truth beyond fiction and of history beyond memory.

Cyber Territories

Another way to interrogate the violent discourse of blood and belonging engages in a free play based on the possibilities offered by new communication technologies to lighten the burden of horror associated with the former Yugoslavia. The authors of the website Cyber Yugoslavia (www.juga.com) are using the form of a mock nation-state to open up the possibility of a constant and fluid sense of belonging for "citizens" ensconced in the de-territorialized constitution of the imaginary state. "The Constitution of Cyber Yugoslavia is variable," they write. This variability consists in the ability of "anyone" to change the constitution, to rewrite it through a "public vote." This lighthearted vision of cyber-democracy relies on at least a partial extraterritoriality of its citizens: As of 2004, only 25.22 percent of its 13,150 citizens resided in the now defunct state of the Federal Republic of Yugoslavia, while the rest were scattered in thirty-seven countries around the globe. The movement away from the violent imaginary inherent in the logic of the nation-state motivates the variability of the law that establishes the basic tenets of the communal bond in the imagined community of post-Yugoslavs.

According to Aleida Assmann, universalist conceptions of culture and identity derive from a fixation with the Hebrew conception of *Ekhad*, a divine sign that dictates the sense of unity in the conduct of personal and communal life established in the Old Testament. The fable of the pure and universal language imagined before the destruction of the Tower of Babel is symptomatic of the projected desire for oneness that underpins most monotheistic concepts of community: "In the original state, the whole earth was united in one language, and this language consisted of one (= invariable?) words; the Hebrew text here uses 'one' in the plural."[18]

This paradoxical positioning of identity expressed by one-in-the-plural encodes the violence of homogenizing cultural projects, reducing the open-ended character of collective temporality to a single source of authority, power, and meaning. For 'the serbs,' the specter of national unity required a sacrifice of ethnic others who endangered the perpetually sacrosanct territory, the latest of which was identified with the common state of the South Slavs. Imagining a horizon beyond ethnic unity was hardly possible after the breakup of the Yugoslav communist federation, since the rise of Milošević relegated the old party internationalism to the museum of failed utopias. The new force of ethnic unity was engendered as a response to the de-legitimized concept of shared Yugoslavia, while the new-old identities were once again consecrated with violence and sacrifice under the sign of One: One Land, One Leader, One People.

When a community reduces its narratives of being and belonging in this manner, the logic of the sacrifice underlying the desire for unity becomes operative in the realm of the political. René Girard reminds us that "there is a unity that underlies not only all mythologies and rituals but the whole of human culture, and this unity of unities depends on a single mechanism, continually functioning because perpetually misunderstood—the mechanism that assures the community's spontaneous and unanimous outburst of opposition to the surrogate victim."[19] The order of the One is supported by the mechanism of transference and substitution that props the community up against external enemies in the guise of the enemy of the nation and its sacred locations. It is not hard to imagine how this sacrificial logic informs the creation of national identity: the elimination of ethnic others depends on imagining surrogate victims whose sacrifice plays a crucial role in the achievement of national unity.

For me, a subject positioned in the constant identity translation between the United States and what used to be Yugoslavia, the psychic space promised by imagining a cyber-nation offered a valuable supplement to a burden that is much like survivor's guilt. Watching mainstream representations of the war between the United States and 'the serbs' engendered a somewhat parodic vision of the Western Empire of Human Rights attempting to drive a stake through the heart of Slobodan Miloševic, the leader of the Last Vampire Republic in Europe. This striving for divine omnipotence by countering yet another bloodsucking operation perpetrated by 'the serbs' incited the global media to view this national assemblage through that old Gothic lens—at least, until the Bulldozer Revolution of October 2000 sent Milošević from the usurped presidency to the international War Criminal Prison and a quiet death in a cell in The Hague.

The burden of guilt accumulated by 'the serbs' throughout the 1990s in Croatia, Bosnia, and Kosovo seemed to suddenly lift as the global media celebrated the triumph of popular democracy among 'the serbs.' Suddenly, the former president became the surrogate victim in the emergence of a new Serbia, with all of the guilt and responsibility transferred by the global media, in the usual manner, to the figure of a single vampire: Milošević. While the legal responsibility for the crimes against humanity still needs to be established, the public discourse about the past needs to come up with new models for imagining a collective identity in the aftermath of Yugoslavia. Each of the ethnic collectives emerging from the former state has an obligation to contemplate the recent past with a cultural double vision—a backward glance at the responsibility for violence and crimes and a forward gaze toward a new form of identity whose boundaries should account for a maximum of fluidity and permeability among its ethnic groups. Imagining identity as a variable assemblage that allows the dissolution of the logic of the One requires letting go of the deadly serious discourse based on homogenous vision of ethnic totality.

Parodic Nations

The tone of benevolent, post-Kafkaesque humor that powers Cyber Yugoslavia creates a culture of laughter and becomes yet another form of a valuable cure for the political misdeeds of the past. The ironic power of the site translates the magnitude of the trauma survived by most of the former Yugoslavia's citizens and uses a specific kind of dark humor to counter the pain. Yet the horizon of nationalism as extraterritorial and nonviolent discourse implies that the playful character of Cyber Yugoslavia could become a model for imagining a nation as a portable cultural project. According to Linda Hutcheon, the postmodern condition has transformed parody into "one of the major forms of modern self-reflexivity," where the intentional performative insignificance of the political helps the subject overcome the burden of past traumas.[20] Cyber Yugoslavia is at once a ridiculing imitation of the nation and a promise to overcome the conflicted legacies of violent cultural imaginary correlated to the Yugoslav tragedies of centuries gone by. The lethally overbearing reach of the political into the everyday during the last decade of the past millennium makes the promise of this type of civil society a particularly alluring one.

As an imaginative Internet project, Cyber Yugoslavia was itself initiated on the ninth day of the ninth month of 1995, as if invoking a vague correspondence to a numerological synergy of several kinds of temporal endings. This sense of global finitude produced its parody of a nation, in which citizens must choose a ministry to head (which they may also name) when they apply for membership. Some choose to head Ministries of Cookies; others aspire to more fundamental kinds of ministries, such as Eric Gordy, a professor of sociology, who is Cyber Yugoslavia's secretary for *kajmak* (a deliciously greasy variety of unprocessed cream cheese). In choosing a barely translatable word for what is yet a very kind of food, Gordy foregrounds a specific locality of post-Yugoslavia that has not withered away with the old state structures. Chinese, Indians, and Americans who have engaged in online communication with post-Yugoslavs located in Cyber Yugoslavia's state-in-deconstruction have been moved by curiosity or by sympathy to become citizens of the parodic nation themselves, which acknowledges the existence of collectivities beyond the imaginary of the nation. One of the ways Cyber Yugoslavia parodies the national form as defined by territory is clear in Article 16 of its constitution:

> When it was founded, CY [Cyber Yugoslavia] had no territory. There were 152 founding citizens. When the number of citizens reaches five million, CY will request membership in the United Nations, and soon after CY will request a territory of 20 square meters, anywhere on the Globe, where it will place its server. This will be the official territory, where its DNS entry will be located: http://www.juga.com.

The gesture toward the creation of the national territory present in the demand for a server set in a diminutive yet global location is mischievous and implicitly critical of the violent imaginary based on the narratives of blood and belonging. The technological extension of this type of cultural imaginary is represented as a meeting place of individuals who have a sense of mutual affinity rooted in narratives of everyday life tied to the memory of the now defunct common state. By projecting the proper name of the Yugoslav collectivity over such a digital territory, the gesture evokes cyber-idealists' longings to extend the technological utopia through a network of possible material relations. Twenty square meters is a minuscule territorial requirement, pointing up what is both ridiculous and earnest about this "nation," as the mechanisms of power are simultaneously laid bare and appropriated for an apparently innocuous "national" cause. Although prone to nationalistic outbursts, the cyber-nationals of the imaginary state share a love of the non-serious as a potential channel of exchange for the simplest everyday practices, from the posting of cooking recipes to attempts to date other citizens. The main "political" preoccupation of Cyber Yugoslavia has been its recent debate about whether to file for United Nations recognition even before the initially imposed quota of five million members is reached.

Post-Yugoslav Identities

This particular version of post-Yugoslavism was imagined by Zoran Bačić, who started managing the Cyber Yugoslavia site after switching his interests from theater to computers. Simultaneously ironic and serious about the question of the nation, Bačić reserves the title "Secretary Webmaster" for himself. "We are looking for active, committed citizens," he said in an interview, "people capable of founding a new kind of country, a new kind of nationality that had laid bare the trappings of the state and placed its future in the hands of humanity."[21] This proclamation of anti-nationalist nationalism may well be rooted in what Mark Poster sees as a new form of messianic discourse initiated by more immediate communications media such as the Internet:

> To the extent that the mode of information restructures language and symbols generally into a configuration that is aptly termed "virtual reality," the particular form of the messianic, of our hope for justice, must go through this technological circuit and must account for the difference between writing and e-mail, dissemination and the Internet, the *parergon* and the World Wide Web.[22]

Compared with print, Benedict Anderson's pillar of the national imaginary, the much higher rate of digital exchange of information promises an accelerated form of virtuality that holds the potential to create utopian effects and transform the very materiality of life through the ability to engage in movement and reach for an outside imagined beyond the digital domain. By using the mathematically based reality of the digital to restructure the realm of human desire, Cyber Yugoslavia's parody of the national exposes the phantoms of collective imagination for what they are: imaginary constructs used by governments, states, and armies to mobilize their citizens for war. This is especially true when governments engage in tweaking ethnic boundaries into the new national ones and set out to destroy multiethnic communities, as was the case in the former Yugoslavia. The unveiling of a "particular form of the messianic" has been especially necessary in the face of the volatility of media representation of the Wars of Yugoslav Succession (1991–95).

It is true: hideous crimes committed both by 'the serbs' and their ethnic rivals. But the hysterical narratives circulated by the global media were preoccupied almost exclusively with 'the serbs' and their "vampiric" desires to appropriate both blood and soil of their ethnic others. The question of guilt and responsibility for all war crimes needs to be addressed by the hardly perfect systems of human rights and global justice. The narratives spun by the global media were pointed at 'the serbs' and their remaining state because they fit perfectly into the mold of the Gothic imaginary. Yet this excessive representation of 'the serbs' may have backfired in the end. Paul Virilio concludes that NATO's intervention in Serbia in 1999 became such a fiasco because "when you claim to prosecute a war in the name of 'human rights'—a humanitarian war—you deprive yourself of the possibility of negotiating a cessation of hostilities with your enemy. If the enemy is a torturer, *the enemy of the human race*, there is no alternative but the extremes of *total war* and unconditional surrender."[23]

The spread of the Gothic imaginary that invokes dismembered bodies, raped women, and death camps has circulated through the global media at the very mention of the names Yugoslavia and 'the serbs' to account for distant and alien forms of violence that require decisive military intervention and peacekeeping. Such volatile media representation of 'the serbs' makes the automatic, surgical interventions by NATO almost obligatory to put an end to barbaric acts against various independence-minded or separatist populations. This approach ultimately always excites more conflict and yields more violence between ethnic communities, providing NATO with an excuse to mount more military interventions under the guise of "peacekeeping." The sacrificial logic used in each particular form of ethnic chauvinism in the Balkans through the manufacture of Girard's "surrogate victims" was ultimately topped by NATO's sacrifice of an entire region through remote-control bombing of 'the serbs' and through radioactive and chemical contamination of the Balkan environment for decades to come.

The escape into the virtual by Cyber Yugoslavia's citizens can be understood as a simultaneous movement away from this type of cultural imaginary, which ultimately will lead to the complete de-legitimation of earthly tyranny and calls for a new project of global identity based on what alternative writers and activists imagined it to be. Therefore, the posited variability of the Cyber Yugoslavia concept is part of the struggle for control over mediated representations and digital translations of the images of violence in the former Yugoslavia. Cyber Yugoslavia represents a site that opens up the possibility of outcomes that take a different course from violence for those who have been labeled with the sign of the vampire within the global cultural economy. By appropriating Western discourses and technologies of virtuality of the imagined community and turning them into a high-tech ruse, Cyber Yugoslavia ends up as the ultimate computer game, a spoof of the neo-nation building that could also act as a channel for interethnic reconciliation while addressing the issues of guilt and responsibility for those who have lost their beloved country.

I Surf, therefore I Serb

The ability to imagine a community of post-Yugoslavs finds one of its digital articulations in the chat rooms of Cyber Yugoslavia, where those who embrace variability are able to engage in discursive practices that reflect their everyday anguish with the destructive, narrow-minded, and boring articulations of the national imaginary. The mixture of nostalgia for my youth and the survivor's guilt of a person who watched the senseless destruction of my native country while becoming an American haunt me as I contemplate entering the site. Because I am laced with utopian and almost secret hopes for a better future for those who will inherit the conflicted and complex legacy of subjects who were unwilling or unable to find their identities in immediate ethnic subcategories after the neo-nationalist takeover of the late 1980s, I resist spending my time as part of this utopian vision projected onto the World Wide Web.

The imaginary core of my true-real experience as a child growing up in Yugoslavia centered on a vision of Titoism as a deviant form of repressive communism that positioned its citizens as participants in an experiment unprecedented in human history. The party policing of the revolutionary gains and the personality cult of Tito himself compromised the messianic vision of revolutionary ideology inherent in the Yugoslav socialist project. The pseudo-totalitarian iconography that represented Tito as a benevolent "almost non-commie commie" served as a paternal metaphor for the masses of workers and peasants engaged in the enforced building of socialism. The extent of Tito's personality soon outgrew reality to such an extent that citizens were forced to either bow to the new idol or subject him to the irony present in such personality-cult excesses as the publication of the coffee-table book *Tito i pčele* (Tito and the bees).

Most of my generation who came of age during the 1970s in the urban cultures of Belgrade, Zagreb, Ljubljana, Sarajevo, Skopje, or Titograd were immersed in further ironies of cultural openness to the Western youth movements paired with constant surveillance by righteous political watchdogs at home. The revolutionary promise was certainly intoxicating to youth who were committed to making a difference, but the creation and continuing existence of the "new class" of communist bureaucrats with almost aristocratic privileges, so aptly described by Milovan Đilas, put a significant damper on the enthusiasm of new generations. Rock culture and new communications media captured the imagination of the postwar, urban, middle-class Yugoslav generations as an expression of protest and passion against any form of authoritarian establishment, including the rapidly laughable discourse of Yugoslav political technocrats in the decade before and after Tito's death. The idea of Cyber Yugoslavia is a logical extension of this kind of youth culture that is compatible with the everyday living practices of urban populations after the real-life tragedies of the 1990s.

The activist motivation and attitude that radiates from Tim Jordan's *Cyberpower* is also present in the promise of a cultural imaginary as a refuge for those whose identifications fit into a particular collective project: "The virtual imaginary always appears to be almost true, because the technology needed to realize a virtual utopia or dystopia always appears to be almost ready."[24] The imaginary promise of fullness, perfection, or totality is there to support the desire for an encounter with those who share the bond of belonging to the same imaginary collective. To form an identity that will be always "almost true" through a communications network requires an imaginary leap of meaning into its transmissible form. The digital revolution enables these "almost ready" realities to coalesce around speech acts sent via computer into the techno-semantic field of others who imagine their own virtual location as a sort of prosthetic nipple of the decaying Mother Yugoslavia.

One of the major nation-building problems of all of the former Yugoslavias was the conflict between the Slavic race as a unifier (pan-Slavic sentiment) and multiple religious cultures (Catholicism, Eastern Orthodoxy, Islam) as dividers of the South Slavic and non-Slavic peoples who inhabit the western Balkans. The latest Yugoslav wars represent the triumph of culture as a factor of difference and separation used by Milošević, Tuđman, and other unscrupulous post-communists who were willing to plunge socialist Yugoslavia into a war of territorial division by activating violence as a form of cultural imaginary. The portable nature of Cyber Yugoslavia both recuperates culture as a possible unifier of citizens across ethnic lines and enables the realm of shared everyday practices to figure into this open form of Yugoslavism.

Those identities that did not fit into the ethnically "cleansed" versions of particular national projects, as well as those whose nationalism was supplemented by the longing for a space of common personal and cultural exchange, were de-territorialized after the breakup of Yugoslavia in 1991. The virtual promise of Cyber Yugoslavia fits perfectly into my own refusal of easy identifications, especially with any form of nation that relies on exclusionary practices and discourses. The Internet's online communities provide a version of the cultural imaginary whose operations have very real existential effects on the identities of those who engage in a particular quest for a shared virtual space of the nation.

However, the cyberscape inhabited by disappointingly sparse digital messaging seems to abrogate anything that might approach the realm of politics, probably due to anxieties about the return of the communist-turned-ethnic war machines that generated the acts of homicidal violence. As is often the case with the Internet, the promise of orgiastic communication between cyber-citizens turns out to be much better than the actual browsing. This digital domain is by definition devoted to the practice of everyday life, which makes it open to criticism regarding questions about those very acts of violence that it would rather escape or forget. The problems of Balkan ethnocides are at least partly rooted in recurring narratives of communal suffering and revenge that are often misused to mobilize masses to commit acts of just and righteous violence.

Online communication extends the possibility of creating a new vision of ethnicity in the region, the one that will create openness despite the Gothic imaginary that dominated the entire last decade of the old millennium. Violent outrages need not be limited to the phantasm of 'the serbs'; they ought to provide a context to examine the legacy of ethnic authoritarianism by opening proper channels for the work of collective mourning to take place. If the Balkans are to overcome the vampire image and legacy in the global cultural marketplace, the digital domain could provide a valuable way to store testimonies of the victims and their loved ones, ensuring that forgetting is not enforced as mandatory in founding the new state entities when the final dissolution of Yugoslavia is over. The traumatic core of identity that informs the sacrificial logic of the One and Only needs to be defused by the formation of a truth and reconciliation process that will operate as a supplement to the work of international justice tribunals.

Those few voices that did not conflate the cosmopolitan orientation with the official Titoist ideology were the most successful in resisting the mindless onslaught of the violent imaginary awakened at the end of Yugoslavia. The post-authoritarian culture continues to struggle with its own vampires of ancient times, trying to find strength and survive in its flights toward the symbolic realm of Europe to come. The irony of that struggle for new forms of collective identity is the recognition of defeat and the resulting deconstruction of 'the serbs' as the resident evil in the Balkans. The role of culture in this process of new collective becoming needs to be redefined away from discourses of exclusion, as was the case in the tunes of Milošević and the Academics in the mid-1980s. The parodic act of the photographer from Požarevac who put the stake through Milošević's grave is a symptom of collective anxiety over the return of violence as cultural imaginary that dominated this part of the world in the final stretch of the last century. If there is a legacy of common life during the times of socialist Yugoslavia, then there must also be a need for imaginative recuperation of those everyday practices that distinguished the region from the rest of divided Europe during the Cold War.

In the meantime, the cultural imaginary tied to the vampire has continued to rise from its cradle in Serbia and spread its ambiguous appeal way beyond its supposed Balkan home. The exemplary violence supplemented by unbridled erotic passion is closer to defining the present temporality of empires than their unpacified fringes. The recognition that the desire exists, especially the one to dominate and violate the minor other, is perhaps the first step in getting closer to Derrida's demand for infinite responsibility.

The Cradle of Vampires in Europe

The extraordinary success of *Twilight* among youth in the United States appears as a global symptom of chronic hunger for attention from others and a craving for freedom that, paradoxically, shrinks under an invisible yet omnipresent force based on consumption and concealed forms of violence inherent in the developed modes of the current economy. Images of vampires have persisted in popular culture as a remnant of that undying demand for the extraordinary established by the Romantics and reveal, with symptomatic ambiguity, ever more powerful yet abstinent revenants who can control their craving for the blood of the ones they love. The disgusting, corpse-like appearance of the vampire has been sublimated into beauty in Goth subcultures, lending esthetic currency to the love of death that is overcome by the ever increasing levels of consumption demanded from ordinary humans.

In fact, the global media gaze that has discovered the cradle of European violence among 'the serbs' continues to act as a stake to put other vampire nations out for good. The skill of the vampire slayer equals that of the exterminator, acting with rational violence against the irrational one of the nations deemed below civilization's dividing line. The imaginary of minor and peripheral cultures of southeastern Europe has been interpellated by the political discourse based on that gaze to produce a variety of strategies of resistance to both domestic and foreign attempts at appropriation. While 'the serbs' face up to the unflattering task of confronting the real crimes committed in their name, the sublimation of the vampire on the global entertainment scene points to the displacement of Balkan topoi to account for the return of imperial desire to its rightful source.

While the U.S.-led West celebrates its techno-masculinity, conspicuous consumption, and superior military strength, the rest of the globe is rapidly undergoing "balkanization" as the fallout of political practices that radiated from the West's unchecked hunger for strategic resources. The global political landscape is being divided ever more sharply between the so-called international community governed by the strategic interests of the United States and its allies and the rest of the world, whose interests are rapidly being de-legitimized: Globalization serves as a discursive screen for the concentration of power and technology within the centers of the West, while the rest of the world has to contend with new forms of economic and political dependence imposed by the insatiable demands of Western consumer-based cultures.

This hunger for increased profits at any cost manifests the global version of the cultural metaphor whose folk roots sprouted in the Balkans—the vampire whose hunger for the life of others knows no national or cultural boundaries. "Capital is dead labor, which, vampire-like, lives only by sucking living labor, and lives the more, the more labor it sucks," wrote Karl Marx to account for the uncanny cultural turn imposed by the increased demand for consumption.[25] The living matter of human life has been altered in the political economy of his age by this insidious demand of the force of death in its fluid incarnations. The return of the vampire as the obverse side of the national discourse points to the roots of the cultural imaginary born out of this structural violence as the new imperial configurations of power use their domination to consume the lesser ones, dispersing the stories of violence onto the "good vampires" present in the discursive cloaks of films such as *Twilight*.

The vampire legends of our age continue to refer to the ancient times that are characteristic of communal origins while appealing to emergent post-human subjects who reproduce the transformations of the latest incarnation of capitalism rooted in consumption. As these new narrative elaborations use Balkan locations to invoke the sinister imaginary potential that originated in the Gothic period, they also create a new breed of uncanny subjectivities lusting for power and recognition. In the global landscape where the force of capital naturalizes its existence to appear as the omnipotent and invisible source of death-in-life, the vampire perhaps remains the only true face of a being lost in the speculations of Western metaphysics. Its imaginary journey from the undead creature of Balkan folklore to the antihero of Hollywood blockbusters tells the story of our post-human future, shared by the most peripheral of European cultures and the political and economic centers of the West, to account for the increasing acceptance of humanity's transformation since mass ideologies of emancipation failed in 1989. The status of the vampire in popular culture suggests that the naturalized state of predation inherent in the global order of consumption marks a transition of humanity to a new stage of development in which it gradually accepts and covertly celebrates the violence whose origins remain hidden by the ruins of Dracula's castle. The notion of the nation as an effect of bourgeois liberalism that originated in the philosophy of the Enlightenment has given birth to a vampire whose current transformations manifest a dawn of a different subjectivity, detaching itself from the nation to enter the global stage of free play, and offer a model of identification that transcends humanism.

The vampire as a theoretical hybrid between political science and psychoanalysis offers a kind of lay philosophy that transcends both the model of the machine and that of the animal commonly utilized by theoreticians of the post-human. The power of this hybrid to incarnate the subjectivity to come builds on the conventions that, in previous centuries, posited the vampire as the opponent of the common human subject. The precognition inherent in the imaginary flights of popular culture speaks the truth about a political unconscious that has found its incarnation in both the phantasm of 'the serbs' as a vampire nation and the vampire as a new model for the global order of being—an order that is all too (post)human.

NOTES

Introduction

1. Erlanger, "Having a Vote in Kosovo Is Requiring Determination," A11.
2. A notable exception is Gibb, *First Do No Harm*.

1. The Great Vampire Swindle

1. Milosz et al., "The Budapest Roundtable," 18.
2. Ibid., 21
3. Todorova, *Imagining the Balkans*, 82.
4. Milosz et al., "The Budapest Roundtable," 20.
5. Ibid., 18.
6. Kiš, *The Tomb for Boris Davidovich*.
7. Milosz et al., "The Budapest Roundtable," 21.
8. Rickels, *Vampire Lectures*, 12.
9. Stoker, *Dracula*, 25.
10. Crnjanski, *Embahade*, 125.
11. Todorova, *Imagining the Balkans*, 19.
12. Stoker, *Dracula*, 29.
13. Clinton, "A Just and Necessary War," 17.
14. Stoker, *Dracula*, 20.
15. Crnjanski, *Embahade*, 134.
16. Zetkin, "Proletarian Women, Be Prepared!," 6.
17. Stern, "Screening Politics."
18. Freud, *Civilization and Its Discontents*, 56.
19. The spelling "vEmpires" in the section heading was first used by Dragan Kujundžić in his essay "vEmpire, Glocalization, and the Melancholia of the Sovereign" to invoke the systemic violence inherent in the insatiable hunger of the economic apparatus draining the planet of its resources under the

global–local binary. An earlier, reverse articulation was coined in the title of Viktor Pelevin's Russian novel, *empireV* (2006).

20. Bhabha, *The Location of Culture*, 5.

21. For an excellent analysis of the relationship between new U.S. imperialism, masculinity, and alterity, see McClintock, "Paranoid Empire."

2. Bloody Tales

1. Andrić, "Razvoj duhovnog života u Bosni pod uticajem turske vladavine," 253.

2. See Said, *Orientalism*, 5. For an excellent presentation of Orientalist themes in the political and cultural discourse of the former Yugoslavia, see Bakić-Hayden and Hayden, "Orientalist Variations on the Theme 'Balkans.'" While the Haydens discuss the ideology of Orientalism in Slovenian and Croatian treatment of the Serbs, I intend to move the argument a step backward (or eastward) and later in this study show how the Muslim figures in the construction of Serbian national identity.

3. See Jelavich, *South Slav Nationalisms*, 231, for a detailed account of the role of education in the formation of nationalist ideologies in the Balkans.

4. See Konstantinović, "Mesto Srba u srednjevropskom krugu kulture." All translations from Bosnian, Croatian, and Serbian are mine.

5. Wolff, *Inventing Eastern Europe*, 42.

6. Deretić, *Istorija srpske književnosti*, 220.

7. Đerić, *Kosovska bitka*, 7.

8. Anderson, *Imagined Communities*, 12.

9. Đurić, "Marko Kraljević i Đemo Brđanin," 303–8.

10. "He deliberately breaks the law, but at the same time, something like a nature gone awry transports him far from all nature; his death is the moment when the supernatural return of the crime and its retribution thwarts the flight into counternature": Foucault, *The History of Sexuality*, 39.

11. For a groundbreaking study of masculinity and its role in the construction of modern nationalism, see Mosse, *Nationalism and Sexuality*, x, 232.

12. For more detail about Marko and his death, see Longinović, "Prince Marko's Death."

13. Đurić, "Marko Kraljević ukida svadbarinu," 316–17.

14. Idem, "Banović Strahinja," 209–29.

15. Barac, *A History of Yugoslav Literature*, 95.

16. Although Michel Aubin and Nikola Banašević both attempt to reconstruct the sequence of historical events linked to "*istraga*" and prove that it had no grounding in reality, the construction of cultural imaginary may treat Njegoš and his attitude toward Islamic domination as an excellent symptom of the problematic relationship to the past as a source of violence and therefore as the foundational discourse of the "vampire nation" as an imaginary construct grounded in the poetic imagination.

17. Njegoš, *Gorski vijenac*, 9. The original edition appeared in Vienna in 1847.

18. Đurić, *Antologija narodnih junačkih pesama*, 343.

19. Njegoš, *Gorski vijenac*, 27–28.

20. It is interesting that, at the same time, Serbian folk culture developed a host of blasphemous, irreverent, and often outrageous treatments of its national(ist) heritage: see the translations of Serbian women's songs in Longinović and Weissbort, *Red Knight*. The title stands for a male sexual organ, a clear parody of the high-flung medieval imagery that was reinvented during the nineteenth-century liberation struggles in the Balkans.

21. Njegoš, *Gorski vijenac*, 56.

22. Ibid., 31.

23. Ibid., 23.

24. Nenadović, "Pisma iz Italije," 371.

25. See Dundes, "The Vampire as Bloodthirsty Revenant," 163.

26. Đurić, *Antologija narodnih junačkih pesama*, 265.

27. Kiš, *Skladište*, 306.

28. Bakhtin, "The Epic and the Novel," 18.

29. Milosz et al., "The Budapest Roundtable," 21.

30. Serbo-Croatian etymology is revealing of the character of self-management techniques. *Ruka*-hand and *vodioci*-leaders—that is, "those who lead you by the hand"—contradicts the self-management ideal of being guided by yourself.

31. For the most successful account of how Eastern Europe was invented by the West during the eighteenth century, see Wolff, *Inventing Eastern Europe*.

32. Handke, *A Journey to the Rivers*, 77.

3. Sounds of Blood

1. Freud, *Civilization and Its Discontents*, 61.

2. Žižek, *The Indivisible Remainder*, 1.

3. Balibar and Wallerstein, *Race, Nation, Class*, 21.

4. Andrić, *The Bridge on the Drina*, 75.

5. Idem, *Na Drini ćuprija*, 282.

6. Benjamin, "Eduard Fuchs," 359.

7. Balibar and Wallerstein, *Class, Race, Nation*, 57.

8. Žižek, *The Indivisible Remainder*, 142.

9. Ibid. German linguistic experts have suggested that Žižek's parallel is mistaken, since the *e* in "*Lueger*" does not stand for an umlauted *ü*.

10. Poggioli, "Scouts without Compasses," 4.

11. Dvorniković, *Karakterologija Jugoslovena*, 429.

12. Ibid., 33.

13. Ibid., 399.

14. Ibid., 376.

15. Ibid., 376–77.

16. Ibid., 191–92. Most of Dvorniković's critique of the superiority of Nordic "racial style" comes from reading Clauss, *Rasse und Seele* and *Die nordische Seele*.

17. Ibid., 17.

18. Ibid., 391.

19. Ibid., 385.

20. Golob, *Neue slowenische Kunst*, 53.

21. Ibid., 43–44.

22. Žižek, *The Metastases of Enjoyment*, 72.

23. Tancig, as quoted in Bakić-Hayden and Hayden, "Orientalist Variations on the Theme 'Balkans,'" 12.

24. Freud used his famous formulation of nationalism as a collective expression of narcissism in *Civilization and its Discontents*, 61.

4. Locations of Horror

Epigraph: "Postoje dva sveta, izmedju kojih nema i ne može biti ni pravog dodira ni mogućnosti sporazuma, dva strašna sveta osuđena na večiti rat u hiljadu oblika": Andrić, *Prokleta avlija*, 75. The original edition was published by *Matica srpska* (Novi Sad) in 1954.

1. Byron, *The Major Works*, 227.

2. Andrić, "Razvoj duhovnog života u Bosni pod uticajem turske vladavine," 51.

3. Said, *Orientalism*, 5.

4. Ibid., 3.

5. Andrić, "Razvoj duhovnog života u Bosni pod uticajem turske vladavine," 255.

6. Ibid., 254.

7. Konstantinović, "O Andrićevom doktoratu," 257–76.

8. Andrić, "Razvoj duhovnog života u Bosni pod uticajem turske vladavine," 201.

9. Ibid., 253.

10. Sekulić, "Istok u pripovetkama Iva Andrića," 57. The original essay was published in *Srpski književni glasnik*, vol. 10, in 1923. For the role of Kosovo myth in Andrić's opus, see also Zjeljinski, "Bosna između Istoka i Zapada."

11. Sekulić, "Istok u pripovetkama Iva Andrića," 58.

12. Ibid.

13. Ibid., 65.

14. Ibid., 69; emphasis added.

15. For more information on the "analytic" discourse of Eastern civilizations, see Nasr, *Islamic Science*.

16. See Tartalja, *Put pored znakova*, esp. 58–74.

17. Andrić, *Na Drini ćuprija*, 119–20.

18. Ibid., 36.

19. Ibid.

20. Ibid., 97.
21. Ibid., 83.
22. Ibid., 145.
23. Ibid., 151.
24. Goldsworthy, *Inventing Ruritania*, 74.
25. Kristeva, *Crisis of the European Subject*, 139.
26. "He deliberately breaks the law, but at the same time, something like a nature gone awry transports him far from all nature; his death is the moment when the supernatural return of the crime and its retribution thwarts the flight into counternature": Foucault, *The History of Sexuality*, 39.
27. The full citation for the verse in this section's epigraph is Dis, "Spomenik," 441.
28. Enriko Josif, a popular Serbian Jewish composer, is credited for resurrecting the Kosovo image of Serbian nationalism as a heavenly construct. It would be interesting to analyze the convergence of Serbian and Israeli constructions of national identity in connection with this "messianic" component. The nations that were singled out for extermination by the Germans during the Nazi Holocaust (1939–45) share a burden of unresolved grief and survivors' guilt. Since revenge feels fully justified to the historically victimized nation, it reserves the full right for itself to get back at the past aggressors but at the same time has a tendency to victimize its others. In both the Serbian and the Israeli case, the other is the Muslim.
29. Andrić, "Razvoj duhovnog života u Bosni pod uticajem turske vladavine," 254.
30. Milošević, "Kosovo i sloga," 6–7.
31. Ibid., 6.
32. Andrić, *Prokleta avlija*, 75.
33. Andrić, *Travnička hronika*, 270.
34. Kiš, *Čas anatomije*, 29–31.
35. Milošević, "Kosovo i sloga," 6.
36. Ibid.
37. Freud's famous definition of nationalism (*Civilization and its Discontents*, 61) describes almost perfectly the evolution of the process of differentiation during the Yugoslav conflict, with a special emphasis on the adjective "minor."
38. Andrić, "Njegoš kao tragični junak kosovske misli, 18.
39. Ibid., 490.
40. Selimović, *Pisci, mišljenja, razgovori*, 373.
41. Redhouse, *A Turkish and English Lexicon*, 1807.
42. Selimović, *Derviš i smrt*, 10.
43. Selimović, *Sjećanja*, 33.
44. Selimović, *Derviš i smrt*, 39.
45. Ibid., 39–40.
46. Ibid., 445.

47. Freudian theories of identity stress that the initial bliss of unity with the mother is interrupted by separation and differentiation, which are chief determinants of subjectivity. For literary origins of this process of subjectification, see esp. Lacan, *Écrits*.
48. Selimović, *Pisci, mišljenja, razgovori*, 302.
49. Selimović, *Sjećanja*, 34.
50. Ibid., 35.
51. Selimović, *Derviš i smrt*, 445.
52. Ibid., 362.
53. Ibid., 363.
54. Ibid.
55. Selimović, *Sjećanja*, 35.
56. See ibid., 34.

5. Quieting the Vampire

1. Ronay, "Vampire Slayer Impales Milošević to Stop Return," 1.
2. Piroćanac, *Izbrisati srpski virus*, 38.
3. Pekić, *Kako upokojiti vampira*, 115.
4. Ibid., 116.
5. Lacan, *Écrits*, 693.
6. Pekić, *Kako upokojiti vampira*, 408.
7. Ibid., 253.
8. Ibid., 254.
9. Ibid., 258.
10. Marković, *Godina dana*, 161.
11. Ibid., 157.
12. Ibid., 162.
13. Freud, *The Standard Edition of the Complete Psychological Works of Sigmund Freud*, 20.
14. Albahari, *Mrak*, 135.
15. Ibid., 37.
16. Albahari, *Mamac*, 51.
17. Ibid., 5.
18. Assmann, "The Blessing or the Curse of Babel," 86.
19. Girard, *Violence and the Sacred*, 299–300.
20. Hutcheon, *A Theory of Parody*, 3.
21. Bruce, "Birth of a Cyber Nation."
22. Mark Poster, quoted in Ryan, *Cyberspace Textuality*, 55–66.
23. Paul Virilio, *The Strategy of Deception*, 8–9.
24. Jordan, *Cyberpower*, 179.
25. Marx, *Capital*, 432.

BIBLIOGRAPHY

Albahari, David. *Kratka knjiga* [Short book]. Belgrade: Narodna Knjiga, 1997.
———. *Mamac* [Bait]. Belgrade: Narodna Knjiga, 1996.
———. *Mrak* [Dark]. Belgrade: Narodna knjiga/Alfa, 1997.
———. *Snežni čovek* [Snow man]. Belgrade: Vreme knjige, 1995.
Anderson, Benedict. *Imagined Communities: Reflections on the Origin and Spread of Nationalism*. London: Verso, 1991.
Andrić, Ivo. *The Bridge on the Drina*, trans. Lovett F. Edwards. Chicago: University of Chicago Press, 1977.
———. *Na Drini ćuprija*. Belgrade: Prosveta, 1945.
———. "Njegoš kao tragični junak kosovske misli" [Njegoš as a tragic hero of the Kosovo idea]. *Kosovski boj u srpskoj književnosti* [The Battle of Kosovo in Serbian literature], ed. Vojislav J. Đurić. Belgrade: Srpska književna zadruga, 1990.
———. *Prokleta avlija* [The damned yard]. Belgrade: Prosveta-BIGZ-SKZ-Nolit, 1991.
———. "Razvoj duhovnog života u Bosni pod uticajem turske vladavine" [The development of spiritual life in Bosnia under the influence of Turkish rule]. *Sveske zadužbine Ive Andrića*, no. 1. Belgrade: Zadužbina, 1982.
———. *Travnička hronika* [The Bosnian chronicle]. Belgrade: Državni zavod Jugoslavije, 1945.
Assmann, Aleida. "The Blessing or the Curse of Babel." *The Translatability of Cultures*, ed. Sanford Budick and Wolfgang Iser. Stanford: Stanford University Press, 1996.
Aubin, Michel. *Visions historiques et politiques dans l'oeuvre poétique de P. P. Njegoš* [Historical and political views on the poetic works of P. P. Njegoš]. Paris: Diffusion de Boccard, 1972.
Bakhtin, Mikhail M. "The Epic and the Novel." *The Dialogic Imagination*, ed.

Michael Holquist, trans. Caryl Emerson and Michael Holquist. Austin: University of Texas Press, 2002.

Bakić-Hayden, Milica, and Robert Hayden. "Orientalist Variations on the Theme 'Balkans': Symbolic Geography in Recent Yugoslav Cultural Politics." *Slavic Review* 51 (1992): 1–15.

Balibar, Etienne, and Immanuel Wallerstein. *Race, Nation, Class: Ambiguous Identities*, trans. Chris Turner. London: Verso, 1991.

Banašević, Nikola. "Pesnička legenda o Badnjem večeru" [The poetic legend about Christmas Eve]. *Prilozi za književnost, jezik, istoriju i folklor* 23 (1957): 1–2.

Barac, Antun. *A History of Yugoslav Literature*, trans. P. Mijušković. Ann Arbor: University of Michigan Press, 1972.

Benjamin, Walter. "Eduard Fuchs, Collector and Historian." *One-way Street and Other Writings*, trans. Edmund Jephcott and Kingsley Shorter. London: Verso, 1979.

Bhabha, Homi. *The Location of Culture*. New York: Routledge, 1994.

Blanchot, Maurice. *The Writing of the Disaster*, trans. Ann Smock. Lincoln: University of Nebraska Press, 1986.

Bruce, Ian. "Birth of a Cyber Nation." *Scotsman*, 30 August 1999.

Bunson, Matthew, ed. *The Vampire Encyclopedia*. New York: Crown, 1993.

Byron, George Gordon. "The Giaour." *The Complete Poetical Works*. Oxford: Oxford University Press, 1970.

Cain, Jimmie E. *Bram Stoker and Russophobia: Evidence of the British Fear of Russia in "Dracula" and "The Lady of the Shroud."* Jefferson, N.C.: McFarland, 2006.

Clauss, Ludvig Ferdinand. *Die nordische Seele: Eine Einführung in die Rassenseelenkunde*. Munich: Lehmanns, 1936.

——. *Rasse und Seele: Eine Einführung in den Sinn der leiblichen Gestalt*. Munich: Lehmann, 1933.

Clinton, Bill. "A Just and Necessary War" (op-ed). *New York Times*, 23 March 1999.

Crnjanski, Miloš. *Embahade*, vol. 4. Belgrade: Nolit, 1983.

——. *Priče o muškom* [Masculine Stories]. Belgrade: S. B. Cvijanović, 1920.

Deleuze, Gilles, and Félix Guattari. *A Thousand Plateaus*, trans. Brian Massumi. Minneapolis: University of Minnesota Press, 1987.

Deretić, Jovan. *Istorija srpske književnosti*. Belgrade: Nolit, 1983.

Đerić, Branislav. *Kosovska bitka: Vojno-istorijska rasprava*. Belgrade: Naučna knjiga, 1989.

Dis, Vladislav Petković. "Spomenik" [The monument]. *Kosovski boj u srpskoj književnosti*, ed. Vojislav J. Đurić. Belgrade: Srpska književna zadruga, 1990.

Dundes, Alan. "The Vampire as Bloodthirsty Revenant: A Psychoanalytic Post-mortem." *The Vampire: A Case Study*. Madison: University of Wisconsin Press, 1998.

Đurić, Vojislav. *Antologija narodnih junačkih pesama*. Belgrade: Srpska književna zadruga, 1965.

——. "Banović Strahinja." *Antologija narodnih junačkih pesama.* Belgrade: Srpska književna zadruga, 1965.

——. "Marko Kraljević i Đemo Brđanin." *Antologija narodnih junačkih pesama.* Belgrade: Srpska književna zadruga, 1965.

——. "Marko Kraljević ukida svadbarinu." *Antologija narodnih junačkih pesama.* Belgrade: Srpska književna zadruga, 1965.

Dvorniković, Vladimir. *Karakterologija Jugoslovena.* Belgrade: Kosmos, 1939.

Erlanger, Steven. "Having a Vote in Kosovo Is Requiring Determination." *New York Times,* 1 February 2001.

Foucault, Michel. *The History of Sexuality,* trans. Robert Hurley. London: Penguin, 2008.

Freud, Sigmund. *Civilization and Its Discontents,* trans. James Strachey. New York: Norton, 1962.

——. *An Infantile Neurosis and Other Works.* Vol. 17 of *The Standard Edition of the Complete Psychological Works of Sigmund Freud,* ed. and trans. James Strachey. London: Hogarth Press and Institute of Psychoanalysis, 1917–19.

——. "Mourning and Melancholia." *A General Selection from the Works of Sigmund Freud,* ed. John Rickman. Garden City, N. Y.: Doubleday Anchor, 1957.

Gibb, David. *First Do No Harm: Humanitarian Intervention and the Destruction of Yugoslavia.* Nashville: Vanderbilt University Press, 2009.

Girard, René. *Violence and the Sacred,* trans. Patrick Gregory. Baltimore: Johns Hopkins University Press, 1977.

Goldsworthy, Vesna. *Inventing Ruritania.* New Haven: Yale University Press, 1998.

Golob, Mario, trans. *Neue slowenische Kunst* [New Slovenian art]. Los Angeles: Amok, 1991.

Handke, Peter. *A Journey to the Rivers,* trans. Scott Abbott. New York: Viking, 1997.

Hutcheon, Linda. *A Theory of Parody.* New York: Methuen, 1985.

Jelavich, Charles. *South Slav Nationalisms.* Columbus: University of Ohio Press, 1990.

Jordan, Tim. *Cyberpower.* New York: Routledge, 1999.

Kafka, Franz. "The Hunter Gracchus." *Short Shorts,* ed. Irving and Ilana Howe and trans. Willa and Edwin Muir. Boston: D. R. Godine, 1982.

Kiš, Danilo. *Čas anatomije* [An anatomy lesson]. Belgrade: Nolit, 1978.

——. *Grobnica za Borisa Davidoviča* [The tomb for Boris Davidovich]. Belgrade: Beogradski izdavačko-grafički zavod, 1980.

——. *Skladište.* Belgrade: Beogradski izdavačko-grafički zavod, 1995.

Konstantinović, Zoran. "Mesto Srba u srednjevropskom krugu kulture." *Književne Novine,* no. 926, 15 March 1996, 1.

——. "O Andrićevom doktoratu." *Sveske zadužbine Ive Andrića,* no. 1. Belgrade: Zadužbina, 1982.

Kristeva, Julia. *Crisis of the European Subject,* trans. Susan Fairfield. New York: Other Press, 2000.

Kujundžić, Dragan. "vEmpire, Glocalization, and the Melancholia of the Sovereign." *Comparatist* 29 (May 2005): 82–100.

Lacan, Jacques. *Écrits: A Selection*, trans. Alan Sheridan. New York: Norton, 1977.

Longinović, Tomislav. "Prince Marko's Death: Text, Performance, and Desire in the Oral Tradition." *Serbian Studies* 3, nos. 3–4 (1986): 65–76.

Longinović, Tomislav, and Daniel Weissbort. *Red Knight: Serbian Women's Songs*. London: Menard, 1992.

Lord, Albert. *The Singer of Tales*. Cambridge: Harvard University Press, 1960.

Lyotard, Jean-François. *Heidegger and "the jews,"* trans. Andreas Michel and Mark S. Roberts. Minneapolis: University of Minnesota Press, 1990.

Marković, Goran. *Godina dana*. Belgrade: Beogradski krug, 2001.

Marx, Karl. *Capital*, trans. Ben Fowkes. London: Penguin, 1976.

McClintock, Anne. "Paranoid Empire: Specters from Guantánamo and Abu Ghraib." *States of Emergency: The Object of American Studies*, ed. Russ Castronovo and Susan Gillman. Chapel Hill: University of North Carolina Press, 2009.

Milošević, Slobodan. "Kosovo i sloga [Kosovo and unity]." *Nedeljne Informativne Novine*, no. 2 (July 1989): 31–32.

Milosz, Czeslaw, H. C. Artmann, Peter Esterhazy, Danilo Kis, Gyorgy Konrad, Edward Limonov, Claudio Magris, Miklos Meszoly, Adam Michnik, and Paul-Eerik Rummo. "The Budapest Roundtable." *Crosscurrents 10: A Yearbook of Central European Culture*, ed. Ladislav Matejka. New Haven: Yale University Press, 1991.

Mosse, George. *Nationalism and Sexuality: Middle Class Morality and Sexual Norms in Modern Europe*. Madison: University of Wisconsin Press, 1988.

Nasr, Seyyed Hossein. *Islamic Science*. Cambridge: Harvard University Press, 1968.

Nenadović, Ljubomir. "Pisma iz Italije." *Kosovski boj u sprskoj književnosti*, ed. Vojislav J. Đurić. Belgrade: Srpska književna zadruga, 1990.

Njegoš, Petar Petrović. *Gorski vijenac*. Belgrade: Prosveta, 1967.

Pekić, Borislav. *Kako upokojiti vampira: A sotija* [How to quiet a vampire: A sotie]. Belgrade: Rad, Narodna knjiga, BIGZ, 1977.

Piroćanac, Zoran Petrović. *Izbrisati srpski virus*. Beograd: Čigoja, 2002.

Poggioli, Sylvia. "Scouts without Compasses." *Nieman Reports* (fall 1993): 4.

Redhouse, James. *A Turkish and English Lexicon*. Beirut: Librarie du Liban, 1974.

Rickels, Laurence. *Vampire Lectures*. Minneapolis: University of Minnesota Press, 1999.

Ronay, Gabriel. "Vampire Slayer Impales Milošević to Stop Return." *Herald Scotland*, 12 March 2007.

Ryan, Marie-Laure. *Cyberspace Textuality*. Bloomington: Indiana University Press, 1999.

Said, Edward. *Orientalism*. New York: Vintage, 1979.

Schevill, Ferdinand. *A History of the Balkans*. New York: Dorset, 1991.

Sekulić, Isidora. "Istok u pripovetkama Iva Andrića" [East in the stories of Ivo Andrić]. *Kritičari o Andriću*, ed. Petar Džadžić. Belgrade: Nolit, 1962.

Selimović, Meša. *Derviš i smrt* [Death and the dervish]. Belgrade: Beogradski izdavačko-grafički zavod, 1983.

——. *Pisci, mišljenja, razgovori* [Writers, opinions, conversations]. Belgrade: Beogradski izdavačko-grafički zavod, 1983.

——. *Sjećanja* [Memories]. Belgrade: Beogradski izdavačko-grafički zavod, 1983.

Stern, Frank. "Screening Politics: Cinema and Intervention." *Georgetown Journal of International Studies* 1, no. 2 (2000): 65–73.

Stoker, Bram. *Dracula*. Philadelphia: Running Press, 1995.

Tartalja, Ivo. *Put pored znakova* [Road by the signs]. Novi Sad: Matica srpska, 1991.

Todorova, Maria. *Imagining the Balkans*. New York: Oxford University Press, 1997.

Virilio, Paul. *Strategy of Deception*, trans. Chris Turner. London: Verso, 2000.

Wolff, Larry. *Inventing Eastern Europe: The Map of Civilization on the Mind of the Enlightenment*. Stanford: Stanford University Press, 1994.

Zetkin, Clara. "Proletarian Women, Be Prepared!" *Lines of Fire: Women Writers of World War I*, ed. Margaret Higonnet. New York: Plume, 1999.

Žižek, Slavoj. *The Indivisible Remainder*. London: Verso, 1996.

——. *The Metastases of Enjoyment: Six Essays on Women and Causality*. London: Verso, 1994.

Zjeljinski, Boguslav. "Bosna između Istoka i Zapada (od kosovskog mita u ideologiji Mlade Bosne do romana Ive Andrića *Travnička hronika*)." *Sveske zadužbine Ive Andrića*, no. 6 (1989): 277–87.

INDEX

Abu-Ghraib (prison), 49

Academics, the, 16, 43, 154, 162, 165–67, 186

"Adam and Eve" (Crnjanski), 79–80

Afghanistan wars, 2

Albahari, David, 17, 153, 168–88

Albanians, 5, 33, 88, 90, 97, 102, 139, 164

Albright, Madeline, 37

alterity, 10, 15, 24, 30, 41, 103, 121–22. *See also* Europe; hybridity; identity; "Orient," the; religion; 'serbs, the'

anal fixations, 131–34

Anderson, Benedict, 62, 181

Andrić, Ivo, 14–15, 52, 92–95, 103, 119–41, 148, 156

animality, 94, 188–89

apologies, 16

Assmann, Aleida, 177

Aubin, Michel, 192n16

Austro-Turkish wars, 55

Bačić, Zoran, 180–81

Bairam (holiday), 122

Bait (Albahari), 174–75. See also *Canadian Trilogy*

Bakhtin, Mikhail M., 51, 53, 56, 64–65

Balibar, Etienne, 91, 95, 112

Balkans. *See* Albanians; Bosnia-Herzegovina; Dinaric highlands; Kosovo; 'serbs, the'; Slovenia

Balkan Wars (1912–13), 40–41

Banašević, Nikola, 192n16

"Banović Strahinja" (song), 74

Barac, Antun, 70

belonging, 4, 6, 8, 12, 29, 36, 52, 70, 75–76, 90, 116. *See also* blood; identity; religion

Benjamin, Walter, 95

Berlin Congress of 1878, 77, 151

Bhabha, Homi, 47–49

Black Hand (secret organization), 40

blackness, 41, 84. *See also* Europe; Islam; Ottoman empire; racism; 'serbs, the'

blood: discourses of, 10, 41; drinking of, 21; folk music and, 106–7; as metaphor for communal unity and purity, 6, 16–17, 25, 43, 68–71, 84, 89–91, 103, 135, 153, 169; tribute, 128; women and, 70–76

Bolivar, Simon, 143

Deleuze, Gilles, 3, 153, 163, 170

Deretić, Jovan, 56

Derrida, Jacques, 1–2, 44–45, 47

Derviš i smrt (Selimović), 144

"Development of Spiritual Life in Bosnia under the Influence of Turkish Rule, The" (Andrić), 121

Đilas, Milovan, 184

Dinaric highlands (as Volk origin), 12, 58, 65, 102, 106, 109, 112, 184

Draculaland (park), 21

Dracula (Stoker), 10, 20, 22, 29–34, 42, 45, 56–57, 78, 105, 143

Dracul Tsepesh, Vlad, 21–22, 31–32

Dumas, Alexandre, 38

Dundes, Alan, 75

Dvornikovic, Vladimir, 13–14, 100–105, 107, 110–12, 115, 126

Enlightenment, the, 6, 11, 19–20, 56, 188

Eothen (Kinglake), 38

epic, 53–54, 59, 65, 67, 78

ethics. *See* conscience; responsibility

ethnic cleansing: attribution of, to 'the serbs,' 41; as rhetorical tool, 4, 9, 34, 36–37, 46

ethnicity. *See* belonging; blood; national imaginaries

European Union, 22, 90–91, 98

Europe (imaginary), 90, 107: boundaries of, 34, 103, 112; ethnic solidarity's importance and, 14–15, 106; humanism of, 35; Islam as anathema to, 38; relation of 'the serbs' to, 9, 21, 65–66, 84, 186; religious identity of, 57–62; violence's legacy in, 8, 22, 27–28, 44–45, 49, 81, 85, 95, 128–31, 156; whiteness of, 91, 105–6, 110, 114, 116. *See also* "Orient," the; 'serbs, the'

Fearless Vampire Killers (Polanski), 42

First World War, 13, 35, 39–40, 79, 83, 94, 103, 135

Foucault, Michel, 63, 134, 192n10, 195n26

Frankfurter Allgemeine Zeitung, 85

Freud, Sigmund, 13, 41, 51, 89, 96–100, 117, 132–33, 159–66, 178, 195n37, 196n47. *See also* guilt; oral tendencies; projection; repression; transference

Gaj, Ljudevit, 105–6

gaze, the. *See* imperialism; Lacan, Jacques; media; U.S.-West

gender, 70–76; marking of, 103, 108, 135; nationalist narratives and, 67; "Orient" and, 52; phallic imagery and, 63–64, 95–97, 132, 134–35, 156–61, 167, 193n20; in Serbian oral tradition and literature, 69, 125–26, 128, 175; in socialist Yugoslavia, 83. *See also* masculinity

Germany. *See* Nazi Germany

Gift of Death, The (Derrida), 45

Girard, René, 2, 177–78, 182

Goethe, Johann Wolfgang von, 38

Goldsworthy, Vensa, 133

Gombrowicz, Witold, 24

Gorbachev, Mikhail, 84

Gordy, Eric, 179

Gorski vijenac (Petrović), 12, 70–76, 124, 143

Gothic (genre), 3, 5, 19; Balkan, 52, 185–88; imaginary of, 16–17, 20, 25, 30, 33, 35; laughter and horror in, 42; manifestations of, in Western military operations, 45–46

Goth (subculture), 187

Guattari, Félix, 3, 153, 170

guilt, 96–98, 167, 178

guslars, 54, 67; neo-, 155, 162; as per-

guslars (*cont.*)
    formers of ritual catharsis, 11, 53,
    58, 64, 77–78
gypsies. *See* Roma

Habsburg empire, 12–15, 21–24, 29–
    31, 35–40, 55–58, 78, 94, 99–100,
    116
Handke, Peter, 88–91
Hegel, G. W. F., 160
"Heidegger and 'the jews'" (Lyotard), 4
Henry, Patrick, 61
Herder, Johann Gottfried, 38, 78, 101,
    105
Herzog, Werner, 2–3, 6
historical imagination, 23–25
history, 20, 23: "extreme durability"
    of, 82; historical imagination and,
    24–25; kitsch and, 141; meta-,
    168–88; monumental, 5, 12, 75, 79,
    131, 135–36; repressed elements
    of, 26, 29, 175; romanticization of,
    in European imaginary, 30, 38; as
    undead, 37–41, 48–49, 57–62, 73–
    76, 142, 171; violence of, 19, 142.
    See also "old centuries"; 'serbs, the';
    temporality; U.S.-West; vampires;
    violence
History of Yugoslav Literature (Barac),
    70
Hitler, Adolf, 100, 106, 109–10, 156
Holocaust, the, 41, 43, 109, 173
Holy Roman Empire, 21, 55. *See also*
    Catholicism
homosexuality, 134
horror (genre), 2–3, 7, 19, 42
How to Quiet a Vampire (Pekić),
    156–62
humanitarianism, 2, 4, 8, 33, 35–36,
    48, 120
human rights, 28, 47, 163, 178, 182
Hungary and Hungarians, 22, 89–90
Huntington, Samuel P., 7, 36, 44

hybridity, 3, 9, 20, 77–78, 80, 105–6,
    111, 119–25, 127–29, 146–51. *See
    also* identity; 'serbs, the'

identity, 2, 12, 62–70, 97, 184; blood
    as basis of, 8, 15, 17, 52, 98–104,
    119–20, 137, 169, 185; Bosnian,
    146–51; culture as basis of, 100–
    104, 115–16; fluid conceptions of,
    174–80; language and, 20, 77–78,
    105–6, 173; music as common basis
    of, 110–13; "new" Europe's perfor-
    mances of, 6, 10, 14, 44, 129; oral
    traditions of 'the serbs' and, 13, 17,
    37–41, 62–70; religion and, 53–57,
    59, 92, 103, 122; territorial bases
    of, 1, 4–5, 13, 89; tragedies of, 146–
    51; U.S. conception of, 26. *See also*
    racism; religion; 'serbs, the'
Iliad, The (Homer), 67
imaginaries. *See* cultural imaginaries;
    national imaginaries; 'serbs, the'
imperialism, 30, 42–43; globalization
    and, 1–2, 36; phallic imagery and,
    131, 133–35. *See also names of spe-
    cific empires*
Independent State of Croatia (nation),
    109
Indivisible Remainder, The (Žižek), 90,
    117
inscription and writing, 51, 77, 172–
    75
Internet, 165, 176–88
Iraq War, 2
Iron Curtain, 23
Islam, 60–77; Bosnian Muslims as
    reemergence of, 137–39, 162–65;
    converts to, 12, 53, 58–59, 124,
    128, 136, 147, 150–51; divine jus-
    tice and, 122–23; historical role of
    'the serbs' in combating, 32, 37–41;
    humanitarian interventions on
    behalf of, 33; in present-day Bosnia,

136–51; racism and, 41, 125; in Serbian literature, 144–51; views of infidels and, 76–77. *See also* "Orient," the; Ottoman empire; 'serbs, the'

Israel, 37

istraga poturica (event), 71

Italian Fascists, 83, 141, 158

Izetbegović, Alija, 91

Janša, Janez, 14

Jasenovac (death camp), 112–13

Jews, 41, 101–2, 109

Jordan, Tim, 184

Josif, Enriko, 195n28

Journey to the Rivers, A (Handke), 88

Judaism, 41

Kako upokojiti vampira (Pekić), 16, 156–62

Kanadska trilogiji (Albahari), 17

Karadžić, Vuk, 11–12, 53, 56, 58, 64, 77–78, 105–6, 155

Karakterologija Jugoslovena (Dvorniković), 100–104

Kardelj, Edvard, 90

Kinglake, Alexander W., 38–39

Kiš, Danilo, 25, 78, 141, 156

kitsch, 141

Konstantinović, Zoran, 123

Kosovka Devojka, 70

Kosovo, 44–45, 53; Albanians in, 88, 97; Battle of (1389), 11, 15, 33, 56–73, 76, 142; bombing of, 4, 9, 164; ethnic makeup of, 139; "humanitarian resettlement" in, 46; in Serbian imaginary, 17, 32, 120, 124, 136, 143, 149, 155, 165, 195n28. *See also* masculinity; national imaginaries; 'serbs, the'

Kratka knijiga (Albahari), 169

Kristeva, Julia, 134–35, 159–60

Kujundžić, Dragan, 191n19

Ku Klux Klan, 91

Kundera, Milan, 23

Kurds, 37

Lacan, Jacques, 48, 63, 90, 96, 99, 117, 153, 157–61

Laibach (band), 113–16

language, 20, 77–78, 105–6, 173

laughter, 173, 179

Lazar (Prince), 59–60

literacy, 12–13, 52, 66–67, 77, 105, 155

literature, 10; as crypt, 57; Gothic, 3, 29–35; Islamic voices in, 145; nationhood and, 51, 53, 56, 62–70; "universal humanism" and, 16. *See also* 'serbs, the'; *and names of specific authors and titles of specific works*

Lithuania, 23

Lord, Albert, 54, 59, 65–67

Lueger, Karl, 99

Lyotard, Jean-François, 4

Macedonia, 98, 101, 108, 111–12

Majka Jugovića, 70

Mamac (Albahari), 176

Marković, Goran, 17, 165–66

Marx, Karl, 159, 188

Masculine Stories (Crnjanski), 79

masculinity, 52, 56–57, 60–76, 155; European, 39; injuries to, 20, 51, 58–59, 79; literary representations of; Milošević and, 91; mourning and, 132–36; nationalism and, 11, 103; Serbian oral tradition and, 77, 126; submission and domination narratives and, 12, 20, 53–55; Tito's versions of, 83. *See also* guslars; Milošević, Slobodan

master-slave dynamic, 130–31, 134

Mažuranić, Ivan, 124

media, 41, 44; hypocritical gaze of, 22, 27, 34; new, 17–18, 103, 168–88;

of, 22; post–Cold War uses of, 37, 165; vampires as motivation of, 21. *See also* U.S.-West

Nosferatu the Vampyre (Herzog), 2–3, 6

novel (genre), 64

Obilić, Miloš, 60, 68
Obradović, Dositej, 12, 78
Oedipal complex, 160–62
"old centuries," 19, 29–32, 38, 78, 146
Operation Merciful Angel, 45
Operation Storm in Croatia, 9
oral tendencies, 28, 131–34
Order of the Drakon, 31, 60
"Orient," the, 6–7, 12, 20, 30, 52, 55, 84, 120
"Orientalism," 121–22
Orthodox Christianity, 43, 55; association of, with Russia and Soviet Union, 113, 120, 131; fusion of, with Slavic dualism, 58–60; literacy and, 52; othering of, 7, 31, 41; Serbian identity and, 70–74, 142; as status marker, 76, 90
othering, 6, 10, 25, 28–29, 102, 133. *See also* blood; identity; religion
Otpor (group), 154
Ottoman empire, 31, 38–41, 45, 52, 58, 120–31; class markers in, 127–31; domination of eastern Europe and, 59, 70–80, 116, 147, 192n16; effect of, on 'the serbs,' 14–15, 54–56, 135; gaze of, 29; musical influences of, 111; torture as tactic of, 21

Palestinians, 37
parody, 42, 178–88
Parry, Millman, 54, 65
Pekić, Borislav, 16, 156–57
Petković Dis, Vladislav, 135–36
Petrović Njegoš, Petar, 12, 70–76, 124

phallic imagery, 63–64, 95–97, 132, 134–35, 156–61, 167, 193n20
Plugojević, Petar, 21
Poggiolo, Sylvia, 99–100
Poland, 22–25
Polanski, Roman, 42
"Political Vampirism" (article), 21
postcolonial theory, 47–49. *See also* Bhabha, Homi
Poverty of Philosophy, The (Marx), 159
Priče o muškom (Crnjanski), 79
projection, 27, 44–45, 47–48, 81, 154
Pulp Fiction (Tarantino), 42

racism, 9, 13, 25–26, 36, 40–41, 81, 84, 90–116. *See also* 'serbs, the'
Ranke, Leopold, 85
rape, 7, 36, 67–69, 182
Reagan, Ronald, 37
regime change, 36
Reissmüller, Johann Georg, 85
religion, 43, 95, 122–24; as basis of communal belonging, 36, 59, 62–73, 103, 140, 184; as distinction between West and Orient, 7, 11, 31, 41, 116
repression, 13, 45, 107, 167
responsibility, 1–2, 25, 44–45, 47, 168, 174, 178
revenge, 20, 25, 68–72, 76, 100–110. *See also* Kosovo; national imaginaries
Rickels, Laurence, 27–28
Rogan, Knez, 74
Roman Catholicism. *See* Catholicism
Romania, 21
Romanticism, 11–12, 20, 38, 73, 100, 107, 112, 127, 187
Roma (people), 101–2, 109

Sacher-Masoch, Leopold von, 24
sacrifice: Battle of Kosovo and, 59–60;

sacrifice (*cont.*)
history's relation to, 20, 23–24; in
Serbian imaginary, 8, 45, 57–60,
65–66
sadomasochism: identity and, 16, 76;
as kernel of vampire nations' cul-
tural imaginary, 6–11, 23–25, 31,
35, 37–41
Said, Edward, 52, 121–22
Schelling, Friedrich von, 101
Second World War, 13, 79, 83, 88, 92–
93, 100, 102, 109, 112, 142, 144,
151, 156
Sekulić, Isidora, 125–27
Selimović, Meša, 14–15, 119, 144–51
Serbia, 48, 96, 101
Serbian Arts and Sciences. *See* Academics, the
Serbian Orthodox church, 77
"Serbian problem," 109
Serbian Revolution, The (Ranke), 85
Serbo-Croatian (language), 140, 157
'serbs, the,' 28–31, 37–41, 53–70, 76,
77, 80–81, 84, 90, 106–12, 116–
17, 119, 122–30; construction of,
in West, 4–5, 7, 9, 85, 181; cultural
memories of, 16, 24–27, 71–75, 82;
cultural profiling and, 21–22, 28;
definition of, 4; desire of, for European belonging, 94, 139, 142, 155,
186; ethnic cleansing and, 9, 44, 46,
89, 136; as "ethnic glue," 46, 144; as
European, 6, 10–11, 14; Gothic literary imagination and, 33–35; guilt
and, 178, 187; hybridity of, 9, 52,
61, 103, 146–51; inferior status of,
under Ottomans, 6, 98–99, 116,
127–31; Islamic converts among,
136, 147, 150–51; literature of, 11,
52, 62–79; marginality of, 33, 42–
43; media representations of, 7–8,
25, 27, 34–36, 84, 100, 117, 181–
82; music and, 100–105, 113–16,

162; national narratives of, 12–13,
53, 73–76, 84; oral traditions of,
10–13, 45, 77, 79–80, 137; "Orientalization" of, 7, 21–22; as original
Indo-Europeans, 165–66; politics
of, 137–39, 142, 165–67; post-
Oriental wounds of, 11, 14, 52, 70–
76, 93–94, 135, 137, 149; pre-
Christian religion of, 146; rebellions
of, against Islamic rulers, 38–41;
religion as belonging and, 11, 84,
97; as resistant to civilization, 19,
34, 85; sado-masochistic self-
concept of, 6–7, 9, 11, 16, 23–25,
31, 76, 90, 103, 117–18, 121–25,
130–36, 142, 149–50, 167–68;
third narratives of, 154, 162–63;
victim narratives of, 11–13, 93–94,
98, 136–44; Western justifications
for attacking, 35–36, 45–47; Žižek
and, 14, 90, 94–100
Sigismund (emperor), 32
silence, 94, 131, 134, 140, 147–48,
167, 172, 175
Sindjelić, Stevan, 38–39
Singer of Tales, The (Lord), 65
Skull Tower, 38–41
Slovenia, 90–91; as "angelic" nation,
22, 98, 110, 114–17; separatist
movements of, 9, 14, 89, 99–100
Smrt Smail-age Čengića (Mažuranić),
124
Snow Man (Albahari), 174–75
socialism, 4, 43, 47, 88–90. *See also*
communism, communists; Tito,
Josip Broz
sotie (genre), 156–62
Soviet Union, 23–25, 43–44, 100
"Spomenik" (Petković), 135–36
Srebrenica massacre, 167
Start, 90
Stern, Frank, 40
St. George, 63, 145–46

Stoker, Bram, 10, 20, 22, 29–34, 42, 45, 56–57, 78, 105, 143, 146
"Svobodijada" (Petrović), 71–72

Tadić, Boris, 16
Takarajima (magazine), 113
Tancig, Petar, 98, 116
Tarantino, Quentin, 42
temporality: history's attempts to overcome, 5, 170–71; literary representations of, 17, 146–47; modernity's attempts to fix, 35; national imaginaries and, 31; relation of 'the serbs' to, 12–13, 30, 75; vampires as metaphorical subversion of, 2, 29
territory, 4–5, 13, 89, 176–88. *See also* blood; gender; identity; women
Tito, Josip Broz, 116; authoritarian socialism of, 15, 26, 82, 88, 98, 103, 109, 136, 183; death of, 89–90; effects of, on art, 113–15; literature under, 162; masculinity and, 83, 95–97; modernizing influences of, 43, 186; in Second World War, 93, 109, 141–42
Tito and I (film), 165
Todorova, Maria, 25, 29
torture, 21–22
Tractatus Logico-Philosophicus (Wittgenstein), 159
transference, 115–16, 178
translation theory, 2, 122, 129–30, 173
Travnička hronika (Andrić), 92, 127–30
Trpković, Adam, 156
truth and reconciliation, 16, 187
Tuđman, Franjo, 91, 184
turbo-folk culture, 76, 102, 111, 162
Turkey, 33, 37
Twilight (Meyer), 186–88

U.S.-West, 37, 45–46, 81–82; "angelic" Balkan nations and, 43; consumerism and, 23; displacement of violence and, 2, 34, 117–18; hegemony of, 47–48; historical imagination of, 25; humanism of, 8, 95; hypocrisy of, 1, 22–23, 163; imperial power of, 7–8, 28, 33–34, 36, 49, 100, 113, 120, 164, 187; mediation of violence and, 4, 84; technological superiority of, 26, 127; vampire as metaphors for, 36, 188
United Nations, 36
Ustaše (group), 25–26, 83, 96, 109–10, 112
Ustinov, Peter, 154–55

Vampire Encyclopedia, The, 48
Vampire Lectures (Rickels), 27
"Le Vampire" (Nodier), 38
vampires, 3, 19–22, 33–38, 188; as cultural hybrids, 28, 95, 121–22, 181; as embodiment of historical violence, 93; in film culture, 2; Gothic imaginary and, 10; historical emergence of, 55; as metaphor for alienated violence, 30, 94, 117, 154; Milošević as example of, 5, 136–37, 142, 153–54; orality of, 133; as reemergence of old centuries, 78; as scientific classification, 6; Serbian converts to Islam and, 72; 'the serbs' as, 9, 16, 40, 44; small nations as reflections of, 25–28, 42; United States as type of, 47, 187
victims, victimization: media's role in declaring, 5, 33; in Serbian mythology and literature, 56, 98; as trope indicating purity and belonging, 31, 92–93. *See also* Kosovo; masculinity; mourning; national imaginaries
Vienna Agreement, 105–6
violence, 2–3, 119–25; alterity and, 3,

21–22, 110; discourses of, 19; displacement of, by imperial powers, 6, 30, 40, 44, 81, 85, 95, 117–18, 156, 175, 188; as endemic to 'the serbs,' 5; ethnic bases of, 26, 43, 90; Europe's self-concept and, 8, 27–28, 85, 105–7; in guslars' oral tradition, 62–70; humanitarianism's deployment of, 19–20; media representations and, 40–41, 89; necessity of, in Serbian imaginary, 60, 75; role of, in identity formation, 23–25, 52; sexuality and, 63–64; sublimation of, by Tito's propoganda, 109–10; transformation of, to melancholy, 79–80

Virilio, Paul, 182

Volksgeist, 12, 78, 101, 105–6, 111

War Criminal Prison, 154

Wars of Yugolsav Succession (1991–95), 4, 42–49, 68, 79–80, 85, 90, 102, 166, 181

werewolves, 57, 166–67

Wiener Diarium, 21

Wittgenstein, Ludwig, 159

Wolff, Larry, 29, 55

Woltmann, Ludvig, 103

women, 67–70, 72–75, 83, 108, 135, 175

writing, 77, 172–75; nationhood and, 51

Yugoslavia (nation and region), 83, 88–92, 109; artistic irony in, 113–16; colonization of, by invading powers, 23; as emblem of violent political practices, 43, 45; ethnic conflicts in, 2–5, 13, 32–35, 37, 46; ethnic makeup of, 37; folk culture of, 38; messianic revolutionary thinking in, 183–84; modernization of, 51; music's importance to, 100–103; political dissolution of, 7–8, 13–14, 20, 80–81, 98, 110, 123; resistance of, to Nazis, 112; Tito's rule in, 82, 95–98; writers of, 9

Zetkin, Clara, 40

Žižek, Slavoj, 14, 90, 99–100, 115–17

Tomislav Z. Longinović is a professor of Slavic and comparative literature at the University of Wisconsin, Madison. His books include *Borderline Culture* (1993) and *Vampires Like Us* (2005), and the edited volumes (co-edited and co-translated with Daniel Weissbort) *Red Knight: Serbian Women's Songs* (1992), and David Albahari's *Words are Something Else* (1996). He is also the author of several books of fiction, both in Serbian (*Sama Amerika*, 1995) and English (*Moment of Silence*, 1990).

Library of Congress Cataloging-in-Publication Data
Longinović, Toma, 1955–
Vampire nation : violence as cultural imaginary / Tomislav Z. Longinović.
p. cm. — (Cultures and practice of violence series)
ISBN 978-0-8223-5022-4 (cloth : alk. paper)
ISBN 978-0-8223-5039-2 (pbk. : alk. paper)
1. Nationalism—Serbia. 2. Serbs—Ethnic identity. 3. National characteristics, Serbian. 4. Vampires—Folklore. I. Title. II. Series: Cultures and practice of violence series.
DR1953.L664 2011
320.54094971—dc22   2011006454